Oratory in the New South

Oratory
in the New
South

EDITED BY WALDO W. BRADEN

Louisiana State University Press

Baton Rouge and London

PS
407
O69

3/1981
gen'l.

LIBRARY OF CONGRESS CATALOGING IN PUBLICATION DATA

Main entry under title:

Oratory in the New South.

  Bibliography: p.
  Includes index.
    1. American orations—Southern States—History
and criticism—Addresses, essays, lectures.
  2. American orations—19th century—History
and criticism—Addresses, essays, lectures
  3. Southern States—Politics and government—
1865–1950—Addresses, essays, lectures.
  I. Braden, Waldo Warder, 1911–
PS407.069   815'.4'09   78–25909
ISBN 0–8071–0472–8

Contents

Acknowledgments

We are indebted to many persons: to the historians for insightful discussions and bibliographies; to Dallas Dickey, first to call attention to southern public address, for inspiration; and to our departmental associates who assisted us in many ways.

I am particularly indebted to my graduate students who participated in my seminars in southern oratory and who have written theses and dissertations under my direction. They have been patient with me as I have struggled in lectures and conversations to clarify my views of the period. They have alerted me to valuable sources and have shared their insights and findings. They have served as willing readers of the essays as they have gone through revision. I have often turned to Harold D. Mixon, always available in a nearby office, for counsel and direction.

I wish to thank Harold Barrett of California State University at Hayward for granting me permission to reprint my essay. Bert Bradley received a research grant from the University of North Carolina at Chapel Hill, and Annette Shelby received one from the University of Alabama. John Pennybacker, chairman of the department of speech at Louisiana State University, has given me considerable support. The staff of Louisiana State University Press has encouraged and helped us. Of course, I could not have completed the editing without the aid of Patricia Webb Robinson, my research assistant, and Virginia Steely, my secretary. Many others have assisted. We extend to all of these persons our appreciation.

WALDO W. BRADEN

Oratory in the New South

Introduction

Upon hearing about the possibility of this book, a professional colleague seriously inquired, "Tell me, what is there to talk about besides Booker T. Washington and Henry W. Grady?" Likewise in his comprehensive *History of Public Speaking in America* (1965), Robert T. Oliver was equally selective and chose to discuss only the same two men. These two reactions are typical views of postwar southern public address. Obviously there must have been many other orators who deserve study and analysis. Who were they? How did they meet the challenges of a defeated society? What does their speaking reveal about southern life? These and similar questions need answers.

This book is a continuation of the project started with the publication of the volume *Oratory in the Old South* (1970). Moving beyond the scope of the first study that covered the years from 1830 to 1860, the present essays look critically at the speaking of the New South (1870–1910). In this context the term *New South* designates a period of time more than a theme or a movement. The contributors focus on speaking that occurred before audiences within the South; hence little is said about how southerners performed before national gatherings, spoke in the United States Congress, or made lecture tours in the North.[1]

The editor has not attempted to impose any predetermined

1. Huber W. Ellingsworth, "Southern Reconciliation Orators in the North, 1868–1899" (Ph.D. dissertation, Florida State University, 1955).

structure or to force the essays into a single mold or to dictate any specific approach to rhetorical criticism. The contributors have set their own courses, but they, of course, have worked within a historical-rhetorical context. Each essay is historical in the sense that it is presented against the backdrop of the unfolding events of the time. It is rhetorical in that it considers public address or oratory.

The word *rhetoric* and the related phrase *rhetorical criticism* may need clarification for some readers. In the present context *rhetoric* is used in its traditional sense to mean the total process of persuasion, and is not limited to language usage or style. In the words of Donald C. Bryant, these terms refer to "the function of adjusting ideas to people and people to ideas."[2] The writer who hopes to qualify as the rhetorical critic investigates how speakers influenced attitudes, thoughts, feelings, and actions. He seeks to assess the speaker as an oral communicator. He may view the orator as a causal force that shapes or directs the course of human events. Or he may study the speaker's rhetoric as a reflection of what listeners want to hear. In making conscious choices, a speaker may respond to feedback and express what is consistent with popular inclinations and prejudices. From this second vantage point speeches provide insight into sociopolitical forces at work and hence into the intellectual and social thought of a period.[3]

The editor has included the first essay to set a theoretical framework for the later presentations and to provide an overview of the public address in the postwar South. To characterize the theme of the period he offers the word *accommodation*. The postwar southern speakers encountered many difficult problems of spirit and morale. They faced listeners whose self

2. Donald C. Bryant, "Aspects of the Rhetorical Tradition: The Intellectual Foundation," *Quarterly Journal of Speech*, XXXVI (April, 1950), 169–76.
3. Ernest J. Wrage, "Public Address: A Study in Social and Intellectual History," *Quarterly Journal of Speech*, XXXIII (December, 1947), 451–57.

concepts and political confidence had been seriously weakened. Furthermore, they had to comply with and cater to outside forces that could coerce, withhold capital for rebuilding, and even exert military pressure. Not free to express their deep feelings or to propose change in policy, they were forced to accommodate. In contrast to the prewar mode of deliberative (i.e., legislative) oratory that considered interpretations of the Constitution and the nature of the Union, many southerners after the war turned to ceremonial speaking because it was safe and it was in demand. Consistent with pressure from within and without, much of this speaking was directed toward creating, promoting, and sanctifying composite social myths,[4] namely those of the Old South, the Lost Cause, the Solid South, white supremacy, and the New South.

Only one of the essays attempts a study of the speaking centered in Reconstruction and Redemption. Perhaps no southern state had a more intriguing or complex story of the "road to reunion" than that of Georgia. Cal M. Logue presents a case study of how certain Georgians battled for leadership, regained state control, and firmly entrenched themselves. He gives special attention to Joseph E. Brown and John B. Gordon, who, moving from different positions, joined forces after 1871 and manipulated their persuasion for home consumption. With others they thereby monopolized the principal political offices in state government and in Washington and dominated business and industry. This climate produced Henry W. Grady.

Picking up the story, Harold Mixon devotes a single essay to Grady. Mixon presents the Atlanta editor as "a rhetorical strategist, an adept practitioner of the rhetoric of accommodation." In a sense Grady holds a special place in the New South similar to that which John C. Calhoun held in the Old South. Through

4. See Waldo W. Braden, "Myths in a Rhetorical Context," *Southern Speech Communication Journal*, XL (Winter, 1975), 113–26.

his editorials in the Atlanta *Daily Constitution* and , more important, through a comparatively small number of speeches[5] delivered in a three-year span (1886–1889), Grady propagandized for the New South on both sides of the Mason and Dixon line. Eminently successful, he became the symbol of reconciliation. Hence today his after dinner speech "The New South," delivered before the New England Society of New York, December 21, 1886, is one of the few southern orations of the period to appear in anthologies.

A foremost motivation of speakers in the New South was to restore the self-image of southerners. The oratory of accommodation prevailed at memorial days, reunions, dedications of monuments, and even in academic assemblies. From these platforms former Confederate generals and politicians gave full vent to rationalizing defeat, to praising heroes, to soothing bruised egos, and to inculcating the young with the romanticism of the Old South and the Lost Cause. Historians, literature teachers, and rhetorical critics are likely to dismiss this genre as excessive, sterile, and ephemeral, but these speakers filled their speeches with what southern listeners craved. W. Stuart Towns discusses how the materials generally thought to be means to further the "cult of the southerner" were actually employed to bring reconciliation closer to reality. In direct contrast, Howard Dorgan studies how speakers who addressed the United Confederate Veterans played upon emotions and sentiment, rationalized the defeat of Confederate arms, and set the myths more firmly into southern consciousness. The two essays reveal the rhetorical strategies of speakers, long forgotten, but most popular in the eighties and nineties: John B. Gordon, John Warwick Daniel, David M. Key, John Temple Graves, John Reagan, William B. Bate, and Thomas M. Logan. These men contributed much to the emerging image of the stereo-

5. Henry W. Grady, *The New South: Writings and Speeches* (Savannah, Ga.: Beehive Press, 1971).

typed southern orator who was known for grandiloquent language, expansive voice, and impassioned delivery.

Discussing in turn blacks, women, and educators, the last three essays uncover certain cross currents that commenced to appear around 1900. Many of these speakers, unhappy with rationalization and eulogies of a dimming past, began to turn away from accommodation and advocate positive programs for social and political change.

No study of the southern public address of this period would be complete without a consideration of Booker T. Washington. Similar to Grady, Washington also became a symbol of the prevailing accommodation, for he publicly accepted an inferior role for Negroes in his efforts to promote his immediate goals. He gained a friendly hearing in the North and the South alike because he provided a point of view that permitted the easing of conscience and stabilizing of race relations. Perhaps no southerner had as much to do with improving the lot of his people as did Washington. But the passing years and improving race relations have cast a shadow over the contribution of the Alabama educator. To provide perspective, Danny Champion contrasts the accommodation of Washington with the defiance of Du Bois. The compassion, patience, and rhetorical effectiveness of Washington stand out in bold relief against the bitterness and anger of his rival.

Scant attention has been given to women speakers of any time or period. Annette Shelby discusses the rise of southern female speakers such as Belle Kearney, Rebecca Latimer Felton, Caroline Merrick, and Julia Tutwiler. The predominant mode of women speakers was ceremonial and as myth-filled as other speaking, but their rhetoric for reform, less prevalent, was more significant in impact. Their adherence to the rhetoric of accommodation had a peculiar twist in that they had to bear indignities and to accommodate their rhetoric to a male-dominated society.

Not all southern speakers felt the compulsion to appeal to the past. With the fading of war memories young, promising leaders, mainly in education, began to demand a hearing. Concentrating upon North Carolina, Bert Bradley discusses the campaigns of Charles B. Aycock, Edwin A. Alderman, and Charles D. McIver, who fought to improve public education in their state and subsequently throughout the South. Bradley's study is indicative of the beginnings of other reform movements.

Many of the speakers of the New South, in facing a defeated people and in coping with pressure and coercion from without, limited their scope and hence the resources upon which they drew and clothed their themes. Regardless of what group is considered, a reader encounters commonality in theme, in supporting material, in language, in visual symbols, and in manner. In short, the postwar southern speakers sounded and acted alike.

In the judgment of this writer (but perhaps not some of the other contributors) these postwar southerners bear a good deal of the responsibility for the uncomplimentary stereotype of the southern orator.[6] Granted that what they said stirred immediate applause and excitement at the moment of utterance, what remains on the cold, printed page now seems trite and insignificant. Herein lies the explanation for why Henry W. Grady and Booker T. Washington are remembered and still quoted. They were more in tune with themes that survived, and what they said had national appeal. In their speeches Americans outside the South found what they wanted to hear as rationalizations and reconciliation.

The opening paragraphs of this essay suggests that speeches

6. See Waldo W. Braden, "The Emergence of the Concept of Southern Oratory," *Southern Speech Journal*, XXVI (Spring, 1961), 173–83, and Waldo W. Braden, "Southern Oratory Reconsidered: A Search for an Image," *Southern Speech Journal*, XXIX (Summer, 1964), 303–315.

expose social and political aspirations. The oratory of the New South suggests why the "cult of the southerner" developed into a strong subculture in the United States. The oft-repeated myths, high in emotional content, gave the southerners a brace of distinction—a kind of nationalism. Once created, the common symbols, rhetorical and visual, took on power and prestige so strong that they defied challenge and made many southerners impervious to certain kinds of social change until well after 1950. Southerners too long repined "over an irrevocable past."

I

Repining over an Irrevocable Past: The Ceremonial Orator in a Defeated Society, 1865–1900*

George B. Tindall urges southern historians to "seek to unravel the tangled genealogy of the myth in order to understand the intellectual history of the South." He argues that "few areas of the modern world . . . have bred a regional mythology so potent, so profuse and diverse, even so paradoxical, as the American South" and that the "various mythical images of the South" should be subjected to a "kind of broad and imaginative historical analysis."[1]

Tindall's advice to the historian has equal significance to the rhetorical critic who deals with one of the chief purveyors of myths: the orator. In this context, wrote Richard Hofstadter, the concept of myth implies "an idea . . . that so effectively embodies men's values that it profoundly influences their way of perceiving reality and hence their behavior. In this sense myth may have varying degrees of fiction or reality."[2] Carefully attuned to sentiments and attitudes of his listeners, the skillful speaker knows the value of incorporating and enlarging the commonly held legends which fuse facts and dreams and often border on fantasy. The belief in certain "mind pictures of his world or of the larger world around him—images that he wants to believe" permitted the southerner to forget and to

---

* This essay was originally published in *Rhetoric of the People*, edited by Harold Barrett (Amsterdam: Rodopi N.V., 1974). Quoted by permission.

1. George B. Tindall, "Southern Mythology," in Dewey W. Grantham (ed.), *The South and the Sectional Image* (New York: Harper and Row, 1967), 9.
2. Richard Hofstadter, *The Age of Reform* (New York: Knopf, 1955), 24.

view the present and the future in a more favorable light. At times this shift in attitude, according to southern historian T. Harry Williams, approached "an ideal dream-world in the past."[3]

I

The postwar South provided a congenial climate in which to exploit the myth. A defeated people, romantically inclined, were seeking a balm for their bruised egos. They could not understand why they were defeated and how they had failed. When they had gaily marched off to fight the Yankees, many southerners thought of themselves as knights, pursuing a holy cause, saving the Constitution, states' rights and the southern way of life. Confident that the God of Hosts was on their side, they had ardently believed that within a few short months they could demolish an enemy made up of what they thought were clerks and foreign-born, naïve draftees led by second-class officers. They had long heard their preachers and politicians tell them that they were superior, a chosen people. They had little reason to doubt their leaders. What they thought was to be a brief romantic adventure turned into four, long, desperate years of carnage that brought fighting deep into the South. Few had escaped privation. Henry W. Grady was quite correct when he pictured the returning Confederate soldier as "ragged, half-starved, heavy-hearted, enfeebled by want and wound." Equally true is Grady's picture of what awaited the returning soldier at home:

He finds his house in ruins, his farm devastated, his slaves free, his stock killed, his barns empty, his trade destroyed, his money worthless; his social system, feudal in its magnificence, swept away; his people without law or legal status, his comrades slain, and the bur-

3. T. Harry Williams, *Romance and Realism in Southern Politics* (Athens, Ga.: University of Georgia Press, 1961), 4–9.

dens of others heavy on his shoulders. Crushed by defeat, his very traditions are gone; without money, credit, employment, material or training; and, besides all this confronted with the gravest problem that ever met human intelligence—the establishing of a status for the vast body of his liberated slaves.[4] (New York, December 21, 1886).

For fifteen years after defeat in war, gloom and despair dominated the South. According to Richard M. Weaver, southerners as a whole "were left groping for an explanation of why their best had failed." Touring the area in 1879 and 1880, Whitelaw Reid said that the South "still sits crushed, wretched, busy displaying and bemoaning her wounds." Cities like Charleston, Galveston, Mobile, Norfolk, New Orleans, Savannah, Wilmington, and New Bern remained dilapidated and desolated.[5] But the scars left by opposing armies fighting across the land disappeared with time. Wrecked property was rebuilt. Far more catastrophic than any physical losses was the destruction of the southerner's view of himself. Shattered dreams, ideals, sentiments, beliefs, and life-styles were not easily recovered or replaced. Hatreds and animosities were intense and remained so for a hundred years. Reestablishing cordial ties with Yankees was humiliating and difficult, and giving allegiance to the federal government was equally galling.

In the excellent essay on Daniel Webster, Wilbur Samuel Howell and Hoyt Hopewell Hudson say that the Massachusetts senator through his ceremonial speaking gave "to his youthful country what it most needed—heroes, shibboleths, and myths.

4. Henry W. Grady, *The New South: Writings and Speeches* (Savannah, Ga.: Beehive Press, 1971), 7.

5. Richard M. Weaver, *The Southern Tradition at Bay: A History of Postbellum Thought*, ed. by George Core and M. E. Bradford (New Rochelle, N.Y.: Arlington House, 1968), 178; New York *Tribune*, October 3, 1879, and August 16, 1880, quoted by C. Vann Woodward in *Origins of the New South, 1877–1913* (Baton Rouge: Louisiana State University Press, 1951), 107, Vol. IX of ten volumes in Wendell Holmes Stephenson and E. Merton Coulter (eds.), *A History of the South*.

... Webster's superiority lay ... in strength of imagination."[6] Herein these two writers point to an oratorical function that is sometimes forgotten; that is, the orator may find that it is more important and desirable to strengthen attitudes and sentiments than to attempt the change of opinions or the implementation of courses of action. For some occasions such as those in the postwar South, the speaker may have only this option.

In contrast to antebellum public address that involved the important issues of the region and nation, the postwar speakers discovered that on many occasions deliberative speaking was pointless, particularly when federal authorities or carpetbagger governments, backed by federal troops, imposed and implemented decisions. Speakers often had to accommodate their proposals to what was acceptable or inoffensive to those who held power. Vote buying, rigged elections, intimidation, coercion, frequent alignment of party factions, harassment by klansmen, tight control by small cliques, and finally disfranchisement of Negroes (especially in the 1890s) were frequently substituted for argument and rational deliberation.[7] Public debate was unimportant when decisions were made beyond public view.

Under these conditions, speakers of the South had left to them as an approach to their listeners what Aristotle has called epideictic speeches or those of praise or blame. Instead of argument, supported by evidence, authority, and rationality, speak-

6. Wilbur Samuel Howell and Hoyt Hopewell Hudson, "Daniel Webster," in William Norwood Brigance (ed.), *A History and Criticism of American Public Address* (2 vols.; New York: McGraw-Hill, 1943), II, 677.

7. Charles Porterfield, "A Rhetorical-Historical Analysis of the Third Party Movement in Alabama, 1890–1894" (Ph.D. dissertation, Louisiana State University, 1965); William I. Hair, *Bourbonism and Agrarian Protest: Louisiana Politics, 1877–1900* (Baton Rouge: Louisiana State University Press, 1969), Chapts. 10 and 11; William Warren Rogers, *The One-Gallused Rebellion: Agrarianism in Alabama, 1865–1896* (Baton Rouge: Louisiana State University Press, 1970); Woodward, *Origins of the New South*, Chapts. 9 and 10.

ers had to turn to their imaginations and build "heroes, shibbo-leths, and myths," intensifying themes through amplification, emotional loading, and appeals to sentiment.

As a central concern, this paper is directed toward a consideration of how the ceremonial orators of the South from 1865 through 1900 attempted to cope with the problems of people in a defeated society. Following Tindall's advice, the writer will analyze how the orators as myth makers encouraged their constituents to retreat into "an ideal dream-world of the past" largely through the development, promotion, and exploitation of four great myths, which may be referred to as those of (1) the Old South, (2) the Lost Cause, (3) the Solid South, and (4) the New South.

II

"The legend of the Old South," according to T. Harry Williams, is "the most appealing and the most enduring" of the mind pictures of the southerner.[8] Much was said about great plantations, the patriarchal master, the genteel lady, and, of course, the happy slaves. After the war, white southerners regardless of position or status commonly accepted the Old South image. Even the poor whites and yeoman farmers dreamed of being a part of the patriarchal aristocracy; it was vogue to associate one's past with a great family, never admitting, of course, that one's forebears might have come from a lower stratum. Families might experience poverty and privation, but they attempted to hold fast to a plantation connection and keep up the appearance of a continuation of the romantic life of a grandfather or even a distant relative. Quite obviously those who found the present unbearable and the future unpromising retreated to the romantic past and preferred to live in fantasy.

Finding the myth of the Old South one of the easiest to arouse

8. T. Harry Williams, *Romance and Realism*, 6.

among the southern people, orators frequently alluded to it in their speeches. Robert Love Taylor, politician, editor, and lecturer from Tennessee,[9] inserted into his lecture "The Old Plantation" the full-blown representation of what his listeners liked to hear:

There, half hidden in the groves of live oaks and magnolia trees, where the mocking birds chuckled and laughed, and the twittering bluebirds built their nests, stood the white-columned mansion of the master, where life reached the high tide of baronial splendor. And stretching away to the horizon were the cotton fields, alive with the toiling slaves, who, without a single care to burden their hearts, sang as they toiled from early morn till close of day. Every sunrise of summer was greeted by the laughter and songs of the darkies as they gathered in gangs and went forth in every direction to begin the labors of the day, and the music floated back to the mansion to sweeten the morning dreams of the drowsy lords and ladies who still rested on their pillows.[10]

In his most popular lecture, "Dixie," delivered many times in both the North and the South, Taylor rhapsodized:

I never shall forget the white-columned mansions rising in cool, spreading groves, where the roses bloomed, and the orange trees waved their sprays of snowy blossoms, and the gay palms shook their feathery plumes.

I have seen pomp and pride revel in banquet halls and feast on the luxuries of every zone. I have heard the soft, voluptuous swell of music, where youth and jeweled beauty swayed and floated in the mazes of the misty dance under glittering chandeliers. There I have seen the lords and ladies of the plantation, mounted on their thoroughbreds, fleet as the wind, dash away like phantoms in the forest in pursuit of the fleeing fox, where the music of the running hounds rose and fell and fell and rose from hill to hollow and from hollow to hill like the

9. My attention was called to Taylor by Raymond W. Buchanan, Jr., who completed under my direction a dissertation entitled "The Epideictic Speaking of Robert Love Taylor Between 1891 and 1906" (Louisiana State University, 1970).

10. Robert Love Taylor, *Lectures and Best Literary Productions* (Nashville, Tenn.: Bob Taylor Publishing Co., 1913), 152–53.

chiming of a thousand bells. Cotton was king and sat upon the ebony throne of slavery. Every day was a link in the golden chain of pleasure.[11]

It was not necessary for an orator to give an extended treatment of a myth in order to invoke the image. For example, Henry Grady and Henry Watterson, more urbane and less saccharine, often stirred memories of the old regime through mention of the cavalier, the southern lady, the happy darky, the snowy cotton fields, or some symbol of the aristocratic mystique. When he spoke of the Negro, Grady suggested the past:

I want no better friend than the black boy who was raised by my side, and who is now trudging patiently with downcast eyes and shambling figure through his lowly way in life. I want no sweeter music than the crooning of my old "mammy," now dead and gone to rest, as I heard it when she held me in her loving arms, and bending her old black face above me stole the cares from my brain, and led me smiling into sleep. I want no truer soul than that which moved the trusty slave, who for four years, while my father fought with the armies that barred his freedom, slept every night at my mother's chamber door, holding her and her children as safe as if her husband stood guard, and ready to lay down his humble life on her threshold.[12] (Boston, December 12, 1889)

The following samples of epideictic rhetoric suggest how easily the Old South myth was activated by a reference to chivalry, an institution, a name, or a sign of the bygone days:

The time will come when the South will build a monument to the old-time black man-servant for his fidelity and devotion.[13]

The blood of one of these men of the Old South shed on yonder fateful field.[14]

No age or country has ever produced a civilization of a nobler type than that which was born in the southern plantation home.[15]

11. *Ibid.*, 166.
12. Grady, *The New South*, 17–18.
13. Taylor, *Lectures*, 169.
14. J. H. McNeilly, "By Graves of Confederate Dead," *Confederate Veteran*, II (September, 1894), 265.
15. John B. Gordon, *The Old South* (Augusta, Ga.: Chronicle, 1887), 7.

What friend of human progress would have deprived him [the Negro] in his original helplessness of the patriarchal care and kind government of the southern master and of holy teaching of southern Christian women upon the southern plantations.[16]

On one side . . . was the South, led by descendants of the Cavaliers.[17]

This constant and growing consciousness of nobleness and justice and chivalry of the Confederate cause . . . constitutes the success.[18]

Shall the blood of the old South—the best strain that ever uplifted human endeavor . . . for the first time falter and be driven back?[19] (Dallas, October 26, 1887)

A kindly, hospitable faithful man was he of the old South, with all the virtues of a rural almost patriarchal, aristocracy.[20]

An artist at weaving references to the past into his speaking, John B. Gordon, a lecturer, senator, and commander of the United Confederate Veterans, found enthusiastic welcomes wherever he chose to speak. He was masterful at establishing common ground and gaining sympathy for the South. In his best-known lecture, entitled "The Last Days of the Confederacy,"[21] Gordon pulled together a series of touching stories in order to "strengthen the sentiment of national fraternity." To cement good feeling between "victors and vanquished," Gordon emphasized how a noble spirit prevailed even during fierce

16. *Ibid.*, 8.
17. R. C. Cave, "Honoring the Private Soldier," *Confederate Veteran*, II (June, 1894), 162–64. Speech delivered May 30, 1894, Richmond, Va.
18. Bradley T. Johnson, "Placing Principle Above Policy," *Confederate Veteran*, V (October, 1897), 507–509.
19. Grady, *The New South*, 37.
20. William Preston Johnston, *Problems of Southern Civilization: An Address Delivered Before the Polytechnic Institute of Alabama, Wednesday, June 10, 1891* (n.p., n.d.), 9.
21. John B. Gordon, "The Last Days of the Confederacy," in Ashley H. Thorndike (ed.), *Modern Eloquence* (15 vols.; New York: Modern Eloquence Corp., 1923), VIII, 169–91. John B. Gordon to George Moorman, April 13, 1895, in the Army of Tennessee Department, United Confederate Veterans Collection, Louisiana State University Archives. It indicates that Gordon delivered this lecture twelve times between March 16 and April 17, 1895. In 1897, he delivered it nine times between March 22 and May 11, 1897.

fighting. A careful reading of Gordon's recitation shows that the Confederate pictured was indeed the romantic figure of the feudal South. Gordon endowed his characters with knightly qualities: courage, compassion, valor, patriotism, respect for women, deep religious feeling, and generosity.

How did the Old South myth serve the persuader? Any answer to this question must, of course, be speculative because of the nebulous nature of the myth, which could affect different people in various ways. But through this particular legend the persuaders were able to develop what Kenneth Burke called consubstantiality, a feeling of oneness or identification.[22] In contrast to the antebellum years when persons often identified more closely with their states, thinking of themselves as Virginians, Georgians, or Texans, now increasing numbers regardless of class or locality spoke of themselves as southerners. The Old South myth permitted southerners to think of themselves as a group apart from other Americans, possessing romantic qualities of a plantation culture.

The power of the myth was that it focused attention on the romantic past, drawing thoughts away from frustration and discouragement. It picked up momentum, of course, when uttered by a prominent personage who had gained fame before the war or who had won acclaim in battle. Former generals and Confederate leaders became living signs of the myth. This myth drew little opposition from within or from without. Even carpetbaggers and young leaders soon became eager to identify with the legend. As the years passed it became romantic and seductive even to northerners who avidly read novels and saw movies about the South. No better representation of the Old South myth can be found than in the novel and later movie *Gone with the Wind*.

22. Kenneth Burke, *A Rhetoric of Motives* (New York: Prentice-Hall, 1953), 21.

III

The second myth frequently used in the postwar period was that of the Lost Cause or the fantasy that soon developed around the demise of the Confederacy. On every side former Confederates encountered signs of their humiliation. Defeat in the field was a severe blow to cherished beliefs concerning superiority. The orator's task, therefore, was to provide escape from guilt and to restore self-respect and self-confidence. Certain accusations repeated often in the newspapers and from the platform were particularly galling to the "hero in gray with the heart of gold" (Grady's phrase). For example, he squirmed at the implication that he had fought for an institution now universally considered immoral—slavery. The label of *traitor* was equally embarrassing. The insinuations that southerners had mistreated Union prisoners and that Jefferson Davis was guilty of treason demanded answers. As the memories of the actual battles dimmed, the participants and their relatives provided more favorable views of the sacrifice of the war years.

Considerable attention has been given to those speakers who accepted speaking invitations in the North—particularly Grady, Watterson, and Gordon, who urged reconciliation, pled for forgetting the past, and concentrated upon establishing common ground where the two sides could meet. In his excellent dissertation, Howard Dorgan clearly demonstrates that these speakers were not typical of the former Confederates who spoke in the South.[23] For disheartened southerners, the speaker had to invent rationalizations that would turn despair into hope and would counter disparagement. Filling these assignments, Con-

23. For much of what I say about the Lost Cause I am indebted to Dorgan, who completed a dissertation under my direction, entitled, "Southern Apologetic Themes, As Expressed in Selected Ceremonial Speaking of Confederate Veterans, 1889–1900" (Ph.D. dissertation, Louisiana State University, 1971).

federate generals and politicians spoke at reunions, dedications of cemeteries and battlefields, funerals, and patriotic gatherings.[24] After its organization in the 1890s, the United Confederate Veterans (UCV) played an active role in arranging these meetings. Much consubstantiality already existed where the participants assembled; consequently, the speaker, aware that rational explanations were unnecessary, gave full range to the amplification of myths.

The themes interwoven into the Lost Cause myth were complex and tangled. The speaker naturally praised the heroism of the soldiers and the self-sacrifice of the home folks, particularly "the martyr-heroine . . . the woman—mother, sister, lover, who gave her life and heart to the cause." In these oratorical flights the participants—gentlemen and Cavaliers—were credited with the qualities of knighthood and chivalry. Listen to General Bradley T. Johnson bring knighthood to life:

> It is this constant and growing consciousness of the nobleness and justice and chivalry of the Confederate cause which constitutes the success and illuminates the triumph we commemorate today. Evil dies, good lives; and the time will come when all the world will realize that the failure of the Confederacy was a great misfortune to humanity and will be the source of unnumbered woes to liberty. . . . This great and noble cause, the principles of which I have attempted to formulate for you, was defended with a genius and a chivalry of men and women never equaled by any race.
> But, while I glorify the chivalry, the fortitude, and the fidelity of the private soldier, I do not intend to minimize the valor, the endurance, or the gallantry of those who led them. I know that the knights of Arthur's Round Table, or the paladine and peers, roused by the blast of that Fuenterrabia horn from Roland at Roncesvalles, did not equal in manly traits, in nobility of character, in purity of soul, in gallant, dashing courage, the men who led.[25]

24. Dorgan isolates ten speakers whom he considers typical of the movement: John Henninger Reagan, Stephen Dill Lee, John Brown Gordon, William Brimage Bate, Edward Cary Walthall, Bradley Tyler Johnson, Clement Anselm Evans, Jabez Lamar Monroe Curry, John Warwick Daniel, Benjamin Morgan Palmer. He actually quotes from thirty orators in all.

25. Johnson, "Placing Principle Above Policy," 508.

Below are some additional examples of how the myth of the Lost Cause became the standard means of amplification at dedications and reunions:

Our American civil war was an advance in the cause of liberty.[26]

Sometimes defeat gives a tragic pathos which lifts the commonplace into the immortal.[27]

It is a joy to the South that its great typical figures . . . such as Davis, Lee, and Jackson were men who wore the white flower of a blameless life.[28]

Every lover of constitutional liberty . . . all over the world begins to understand that the war was not a war waged by the South in defense of slavery but . . . to protect liberty won an bequeathed.[29]

The war of the South was a war of self defense. . . . Not one man in a thousand in the Confederate army had any property interest in slavery. Every man had a home and a mother.[30]

Poorly equipped, poorly clad, poorly fed . . . they confronted at least three times their number.[31]

The Southern troops . . . merited tribute when he [a Pennsylvania farmer] said of them: "I must say they acted like gentlemen."[32]

I need not name him [Lee] for his name is written in ever-enduring letters throughout the civilized world.[33]

Tell me not that the cause is lost when hosts of Americans are marshalling in defense of these rights and that flag . . . of the old Confederates typifies the fight.[34]

26. John B. Gordon, "The Chickamauga Battlefield Dedication," New York Times, September 20, 1895, p. 3.
27. Stephen D. Lee, "A Noble Tribute to President Jefferson Davis," in Minutes of Sixth Annual Meeting and Reunion of the United Confederate Veterans (1896), 155.
28. Ibid., 158.
29. Johnson, "Placing Principle Above Policy," 507.
30. Ibid., 509.
31. Cave, "Honoring the Private Soldier," 163.
32. Ibid., 163.
33. Ibid., 164.
34. George Clark, "Reunion of Texas Veterans at Waco," Confederate Veteran, II (April, 1894), 122.

The cause is triumphant and the Confederate soldier will go down into history occupying the proud page he should occupy.[35]

It was defensive and not offensive war. The Confederates asked to be let alone—only that.[36]

Into this type of speech speakers frequently inserted such words as *fortitude, fidelity, valor, endurance, gallantry, nobility,* and *purity.* As symbols, heroes were much a part of the legend. Robert E. Lee, Stonewall Jackson, and Jefferson Davis were canonized and held up as the personification of the Confederate spirit. William C. P. Breckinridge said, "Lee . . . was a great captain and pure gentleman; Jackson . . . was a Christian soldier of superb gifts and stainless life."[37] Davis soon became a martyr because of his imprisonment and the denial of his citizenship.

But hero worship and accounts of the battles of the war were insufficient to counter disillusionment. What was needed was a positive stand to succor self-respect and confidence. A burning question was what interpretation would posterity—particularly their own children—place upon the struggle. Southerners craved rationalizations to explain that the war was not fought to preserve immoral slavery. Many admitted publicly that emancipation was desirable and that the South was better off without the peculiar institution. But this admission made more important a justification of the four years' fighting and sacrifice, a device that let the southerner regard defeat as victory. Judge George Clark made this point clear:

It is sometimes said that our cause is lost. Some causes are never lost. They may be crushed in defeat, they may go down in seeming

35. *Ibid.,* 123.
36. William B. Bate, "Word for the South," *Confederate Veteran,* III (November, 1895), 344.
37. William C. P. Breckinridge, "Who Were the Confederate Dead?" in Thomas Watson (ed.), *History of Southern Oratory* (Richmond, Va.: Southern Historical Publication Society, 1909), 418–40.

ignominy, but in the end, like truth crushed to earth, they rise again. The Confederate soldier is always and under all circumstances true to principle. There was no selfishness in his heart, no thought of the morrow with him. He put all upon his country's altar, and went forth and gave his time and his heart and his life to the cause. What did that cause represent? I said it was not lost, and I repeat the assertion. It could not be lost.[38]

To accomplish what seemed an almost impossible reversal of positions, the speaker shifted ground and magnified certain virtues. To move away from charges concerning the defense of an immoral institution, the apologists argued that the South's primary goal had not been to preserve slavery but to preserve liberty, freedom, the Constitution, and the Union. Likewise they argued that the southerner struggled to protect and preserve benefits for the Anglo-Saxon race. Closely related to these themes were the assertions that the Yankee traders had brought slaves to the South for profit. Furthermore, the southerner had Christianized and civilized the ignorant blacks and had produced a superior way of life. In other words, the slave users were less guilty than the slave traders. William Preston Johnston, at the time president of Tulane University, said in a commencement address at the Polytechnic Institute of Alabama, June 10, 1891:

Apply this test. A barbarous, yea, a savage race, heathens and cannibals to this day in their own land, as travelers tell us. . . . superstitious and cruel. . . . We have inspired a static race, and converted it into a progressive one.[39]

Involved herein was the shift of blame to the enemy and the laying claim to virtues.

The magnification of virtues of course provided a means to dismiss defeat. A whole series of enthymemes was developed around the position that the defeat was God's way to test the

38. Clark, "Reunion of Texas Veterans at Waco," 122.
39. Johnston, *Problems of Southern Civilization*, 7.

character and Christianity of the southern people. Many speakers found parallels between the Christian martyrdom and the misfortune of southerners. Said one speaker, "I believe that God brings such crises into the history of nations and into the lives of men to test them."[40] Henry Savage, Jr., observes that the Old South and the Confederacy myths became a religion "replete with unchallengeable tenets, ritual, hallowed saints and sacred shrines. Any criticism, even any factual derogation of those enshrined concepts came to be regarded as blasphemy."[41] The participants in the Lost Cause were declared brave, gallant, pure, law-abiding, and God-fearing; they stood for freedom, the Constitution, and the Anglo-Saxon race. The victors —the enemy—were presented as crass, unprincipled, cruel, unyielding, unwise, and un-Christian; besides, they attacked the South, sold slaves for profit, destroyed the Constitution, and persecuted Jefferson Davis.

IV

A third popular myth prominent in the ceremonial oratory of the period was that of the Solid South. This myth advanced the concept that Anglo-Saxon southerners must stand united in order to meet threats from without and the uprising of the Negroes from within. Another name for or perhaps a dimension of the myth is white supremacy. The excesses of blacks during Reconstruction, the distaste for military occupation, the appearance of the Republican party in Dixie, the Populist campaigns, and finally the threats of a second federal intervention nurtured an atmosphere for this image. The Bourbons, that is agrarian aristocrats, and the Confederate leaders (both often embodied in the same person), found in this myth a means to hold power and thwart reform. The legend was given physical

40. J. H. McNeilly, "By Graves of Confederate Dead," 265.
41. Henry Savage, Jr., *Seeds of Time* (New York: Holt, 1959), 198.

reinforcement by the hooded horseman, the fiery cross, and lynchings.

The myth of the Solid South was not difficult to arouse because of the chaotic conditions that resulted from Reconstruction. Below are some examples:

The South is solid now in a sense not dreamed of in antebellum days.[42] (Augusta, Ga., November 24, 1887)

When the Negro was enfranchised, the South was condemned to solidity as surely as self preservation is the first law of nature.[43]

The question was not whether the negro should be freed or held in servitude, but whether the white man of the South should have the same privileges enjoyed by the white man of the North.[44]

The great crime of the century was emancipation of the negroes. They are an affectionate, trustworthy, race.[45]

But believe me, the Anglo-Saxon race, has set itself, with all its power, to face it [race problem] and to overcome it, to solve it in some way, and in the wisest way.[46]

We have clearly seen that the salvation of this section is in white rule.[47]

Some persons may think that the myth of the Solid South and white supremacy was the creation of local orators in rural Georgia, the Mississippi Delta, and the flat lands of north Louisiana; but such was not the case. The call for the continued dominance of the so-called Anglo-Saxon and suppression of the Negro was the major thesis among the Establishment. In defense of the Solid South, L. Q. C. Lamar told the Senate that

42. Grady, *The New South*, 46.
43. *Ibid.*, 50.
44. Cave, "Honoring the Private Soldier," 162.
45. Johnson, "Placing Principle Above Policy," 509.
46. Thomas Nelson Page, "The Torch of Civilization," in Thomas B. Reed (ed.), *Modern Eloquence* (15 vols.; Philadelphia: John D. Morris, 1900), III, 869.
47. Johnston, *Problems of Southern Civilization*, 11.

southerners were "solid in defense of and for the protection of their civilization, their own society, their own religion against the rule of the incompetent, the servile, the ignorant, and the vicious."[48]

In an address delivered at the Texas State Fair in Dallas, October 26, 1886, Henry W. Grady gave voice to the myth in a full-blown form. To read only the much quoted "New South" speech is to miss what the Atlanta editor said to fellow Southerners. In New York, exuding charm and good humor, Grady told his Yankee listeners what they wanted to hear. But Richard M. Weaver, a fellow southerner, observes that when one examines the whole body of the utterances of Jefferson Davis and Grady, "he finds that they stood fairly close together in support of orthodox Southern ideals."[49] This statement is not surprising when it is remembered that Grady was the spokesman for and allied with the dominant white political faction in Georgia —John B. Gordon, Joseph E. Brown, and Alfred H. Colquitt, sometimes called the "Bourbon Triumvirate."[50]

Consistent with his interests, Grady knew the power of the myth of the Solid South. At Dallas, Texas, Grady argued:

The worst thing, in my opinion, that could happen is that the white people of the South should stand in opposing factions, with the vast mass of ignorant or purchasable votes between. Consider such a status. If the negroes were skillfully led,—and leaders would not be lacking, —it would give them the balance of power, a thing not to be considered. If their rule was not compacted, it would invite the debauching bid of factions, and drift surely to that which was the most corrupt and cunning. With the shiftless habit and irresolution of slavery days still possessing him, the negro voter will not in this generation, adrift from war issues, become a steadfast partisan through conscience or conviction.

48. Speech delivered to U.S. Senate, April 1, 1881, *Congressional Record*, 47th Cong. Special Sess., 158–59.
49. Weaver, *Southern Tradition at Bay*, 343.
50. Woodward, *Origins of the New South*, 14–15.

He left little doubt of his position a little later, saying:

It is a race issue. . . . There is not a white man, North or South, who does not feel it stir in the gray matter of his brain and throb in his heart, not a negro who does not feel its power. . . . It speaks wherever the Anglo-Saxon touches an alien race. . . . The Anglo-Saxon blood has dominated always and everywhere.

Grady put his argument for white supremacy boldly when he said:

But the supremacy of the white race of the South must be maintained forever, and the domination of the negro race resisted at all points and at all hazards, because the white race is the superior race. . . . The races and tribes of earth are of divine origin. Behind the laws of men and the decrees of war, stands the law of God. What God hath separated let no man join together. The Indian, the Malay, the negro, the Caucasian, these types stand as markers of God's will. Let no man tinker with the work of the Almighty.[51]

Throughout the speech the Atlanta editor reinforced his position by incorporating the Old South myth, particularly mentioning the happy darky on the old plantation. In spite of urging kindness for and understanding of former slaves, Grady argued for a continuation of the attitudes and values of the Old South. Surprising as it now appears, Booker T. Washington likewise implied that he accepted an inferior role for the blacks.[52] It is true the southern whites, imbued with myths of white supremacy and the Solid South, read meanings into Washington's speeches that the Negro educator probably did not believe, but which he let stand as a means of accommodation.[53]

The power of the myth of the Solid South and its companion white supremacy rested often upon the strategy of fear and terror. "This technique," explain Brembeck and Howell, "seeks to

51. Grady, *The New South*, 47.
52. E. D. Washington (ed.), *Selected Speeches of Booker T. Washington* (New York: Doubleday, 1932), 32–33.
53. Louis R. Harlan, "The Secret Life of Booker T. Washington," *Journal of Southern History*, XXXVII (August, 1971), 393–416.

lessen resistance and gain acceptance by creating anxieties, panic, hysteria, confusion, dissension, and futility."[54] The "nigger," the "nigger lover," the carpetbagger, and scalawag were made the scapegoats. When in an oral form the myth alone failed to produce sufficient response, the orator held up in lurid terms miscegenation and rape.[55] Or, he might repeat overworked rhetorical questions, such as "Would you want your daughter to marry a nigger?" At intensely charged moments such language flaunted before emotionally wrought listeners could turn a peaceful assembly into a lynch mob. When an opponent could not be answered or when he dared challenge the Establishment, he was dismissed as a "nigger lover," or integrationist, or even Yankee. This myth played an important part in the defeat of populism and the delay of educational and social reform.

V

The three myths so far discussed were developed primarily for home consumption: the Old South myth promoted loyalties to the romantic past; the Lost Cause salved hurts and soothed bruised egos associated with defeat; the Solid South and white supremacy, drawing upon the first two, provided a means to destroy dissension that threatened the entrenched leadership. In a sense, this triumvirate drew sustenance from the past and was most effective with persons who had vivid memories of the plantation South and the Confederacy. But the forced re-

54. Winston Lamont Brembeck and William Smiley Howell, *Persuasion: A Means of Social Control* (Englewood Cliffs, N.J.: Prentice-Hall, 1952), 181.

55. Among the most flagrant in intensifying Negrophobia were Pitchfork Ben Tillman and Coleman L. Blease of South Carolina, Tom Watson of Georgia, James K. Vardaman and Theodore Bilbo of Mississippi. A particularly lurid example is Vardaman's 1903 campaign; see William F. Holmes, *The White Chief: James Kimble Vardaman* (Baton Rouge: Louisiana State University Press, 1970), Chap. 5.

turn of the southern states to the Union, the upset of the labor supply and the plantation system, the need for capital to develop resources and industry, and the emergence of a new generation who knew the Old South and the war largely through secondary accounts demanded a different strategy of persuasion; the old myths began to lose vitality in meeting pressures from without and desires for progress from within the region. As a result, ceremonial orators helped to create and promote a fourth myth: the New South.

This fourth myth played a significant role in the oratory of accommodation and reconciliation, for it gave the politicians who came forward after 1885 a means to persuade the Yankee industrialist and banker to risk investments in the South. Furthermore, it served as a means to stir hope of the new generation who had no direct experience with the war and at the same time to sooth the restless farmers and wage earners who flirted with the Populists. In addition, it was useful in starting backfires on the Radical Republicans who continued to wave the bloody shirt and to harass the South through threats in the form of such legislation as Henry Cabot Lodge's "force bill" of 1890.

The phrase New South appeared frequently in newspapers and magazines and on the platform. Referring enthusiastically to the southern development as "a commercial evolution unparalleled in the annals of American progress," a New Orleans editor gave a full-blown version of the myth: "The stagnation of despair has, by some magic transformation, given place to the buoyance of hope, of course, of resolve. The silence of inertia has turned into joyous and thrilling uproar of action. We are a new people. Our land has had a new birth."[56]

Atticus Green Haygood, president of Emory College, developed the theme in his Thanksgiving Day sermon to Emory students

56. New Orleans *Times Democrat*, December 4, 1881.

on November 25, 1880.[57] Endowed with a rugged, courageous constitution, this Methodist minister and former Confederate Army chaplain was a realist who frankly admitted the limitations of the South. Wasting no time in unnecessary lamenting, he told his listeners: "We of the South should both 'thank God and take courage.'" As blessings, he pointed to the progress of the past fifteen years: the restoration of "relations to the general government," and the abolishment of the African slavery. He dared say, "As a people, let us of the South frankly recognize some of the faults and lacks, and try to reform and improve." This advice indeed was strong medicine for 1880. Refusing to advance rationalizations for his listeners, he made a plea for overcoming provincialism and illiteracy, for improvement in character and industrialization. In closing he said:

> There is no reason why the South should be despondent. Let us cultivate industry and economy, observe law and order, practice virtue and justice, walk in truth and righteousness, and press on with strong hearts and good hopes. . . . There is nothing weaker or more foolish than repining over an irrevocable past, except it be despairing of a future to which God invites us. Good friends, this is not 1860, it is 1880. Let us press forward, following the pillar of cloud and of fire always.[58]

Unlike the orations of Grady and others, this speech, positive and realistic, relied little upon myths for power. Perhaps this bold and fearless stance explains why one violent critic wrote of Haygood: "He is today doing the South and his people more harm than even Sherman and his torch."[59] Refusal to listen to men such as Haygood is another indication of why fantasy was more acceptable than realism. Unfortunately, many years would pass before southerners could realistically view their problems.

The New South myth became standard fare of those south-

57. Atticus G. Haygood, *The New South: Thanksgiving Sermon, 1880*, ed. Judson C. Ward (Atlanta: Emory University Press, 1950). Ten thousand copies of the sermon were printed and circulated.
58. *Ibid.*
59. Editorial from Athens (Ga.) *Banner-Watchman* (n.d.) cited in *ibid.*, ix.

erners who journeyed north to encounter Yankee audiences. Some, of course, went forth as missionaries, but others found the lecture fees attractive. Finding the occasions novel, many northern listeners came out of curiosity to hear what a real-live ex-Rebel would say. One of the earliest reconciliation speakers was Benjamin Hill of Georgia, who addressed the Young Men's Democratic Union Club of New York as early as October 6, 1868, and the Society of New York Editors of June 6, 1874.[60] In his excellent dissertation, Huber W. Ellingsworth identified twenty-seven southern reconciliationists who delivered fifty-nine speeches in the North between 1868 and 1899. The great majority of speeches, forty in fact, were presented after 1880 and twenty-six in the final decade of the century.[61] Ellingsworth located fifteen appearances of John B. Gordon, nine of Henry Watterson, four for Fitzhugh Lee, and three each of Wade Hampton and Henry W. Grady. Others who spoke once or twice included Benjamin H. Hill, L. Q. C. Lamar, Alfred H. Colquitt, Simon Bolivar Buchner, William Gordon McCabe, Thomas Nelson Page, Roger Pryor, Joseph Wheeler, and Bennett Young.

The majority of these speeches were delivered at centennials, banquets, fairs, veterans reunions, decoration days, and lyceum meetings. In Congress, L. Q. C. Lamar won acclaim for a eulogy of the once-despised Charles Sumner. John B. Gordon, who led in the number of reconciliation speeches delivered, was in demand for his "The Last Days of the Confederacy." Robert Love Taylor of Tennessee made his pitch with his entertaining piece called "Dixie." Of course no one attracted the acclaim afforded Henry W. Grady for his speech "The New South" delivered to the New England Society in New York, December 21, 1886, and his speech "The Race Problem" de-

60. Benjamin H. Hill, Jr., *Senator Benjamin H. Hill of Georgia: His Life, Speeches and Writings* (Atlanta: T. H. P. Bloodworth, 1893), 320–31.
61. Huber W. Ellingsworth, "Southern Reconciliation Orators in the North, 1868–1899" (Ph.D. dissertation, Florida State University, 1955).

livered in Boston, December, 1889. Among the most urbane, Henry Watterson, editor of the Louisville, *Courier-Journal*, delivered several speeches on the New South theme as well as a eulogy of Abraham Lincoln.

Excellent storytellers, many reconciliationists—particularly Grady and Watterson—knew how to insert humorous stories at tense moments. Very often they spent considerable time in establishing rapport and common ground with their listeners. Eager to win favor, these orators exuding ethos, were polished and good-natured, and were seldom flustered by the chiding of toastmasters. Not even the playing of "Marching through Georgia" could make Grady, for example, forsake his cordiality. His retort that General Sherman was considered "an able man though some people [thought] he [was] a kind of careless man about fire" brought cheers from his listeners and admiration from those at home.

Excellent at adaptation, most of these speakers pursued a common line of development, stressing that war had settled the issues of slavery and disunion, that there were no longer Cavaliers and Puritans, only Americans, that Abraham Lincoln was a typical American, and that harmony prevailed in the South. In the most notable example, Henry W. Grady told the New York group:

> Neither Puritan nor Cavalier long survived such. . . . [They] were lost in the storm of the first Revolution. . . . The typical American . . . has already come . . . from the union of these colonist Puritans and Cavaliers. . . . He who stands as the first typical American . . . [is] Abraham Lincoln. He was the sum of Puritan and Cavalier. . . . He was greater than Puritan, greater than Cavalier, in that he was American.[62] (New York, December 21, 1886)

After referring to the Georgia editor's speech, Henry Watterson advanced this same thought before the same group in 1894 (also at the World's Fair in Chicago, October 21, 1893).

62. Grady, *The New South*, 5.

30

Why, in that great, final struggle between the Puritans and the Cavaliers . . . there had been such a mixing up of Puritan babies and the Cavalier babies during the two or three generations preceding it, that the surviving grandmothers of the combatants could not, except for their uniforms, have picked out their own on any field of battle! . . . and I appeal in the name . . . of that common origin—back both of the Puritan and the Cavalier. . . . Let the dead past . . . bury its dead.[63]

Judge Henry C. Caldwell, a distinguished jurist, gave voice to the same message before the New England Society of St. Louis, December 21, 1895:

The Cavalier learned much that was good from the Puritan and the Puritan learned something from the Cavalier, and they have so mingled together that today there remains neither Cavalier nor Puritan, but in their stead the broad-guage, brave and patriotic American.[64]

Again in 1899, the New England Society of New York heard William Gordon McCabe (1841–1920), Virginia orator, rephrase these same themes:

What you call the puritan spirit, of which you are justly proud, has never, I think, been confined to New England alone; nor do I believe that Virginia can claim exclusive heritage in the gracious and generous qualities of the Cavalier. Isn't it after all, the *American spirit*, differentiated by environment?[65]

As a part of the strategy of reconciliation, southern orators sought financial support to rebuild industry and develop resources—mines, timber, and railroads. Before banquets, Lincoln Day dinners, expositions, unveiling of monuments, and in Congress, they pictured the changes taking place, the prevailing harmony, and progress in education, government, racial relations, agriculture, and industry. This point was centermost

63. Henry Watterson, "The Puritan and the Cavalier," in *The Compromise of Life* (New York: Duffield, 1906), 320.
64. Henry C. Caldwell, "A Blend of Cavalier and Puritan," in *Modern Eloquence* (15 vols.; Philadelphia: John D. Morris, 1900), I, 118.
65. William Gordon McCabe, "Puritan and Cavalier," in Edwin Du Bois Shurter (ed.), *Oratory of the South* (New York: Neal, 1908), 21–22.

in Grady's famous New South speech, but this theme was stated or implied by Alderman, Watterson, Haygood, and Page. Grady quoted Hill, who said: "There was a South of slavery and secession—that South is dead. There is a South of union and freedom —that South, thank God, is living, breathing, growing every hour."

Henry Watterson put the argument as follows:

The whole story of the South may be summed up in a sentence: She was rich, and she lost her riches; she was poor and in bondage; she was set free, and she had to go to work; she went to work, and she is richer than ever before. . . .

The South never knew what independence meant until she was taught by subjection to subdue herself. We lived from hand to mouth. We had debts and our niggers. Under the old system we paid our debts and walloped our niggers. Under the new we pay our niggers and wallop our debts. We have no longer any slaves, but we have no longer any debts, and can exclaim, with the old darky at the camp-meeting, who, whenever he got happy, went about shouting: "Bless the Lord! I'm gittin' fatter and fatter!"[66]

The persuasiveness of this chain of enthymemes developed out of the blending of two attractive myths (Puritan and Cavalier), each greatly revered in its region, into an even more impelling myth (the American). Of course, associating this linkage with the martyred Lincoln ensured acceptance by the northern listeners. At first glance this line might seem to be only an attempt to establish common ground, but it was much more because it moved the listener toward acceptance of a new position. Grady "eloquently proclaimed the new gospel," says Savage, "and attracted nationwide attention . . . and spread abroad the term 'new South' to emphasize the change."[67] Grady's concept was expressed in statements such as these:

66. Henry Watterson, "The New South," in *The Compromise of Life*, 288–93.
67. Savage, *Seeds of Time*, 206.

We have found out that in the summing up the free negro counts more than he did as a slave.[68] (New York, December 21, 1886)

Hardly more is the South profited when, stripping the harvest of her cotton fields, or striking her teeming hills, or leveling her superb forests, she sends her raw material to augment the wealth and power of distant communities.[69] (Dallas, October 26, 1887)

Every man in the sound of my voice, under the deeper consecration he offers to the Union, will consecrate himself to the South.[70] (*Ibid.*)

But, sir, backed by a record on every page of which is progress, I venture to make earnest and respectful answer.[71] (Boston, December 12, 1889)

Many other speakers, of course, spent considerable effort in both the North and the South amplifying the New South image.[72] Below are some examples:

This is especially true here in Alabama, where your vast minerals have invited capital, immigration, manufacturers and railroad and every sort of corporate action, in an unprecedented way.[73]

Overwhelmed by all these calamities, that the people should have been able to reorganize society . . . furnishes the strongest possible proof of the capacity of our people for the preservation of social order and self government, and cannot fail to secure for them the good opinion of the civilized world.[74]

The new robust life upon which through the ashes and ravages of war, the South has already entered inspires our hearts with the most buoyant hopes of the future.[75]

The more we shall be able to incorporate into the South's new life

68. Grady, *The New South*, 8.
69. *Ibid.*, 32.
70. *Ibid.*, 40.
71. *Ibid.*, 93.
72. Paul M. Gaston, *The New South Creed: A Study in Southern Mythmaking* (New York: Knopf, 1970).
73. Johnston, *Problems of Southern Civilization*, 11.
74. John A. Reagan, "The Causes of the War," *Confederate Veteran*, IV (March, 1896), 79.
75. Gordon, *The Old South*, 12.

the chief characteristics developed by the old, the better, the higher, and the purer will the new life become.[76]

After reviewing in some detail the writings of the New South historians, Paul M. Gaston asks why "the original New South idea . . . had such appeal and persistence, what gave its spokesmen their persuasiveness and ability to deceive others as well as themselves."[77] The answer is found in the tendency of the southerners of this period to prefer the world of fantasy to that of reality; consequently, the New South myth was acceptable at home as well as it was in the North. In contrast to the Old South myth which promoted regional solidity and pride, the New South myth stimulated hope and expectation, particularly among the have-nots.

Like other Americans, the southerner could not resist appeals that suggested Progress: that is, that life was getting better day by day. In addition the myth enabled the orator to assert that the southerner was superior because he had promoted Progress in spite of adversity and the burden of coping with the freed slaves. Henry Savage, Jr., explains the motivation back of linking the New South with the hope and change:

The three decades of activity in new directions, of conflict and contrast, of pride and disgrace, which were ushered in by those espousers of hope came to be known as the era of the new South, a misleading title connoting an unwarranted assumption of entity and an exaggerated degree of change. Actually, the only common denominator inherent in that era of contrast was the spirit of hope. And that hopefulness was about the only thing new in the new South.[78]

Herein was the suggestion that the southerners were a chosen people. It was not long until orators actually were telling their listeners how fortunate they were to have faced adversity be-

77. Paul M. Gaston, "The 'New South,'" in Dewey W. Grantham, Jr. (ed.), *The South and the Sectional Image* (New York: Harper and Row, 1967), 34.
78. Savage, *Seeds of Time*, 202.

cause it had forced them to change. This rationalization became another link in rebuilding the southerners' ego and another part of the fantasy which dominated much of the southern
consciousness. The tragedy of this rationalization—like any
self-deception—was that it interfered with the citizen's ability
to compare his own condition with that of others outside the
region. In spite of the assertions about progress, the South in
1904 had only 15 percent of the nation's manufacturers, 2 percent less than in 1860. And as Woodward has pointed out, the
masses were exploited, resources were wasted, and personal
fortunes for a few were accumulated at the expense of reform
in education and social services.[79] Holding fast to the fantasy,
many persons continued to "enjoy" poverty. Even the upper
classes yielded to self-deception and failed to see clearly that
they were not solving the problems at hand—only postponing
them until a much later time.

VI

Having a tangled genealogy, the four myths are sometimes difficult to isolate because they seldom appeared alone or in a
simple or pure form. They were activated by common termi-
nology and were triggered with a minimum of critical thought
and by a phrase such as "nigger lover," or the playing of Dixie,
or the unfurling of the stars and bars. They appealed to common states of readiness and drew support from revered events
and sentiments. Because they shared common sub-myths, they
were multidimensional, overlapping, and intertwined. Used so
often, they found their way into the popular vocabulary and
were accepted as fact by historians, journalists, novelists, and
literary critics.

Once energized, these four myths became so emotionally
loaded that they defied rational analysis, challenge, or oppo-

79. Woodward, *Origins of the New South*, Chap. 5.

sition. The mere mention of a myth could destroy an opponent's ethos, smother arguments, drive underground a counter thought, and stifle reform. They dominated the southern forum for more than a hundred years and remain potent forces in southern politics even today. In fact, George Wallace of Alabama, Lester Maddox of Georgia, and John Bell Williams of Mississippi recently revived these myths when opponents threatened to overturn them. And the charge that a candidate received a "block vote"—meaning that he received support in predominantly black areas—is a sure way to stir up determination to maintain white supremacy.

The ceremonial orators in the postwar South more nearly approached the commonly held stereotype of the "southern orator" than the deliberative speakers of the antebellum period. Because of the nature of the postwar times, speakers in the South were limited in the stances they could take. The frequent use of the four myths and related sub-myths, often cast in much the same language, narrowed their purview. These speakers often repeated themselves. Facing uncritical and sometimes overwrought listeners, the myth users relied heavily upon pathetic appeals. Consistent with the demands of ceremonial speeches, they resorted to stylistic flourishes, commonality in tone, and expansive delivery. Indulging in what is known as spread-eagle or high-flown oratory, they soothed their listeners, encouraging them to remain in the euphoria of a romantic past.

BIBLIOGRAPHICAL NOTE

Much has been written about the social myth. In addition to items cited in the footnotes of this article I have found helpful in gaining understanding the myth in the present context the following books: Wilbur J. Cash, *The Mind of the South* (New York: Alfred A. Knopf, 1941); Paul M. Gaston, *The New South Creed* (New York: Alfred A. Knopf, 1970); Richard Hofstadter, *The Age of Reform: From Bryan to F.D.R.* (New York: Vintage Books, 1955); R. W. B. Lewis, *The American Adam: Innocence, Tragedy and Tradition* (Chicago: University of Chicago, 1955); Leo Marx, *The Machine in the Garden: Technology and the Pastorial Ideal in America* (New York: Oxford University Press, 1964); Rollin G. Osterweis, *The Myth of the Lost Cause, 1865–1900* (Hamden, Conn.: Archon Books, 1973); Henry Nash Smith, *Virgin Land: The American West As Symbol and Myth* (Cambridge: Harvard University Press, 1950); George B. Tindall, "Mythology: A New Frontier In Southern History" in *The Ideal of the South*, ed. Frank E. Vandiver (Chicago: University of Chicago Press, 1964), 1–16; Richard M. Weaver, *The Southern Tradition at Bay* (New York: Arington House, 1968).

The subject is also discussed meaningfully in the following journal articles: Patrick Gerster and Nicholas Cords, "The Northern Origins of Southern Mythology," *Journal of Southern History*, XLIII (November, 1977), 567–82; Bruce Kuklick, "Myth and Symbol In American Studies," *American Quarterly*, XXIV (October, 1972), 435–50; Lawrence Veysey, "Myth and Reality in Approaching American Regionalism," *American Quarterly*, XII (Spring, 1960), 31–43.

Restoration Strategies in Georgia, 1865–1880

The Civil War left Georgia in social, economic, and political turmoil.[1] Herschel V. Johnson wrote that "our beautiful region has been desolated, all our capital sunk, our people impoverished, and our slave property . . . confiscated by the act of emancipation."[2] Radical Reconstruction enfranchised former slaves and disfranchised many Confederates, disrupting the political control of native whites. Some blacks voted, campaigned, held office, and openly challenged the slavery image created for them by whites.[3] Reacting to these racial changes, the Atlanta *Constitution* warned that "you have seen the Government under which you had lived swept away, and a monster despotism erected in its stead." These sociopolitical conditions caused "a new class alike of duties and of dangers." Whereas outsiders

1. See Charles Stearns, *The Black Man of the South and the Rebels; Or the Characteristics of the Former and the Recent Outrages of the Latter* (New York: American News, 1872); Frances B. Leigh, *Ten Years on a Georgia Plantation Since the War* (London: Richard Bentley, 1883); reprinted by Negro Universities Press, 1969); and Eliza Frances Andrews, *The War-Time Journal of a Georgia Girl, 1864–1865* (New York: D. Appleton, 1908).

2. Milledgeville *Southern Recorder*, August 27, 1867; Savannah *Daily News and Herald*, September 8, 1866, and July 17, 1867.

3. For political speaking by blacks see Savannah *Daily News and Herald*, March 22, 1867, March 28, 1867, April 2, 1867, May 25, 1867, July 8, 1867, August 22, 1867, October 30, 1867, December 20, 1867; Atlanta *Constitution*, August 12, 1868, September 14, 16, 21, 25, 26, and 29, 1880, October 1, 1880; Augusta *Weekly Chronicle and Sentinel*, July 18, 1866; *Weekly Atlanta Intelligencer*, September 2 and 9, 1868; Savannah *Morning News*, July 29, 1870; Augusta *Chronicle*, September 23, 1880, October 5, 1880; Columbus *Enquirer*, August 31, 1880; Thomasville *Southern Enterprise*, May 9, 1866.

perceived the postwar situation in terms of victory and defeat, white southerners redefined the results in reference to their own regional interests. The Macon *Journal and Messenger* warned that "the white wives, mothers, and daughters" would be "dragged down to the level of the negro women, and their children made the associates on terms of forced equality with negro children. It is not a question of 'peace,' and 'quiet,' and 'getting back into the Union.' It is the Constitution of our country and white supremacy against negro rule." War scars further solidified the region and marked the perception of whites: "Graves which, amid the confusion and excitement of the closing scenes of the war had been neglected, were searched out, renovated, and dressed with flowers by fair hands."[4]

This explosive situation hardened the minds and hearts of whites to any dispassionate discussion of social and political problems and solutions. "Our people," proclaimed an editor, "are well informed on all the issues, and decided." "The same spirit" prevailed "which caused the late disastrous bloody war." Neither whites nor blacks were safe voicing opinions at variance with the conservative consensus of the white citizenry. When George P. Burnett, a white merchant and planter who had lived in Georgia thirty-one years, ran as a Republican candidate to Congress, the Ku Klux Klan sent him "a note" telling him he "could not . . . make a speech" in Summerville.[5]

This emotional scene spawned more pathos than reason, which served as a kind of rhetorical relief for whites cornered by an Old South culture and threatened by Radicalism. In adjusting to this conflict, many spokesmen turned to the past.

4. Atlanta *Constitution*, July 23, 1868; *Weekly Atlanta Intelligencer*, September 20, 1865; Macon *Journal and Messenger*, October 30, 1867; Savannah *News and Herald*, April 30, 1866.

5. Atlanta *Constitution*, September 7, 1870; Augusta *Chronicle and Sentinel*, August 16, 1865; *Testimony Taken by the Joint Select Committee to Inquire into the Condition of Affairs in the Late Insurrectionary States*: Georgia (13 vols.; Washington: Government Printing Office, 1872), Vol. VI, Pt. I, pp. 64–65.

"Recuperation" was envisioned in orations and in the press as a commemoration of "the good old days of peace and prosperity."[6] Under these conditions, when southern whites communicated among themselves, style was more important than substance, ritual more valued than analysis, and empathy more influential than objectivity. The people were led more by regional legend than critical argument, with particular celebrants confirmed to lead the regional ritual. Spokesmen were required to identify their words and acts with the social structure of the Old South and the martyrdom of the sacred war, mythic symbols capturing the sectional mood. This ritual reasoning resulted in some curious communicative choices difficult for nonbelievers to comprehend. For example, in this seditious setting it was quite appropriate that "the anniversary of the surrender of Gen. Lee's army" would be "observed by the patriotic ladies of the South as the day on which to pay a tribute of honor and affection to the brave men who fell in defence [sic] of the Confederate Cause." Based on traditional standards of appropriateness, an outsider would have suggested a more "suitable" occasion, missing the sacredness of that martial sacrament to white southerners and the conviction that salvation followed suffering, victory defeat. Robert Toombs understood: "Purification in the crucible of adversity, in the fiery furnace of individual and national sufferings, seems to be the price of the penalty of national greatness." This blending of secular events with sacred creed generated complex rhetorical crosscurrents which were hazardous for the uncommitted and instructive to believers. In practical terms communicative maneuvers during this period took on the appearances of what even a friendly editor saw cynically as a new rhetorical form: "Politics like everything else shows in its *devil*-opment genius of the age. . . . Its new system is to profess one set of principles and practice

6. Savannah *Daily News and Herald*, December 17, 1866.

openly the very opposite; while it ingeniously convinces both parties that it is true to each and opposes the other."[7]

Who in Georgia, then, was qualified to represent the feelings and conviction of whites? One editor asked that men be chosen, "not for their . . . talent to rhetorica or bombastic display, but for their plain, common sense and every day business capacity," hardly the communicative requisites demanded by whites. One citizen suggested men "trained in argument," which was adequate advice considering what "argumentation" meant to many prideful spokesmen.[8] The Savannah News and Herald defined best the rhetorical criteria for consorting with people[9] in the South: "pride of the past, the honor of the present," and "the hope of a brighter future to guide their action."[10] To find spokesmen who could articulate their "rhetorical vision"[11] of southern culture, white Georgians turned to established leaders, most of Confederate fame: "the Toombs, the Cobbs, the Johnsons, the Hills, the Colquitts, the Stephenses, the Gordons, the Bennings. . . . At their call they will rally again." Although many of these prominent persons were banned from official office, they continued to "create public sentiment" and "control the State." P. M. Sheibley explained to a congressional committee that the credibility of Robert Toombs and "that class of men" derived not from law but from empathy with people: "General Toombs, with his powerful intellect, with the influence he has in the State, and having been connected

7. Savannah News and Herald, April 30, 1866; Atlanta Constitution, August 23, 1868, and September 16, 1869.

8. Augusta Chronicle and Sentinel, August 26, 1865; Atlanta Constitution, July 21, 1871.

9. I have been influenced by Michael C. McGee "In Search of 'The People': A Rhetorical Alternative," Quarterly Journal of Speech, LXI (1975), 235–49.

10. Savannah News and Herald, June 22, 1867.

11. Ernest G. Bormann has argued that in public communication "composite dramas which catch up large groups of people in a symbolic reality can be termed a rhetorical vision"; see "Fantasy and Rhetorical Vision: The Rhetorical Criticism of Social Reality," Quarterly Journal of Speech, LVIII (1972), 396–407.

with the State and national politics for a very long time, with his particular line of politics, could control it, independent of any official position, of any support of law."[12]

After an initial conspiracy of silence against making "sensational speeches" which could be "used against" them, citizens entered a vigorous discussion of how Georgia should be redeemed. Provisional Governor James Johnson said that citizens "should all lay aside" their "animosities and meet the North again as friends and brothers. You need allow no pride to influence you against it."[13] After initially refusing to comment on the "present situation" because he believed nothing he "could say or do could possibly effect any good," Alexander Stephens eventually recommended "patience" and "a liberal spirit of forbearance amongst ourselves." He would not "stir up the discords of the past." Later he warned that only "the people" could stop the country from "drifting to consolidation and empire."[14] Faced with what he perceived as a choice "between a mob and a master," Alfred H. Colquitt supported euphemistically "a return to our duty under the Constitution" as "the only hope and solace left us in this evil day."[15] Robert Toombs ridiculed Radical rule as "nigger Government," "plunder," "fraud," and "despotism." Georgians, he argued, should "make new sacrifices" to "redeem" their "country from bondage," for the "noblest and holiest cause for which patriot blood was ever shed."[16] Benjamin H. Hill, a second violent spokesman of the period, warned of "native traitors and immigrant spies," and was particularly critical of compromisers: "They said they were

12. Atlanta *Constitution*, July 25, 1868, and June 20, 1868; *Testimony Taken by the Joint Select Committee*, 21–39, 44–58.

13. Atlanta *Constitution*, August 18, 1870, September 7, 1880; Savannah *Daily Republican*, July 3, 1865; Augusta *Chronicle and Sentinel*, July 26, 1865.

14. Atlanta *Constitution*, January 20, 1870; Savannah *Daily Herald*, February 26, 1866; Atlanta *Constitution*, June 24, 1869.

15. Atlanta *Constitution*, October 10, 1868.

16. Atlanta *Daily Constitution*, July 24, 1868; Atlanta *Constitution*, August 23, 1868.

not going to be Radicals . . . but they said 'let us *seem* to go into this thing, let us get back into the Union and then we'll turn it all over and do as we please.' " Hill interpreted such reasoning to be "based upon treachery." Patriots should again be willing "to fight and die for" their "rights." "Never go half way with a traitor, nor compromise with treason or robbery."[17]

Two white Georgians who entered the postwar situation with contrasting rhetorical styles and strategies were former governor Joseph E. Brown and Confederate general John B. Gordon. Because they confronted Reconstruction with dissimilar styles and strategies, analysis of their public discourse should contribute to a further understanding of the social and political forces at work in Georgia after the war. By considering the nature of the public performances of Brown and Gordon within the conflicting constraints of Radical rule and southern purpose, one should also discover something of how public communication works in a volatile setting. Joseph E. Brown best represents the minority belief in Georgia that whites should accept Reconstruction voluntarily. Although many white Georgians opposed Radicalism, John B. Gordon was selected for study because he publicly confirmed the mood of the masses of whites for regional celebration and independence. Also Gordon played a significant role in Georgia's departure from the Old South culture to the New.

Underlying this analysis is the conviction that for some years after the Civil War there evolved in the Southeast not only an increased public pride among whites in a way of life peculiar to the South but also a renewed dedication to its preservation and promotion. In addition, white southerners devised a public discourse indigenous to their region. What distinguished this pe-

17. Columbus *Daily Times*, February 22, 1865; Benjamin H. Hill, Jr., *Senator Benjamin H. Hill of Georgia: His Life, Speeches and Writings* (Atlanta: H. C. Hudgins, 1891), 308–319; Savannah *Daily News and Herald*, July 22, 1867.

riod's communication was the "rhetorical vision" which that discourse both generated and reflected, a communal commitment to a way of life purified by Old South principle and war sacrifice and called into celebration. Increasingly after home rule was restored to white Georgians in the early 1870s as a means of improving their own economic condition, southern spokesmen helped re-create the region's vision of values into a rhetorical image of the national pantheon of prosperity, a social-rhetorical phenomenon which saw southern society in general and the nature of public communication in the South in particular significantly changed.

A Strategy of Submission

Joseph Emerson Brown (1821–1894), governor of Georgia during the Civil War, retired to private life on June 29, 1865, and urged whites to "abandon resistance" and "do whatever was necessary and proper to place themselves in constitutional relations" with the federal government. Using defeatist language highly offensive to conservative whites, Brown called for "submission to the 'powers that be.'" Ignoring the hurt and pride of fellow Georgians, the former governor "took the position at once . . . of acquiescing"[18] to northern demands. In arguing that white Georgians should accept the will of war, Brown advised audiences "contrary to every instinct, impulse, and passion of their nature."[19] A former circuit judge, state senator, and governor from 1857 to 1865, this self-made millionaire had previously earned high credibility among the people; thus, to impede his influence critics attacked not only his argument but him personally. Critics portrayed Brown as a traitor to his countrymen. The *Daily Rebel* concluded, "We do not remember

18. Savannah *Daily News and Herald*, November 3, 1866,and April 19, 1867; Atlanta *Constitution*, September 19, 1868.
19. Herbert Fielder, *A Sketch of the Life and Times and Speeches of Joseph E. Brown* (Springfield, Mass.: Springfield Printing Co., 1883), 435.

ever to have witnessed a parallel to the almost universal aston-
ishment and indignation which has been produced by Governor Brown's message to the Georgia Legislature." The *Weekly
Atlanta Intelligencer* judged that "a more artful politician and
a greater political demagogue does not live in the State than
Joseph E. Brown." In a speech at Valdosta, Colonel William B.
Gaulden named Brown "The chief of Southern Radicals." So
unpopular was Brown that opponents even fabricated stories
about how he was involved in "amours with another man's
wife."[20]

What moved Joseph Brown to advocate the repugnant position
that white Georgians should surrender politically? A practical-
minded businessman and lawyer, Brown was motivated by expediency and pecuniary interests. When accused of abandoning
Georgia to save his own property, he responded: "I know my
own heart, a nobler object prompted me," but he readily admitted that it was better to save his property than to gratify his
"prejudice."[21] While in Washington after the war, in an attempt
to win his own parole, Brown secretly promised President Andrew Johnson he would "use his influence" to induce Georgians "to return to their loyalty." During his public campaign
for a prideless peace, Brown reported to Johnson the conditions
in the state, asking that this contractual arrangement not be
revealed because it would further lower his persuasive credibility.[22] One should know, however, that Brown had recommended a conciliatory posture before going to Washington. In
his Governor's Message in 1864, he warned of "extremists on
the Southern side whose morbid sensibilities are shocked at
the mention of . . . negotiation," asking for "cool-headed think-

20. Quoted in Columbus *Daily Times*, February 26, 1865; Quoted in Atlanta *Constitution*, August 21, 1870; Savannah *Daily News and Herald*, October 21, 1867; Atlanta *Constitution*, August 30, 1868.
21. Savannah *Daily News and Herald*, April 19, 1867.
22. Joseph H. Parks, *Joseph E. Brown of Georgia* (Baton Rouge: Louisiana
State University Press, 1977), 338–39, 347–49.

CAL M. LOGUE

ing men on both sides . . . including the scar-covered veterans of the army." What changed most was the tone of Brown's public discourse. Early after the war he supported submission, but not the "sacrifices of interest and of principle which magnanimity would not exact and self-respect could not make." Brown quickly abandoned this ritual rhetoric for a practical discourse of "unwelcome truth" highly inappropriate for the turbulent setting. Hoping that personal candor would appeal to audiences devastated by war, Brown stated that he would speak "with perfect frankness without regard to the effect which the communication of truth may have upon" his "present or future popularity." He was "aware that the facts which" he felt it was his "duty to communicate" were "unacceptable to the good people of Georgia."[23]

In numerous speeches and in letters to the press, Joseph E. Brown developed two affirmative arguments in support of his strategy of submission. At the same time, Brown refuted three attitudes prevailing among white Georgians which he knew constrained them from accepting Reconstruction realistically. Brown first argued that Georgians had no choice but to obey Union regulations. To "settle the question," southerners should simply adopt the Reconstruction acts and the Thirteenth and Fourteenth amendments. "Nothing less ever will." Although his speeches were met with "many violent and unguarded words," Brown confronted audiences directly, convinced that to delay submission would be futile. He insisted that Georgians "recognize" they were "a conquered people, and that they must submit to whatever terms the conqueror imposes." The "sword" had "decide[d] the question."[24] Georgians "were at

23. Columbus *Times*, March 15, 1864; Savannah *Daily News and Herald*, November 3, 1866; Atlanta *Constitution*, January 5, 1870.
24. Savannah *Daily News and Herald*, February 28, 1867; Atlanta *Daily New Era*, March 6, 1867, a Radical Republican newspaper. Because of "advance orders for Ex-Governor Brown's speech" "one thousand extra copies" of the *Daily New Era* were printed. Savannah *Daily News and Herald*, April 19, 1867.

46

the mercy of the conqueror." Reconciled within himself to accept what had to be rather than what he preferred, Brown "acquiesced," not "as a matter of choice, but as matter of necessity." He developed his "no choice" argument through threat appeals. By envisioning the dangers inherent in a policy of resistance, Brown attempted to frighten whites into submission, a relevant appeal for persons impoverished by war and suppressed by Reconstruction. If citizens did not "act promptly," he warned, "all is lost." Would they "stubbornly . . . sacrifice the little that is left?" Brown contrasted the region's choices in a manner favorable to his own proposition: "Persistent opposition may lead to confiscation. . . . A speedy acceptance of the terms offered will lead to an early restoration." Rejection would lead to "years of darkness, confusion, prostration in business and financial wreck."[25]

In his second argument Brown contended that political submission would bring economic benefits, a position with which this successful businessman was most comfortable and probably, to some degree, convincing. Eventually even conservative leaders echoed this appeal. Certainly the effects of the war on currency, bonds of the state, stocks of banks and railroads, land value, and personal debts created a market for Brown's promise of economic recovery, an argument he packaged in the "motto" of "action, reconstruction, and relief." Unlike most Georgians, Brown ranked prosperity above regional pride. Ignoring the people's preoccupation with their past, Brown emphasized "a new era" in "need" of "capital and labor," reminding whites of their "vast fertility and great natural resources." "Peace, harmony and prosperity," Brown insisted, "can only be obtained by a rapid reconstruction and the consequent development of our

25. Atlanta *Constitution*, September 24, 1872; Atlanta *Constitution*, September 19, 1868; Atlanta *Daily New Era*, January 9 and 10, 1868; Savannah *Daily News and Herald*, February 28, 1867; Savannah *Daily News and Herald*, April 29, 1867; Atlanta *Daily New Era*, January 9 and 10, 1868; Atlanta *Constitution*, September 19, 1868.

national resources." "The *interest* of the State imperatively demands that our relations with the national government shall
be reestablished and peace and harmony restored. . . . Heretofore the watchword has been non-action. In future it should be
Action, Action, Action."[26] By detailing how segments of society would profit from immediate reunion, Brown exploited the
chronic financial needs of his audiences:

We must accommodate ourselves to circumstances. . . . We lack labor. We lack capital. Let us invite both. . . . Let us do all in our power
to heal the wounds opened by the war and as little as possible to irritate. This is the only way to advance our own prosperity. The more
population we have, and the more thrifty, the more valuable is the
farmer's land, the better the merchant's trade, the more patients the
doctor has, the more cases for the lawyer, the better the freights on
the railroad and, indeed, the better for every interest of the whole
State.[27]

In addition to arguing that southerners of necessity must accept Reconstruction and that such a policy would mean economic security, Brown attacked three attitudes which caused
obstinacy among whites: that to submit to Radical Republicans would mean a loss of self-respect, that to cooperate with
the enemy was to repudiate southern principles, and that to accept the participation of blacks in state politics would result in
a loss of white control.

Concerned that the obstinate pride of southerners would be
an obstacle to rational action, Brown pleaded that Georgians
should "know no North, no South, no East, no West but" only
a "re-united country." This businessman called for "habits of
industry and energy instead of habits of effeminacy and false
pride." The "stubbornness" of southerners would be "ruinous"

26. Atlanta *Daily New Era*, April 24, 1867; Savannah *Daily News and Herald*, February 28, 1867; Savannah *Daily News and Herald*, April 19, 1867; Atlanta *Constitution*, January 5, 1870.
27. Atlanta *Daily New Era*, March 6, 1867. Brown continued this line of
reasoning in his speech on April 18, 1867; See also April 24, 1867.

and "folly." Brown argued that "reason and judgment were dethroned by prejudice and passion,"[28] strong words for audiences recovering from war. This lawyer stated that to obey federal laws was not a sign of weakness but a recognition of duty. In a speech at Rome, Georgia, on April 10, 1868, Brown appealed for a *national* patriotism: "I came to the deliberate conclusion that it was my duty either to quit this country and seek a home in a foreign land, or to remain, accept the amnesty tendered, claim the protection of the government, and yield to it in good faith my obedience and support."[29] By identifying his thinking with men that white Georgians admired, and scolding the citizenry for their regional doggedness, Brown hoped to awaken audiences to the realities of their postwar predicament:

General Lee did not put himself upon his *dignity* and say, I am conquered: I will never disgrace myself by doing what the conqueror requires. . . . When the terms were ordered, General Lee and his gallant veterans accepted them, and acted upon them, as the best they could do under the circumstances. . . . Why did not gentlemen put themselves upon their dignity and manhood when required to abolish slavery, repudiate the war debt, and abrogate the ordinance of secession, which we had passed with so much defiance? If we could take all that, and maintain our "self-respect." I think we may take the balance of the dose, which we are informed shall be the last, without making as ugly faces as some of us now make.[30]

Brown refuted a second belief, that cooperation with the enemy would mean violating sacred southern principles. Insistent that whites not "quibble about terms," Brown asked that citizens measure persons or parties by what they actually represented, not what they claimed in exaggerated rhetoric. Concluding that all Georgians wanted the "Republican simplicity practiced by our fathers," Brown maintained that southerners

28. Atlanta *Daily New Era*, January 11, 1868 and January 1, 1871; Savannah *Daily News and Herald*, February 28, 1867; Atlanta *Constitution*, January 5, 1870; Savannah *Daily News and Herald*, April 19, 1867.
29. Atlanta *Daily New Era*, April 14, 1868.
30. *Ibid.*, March 6, 1867.

owed no obligation to any party: "The Republicans were openly against us at the commencement of the war, and the Democrats who had promised that there should be no war soon deceived us and joined the Republicans and poured their leaden hail into the ranks of our brave Southern defenders. . . . I think we have had enough of war for this generation. I long to see quiet and repose restored once more to the country. This can never be till we are reconstructed and readmitted."[31] Speaking in Marietta in 1868, Brown argued that Benjamin Hill and the "National Democratic Party of Georgia, so-called" were foolish to continue preaching the "principles of the old State Rights Democracy" such as "State Sovereignty, the right of secession, opposition to high tariff, internal improvements, etc." Brown "predict[ed] that within four years from this date Ben. Hill will be making as loud speeches in favor of negro office holding as he now makes against their right to vote . . . as the negro vote of the South will entitle us to over twenty more members of Congress." Brown further explained, "I make the above allusions to the present Democratic party and its leaders as a set off to the attacks made by those who now claim the name Democrat upon old line Democrats who do not see the old issues in this new organization and do not feel bound by party allegiance to fall down and worship these strange gods." Brown likened those who claimed to don the cloak of Democratic respectability to "the Jackass with the Lion's skin on, they frighten us for a time, but when we hear their voice and see their ears we are no longer deceived."[32]

The former governor counteracted a third fear of Georgians, that black voters in a reconstructed state would rule white citizens. As was true of most spokesmen, Brown recited the stock pretention that "white men" should "see that the black man

31. Atlanta *Constitution*, September 24, 1872; Atlanta *Daily New Era*, January 10, 1868.
32. *Ibid.*, March 18, 1868, and April 14, 1868.

has full, equal, even-handed justice before the law." Brown believed, however, that former slaves were not equipped to threaten white power; thus, he recommended obeying minimal reconstruction requirements as a means of restoring local government to whites. Brown held that blacks were not full citizens. While in Washington after the war, the former governor warned that the effect of bills passed in Congress "will be to make the slaves of the South the political masters of their former owners."[33] In his much discussed Marietta speech in 1868, Brown argued that the Constitution did not "give . . . the negro the right to hold office." "The civil rights bill passed by Congress . . . only conferred upon them civil rights, not political rights, and he can have none, except such as are conferred or granted to him." In his speech to a Republican convention in Georgia, Brown even criticized fellow Radicals for being "more Radical than Congress" in attempting to confer upon blacks the "right to hold office in Georgia." Later Brown infuriated whites when, as chief justice of the Georgia Supreme Court, he ruled that the "Code of Georgia and Acts amendatory" conferred "upon all citizens the right to hold office."[34]

To appease the fears of whites, Brown stressed the superior experience and ability of white voters. He also predicted that continued resistance would make the racial situation worse. "If we accept" the black man's right to vote and "act upon it, the ballot will remain in the hands of nine-tenths of the white men of the south. If we refuse to do so, it will be taken from them and given to a very small class of white men and the negroes."[35] Answering the arguments of antireconstructionists, Brown assured his audiences that as always a white coalition would govern Georgia:

33. *Ibid.*, April 24, 1867; New York *Herald*, quoted in *Daily Columbus Enquirer*, March 7, 1867.
34. Atlanta *Constitution*, August 11, 1868, September 19, 1868, and June 19, 1869.
35. Atlanta *Daily New Era*, March 6, 1867.

We have been told again and again by the newspapers of the State and by popular orators who oppose reconstruction that the reconstruction acts of Congress, if carried out, establish negro government and negro supremacy in Georgia. There is not one word of truth in this. . . . The very men who make it object to giving the negro the ballot, because they say, he has not intelligence and capacity enough to know how to use it. . . . All know that we have more experience, and that what property is left is almost exclusively in the hands of the white race. . . . All know that intellect, education, experience and property control numbers in all communities. Intelligence and capital control alike labor and the ballot box among the blacks or whites.

Characteristically candid, this self-made businessman argued that "dishonest demagogues" not only were opposed to black voters but also were "against *universal* white suffrage," following "the old doctrine that only those born of the aristocracy should govern." "But in this new era," Brown predicted, "it will be a failure."[36] Finally Brown recommended that whites work to win the black vote. After all, he insisted, former slaves had a natural allegiance to southern whites: "Do all you can to elevate him. Encourage his education. He is now a citizen, and your interests require that he exercise the rights of a citizen intelligently and wisely. Cultivate friendship between the races."[37]

Joseph E. Brown spoke with energy, intelligence, clarity, and good reason, but predictably Georgians refused to be reconstructed voluntarily. In retrospect Brown's candid strategy appears to have been feasible but unrealistic. Ravaged by war and angered by Radicalism, white Georgians never seriously considered sharing political decision making with former slaves. Instead, whites listened to voices sympathetic with their sorrows, sacrifices, and desire for self-government. Instead of fulfilling these rhetorical expectations, Brown responded brusquely in a vocabulary whites perceived to be defeatist and repulsive. Rhetorically reckless, Brown spoke such words as: *acquiesc-*

36. *Ibid.*, January 10, 1868.
37. *Ibid.*, April 24, 1867.

ing, submission, abandon resistance, conquered, obedience and support. Probably most telling, Brown defined the pride of southerners as being merely "prejudice," "morbid sensibilities," and "stubbornness." Even Brown's potentially appealing argument, that submission would bring prosperity, when communicated in symbols of surrender appeared to whites more like political blackmail than reasonable advice. Until after 1880, whites responded to Brown's minority views with verbal abuse, physical threats, and political ostracism. In the United States Senate election of 1868, Joshua Hill was elected over the former governor. This news was "received in the gallery with a tornado of applause." Representing the reaction of many whites, on August 25, 1868, Robert Toombs suggested that Brown had "betrayed his natural and foster mother. More bitter than a serpant's [*sic*] tooth it is to have a thankless child! He is false to nature. . . . Ignoble villain! Buoyant solely with corruption, he only rises as he rots." [38]

Call to Celebration

General John B. Gordon (1832–1904) preached the faith of southern fellowship against the "diabolism" of Radicalism. His "State *destroyed—conquered?*" Proclaimed Gordon, "Never." In his public communication, Gordon promised to "blink at no issue" and "indulge in no spirit of apology." "Oh, who can tell the length and the breadth, the height and the depth of *Fiendish Radical* hate. Confirm these men in their ill-gotten power and . . . lost is the South—Liberty is lost." [39] A distinguished Confederate general, Gordon was considered by many to be "a brilliant and captivating orator," "endowed with a clear mind, a

38. I. W. Avery, *History of the State of Georgia from 1850 to 1881* (New York: Brown and Derby, 1881), 397; Mrs. William H. Felton, *My Memoirs of Georgia Politics* (Atlanta: Index Printing, 1911), 64–65.

39. Atlanta *Constitution*, May 28, 1872; *Daily News and Herald*, October 16, 1867; Atlanta *Constitution*, August 24, 1872; Savannah *Daily News and Herald*, July 30, 1866.

strong honor, and a pulsing public spirit, backed by a rare physical vigor." Not all Georgians agreed. One lone listener was appalled by Gordon's "appeals to the emotional senses of the audience" and described how he "just wilted and became completely hushed"[40] when confronted with questions from the audience.

In representing the convictions of white Georgians, General Gordon discussed three features of the inflated sentiment they felt for themselves: the southern cause, southern principle, and white superiority. First Gordon identified rhetorically with the southern cause, a mythic commitment to a way of life combining Old South culture and Civil War legend. The general heightened southern consciousness through symbols of shared suffering, an experiential bond more binding than blood lines. Gordon preached that southerners "are bone of our bone, and flesh of our flesh. They are bound to us by stronger ties than those of consanguinity. We are linked to them—heart to heart —by that strongest of all bonds, the bond of a common sorrow, and an immortal sympathy."[41] This sacrificial communion honored any white person "born upon our soil or" who "identified with our people" in a common cause of "light and truth." Gordon taught youth the regional values as a protection against foreign influences: "Would that I had the power to kindle in the hearts of these boys before me . . . the feeling which animates me, as I contemplate the day when there shall no longer remain in Georgia anything to remind us of Radical usurpation or Federal intervention in the affairs of the States." Concerned that some persons "talked disparagingly of our cause," Gordon spoke in order to keep the mission in march: "Let that sentiment be generated here tonight. Let all cherish it. It will give

40. Allen P. Tankersley, *John B. Gordon: A Study in Gallantry* (Atlanta: Whitehall, 1955), 76; Avery, *History of the State of Georgia*, 505–556; Columbus *Enquirer*, September 11, 1880.
41. Atlanta *Constitution*, August 24, 1872.

vigor to our youth, strength to our manhood, just pride to our State, and a sustaining self-respect to our people. . . . Without it, patriotism has no inspiration, hope languishes, industry loses its nerve, eloquence its fire, and civilization its chiefest ornament. . . . Cultivate this feeling, young men of Georgia. Cultivate a pride in your State."[42] Gordon mastered a vocabulary forged from the sounds and sympathies of southern experience, creating a regional symphony of defiance. He spoke of "Dixie," "southern tongues," "honorable," "southern man," "rights of the States," "local government," "liberty," "God," "unity," "our soil," "our people," "truth and right," "hardship and humiliation," "flourishing antebellum days," "heroic days during the war," "spirit of Lee," "Georgia democracy," "our fathers," "fundamental faith," and "sacrifice."

Gordon spiritualized the cultural cause as a means of rallying with whites in defense of southern traditions. He manufactured martial and sacred metaphors as a way of extolling their common commitment: "I shall keep steadily in view of the goal of deliverance. I shall allow nothing to divert me. Perish pride of opinion; perish hatred of former enemies who strike for liberty now; perish prejudice and all considerations of personal preferences or personal comfort; let all be subordinated to the higher and holier and braver determination to lock shields for this final charge." Gordon elevated public discourse above politics to a calling comparable to the saints of old: "Oh! for that patriotism, the lofty self-sacrificing patriotism, which in this crucible of political fires, shall refine itself into martyrdom . . . like the stoned Stephen of Bible memory, ready to die for the faith." The general asked for volunteers from "your best and your truest men, men who . . . remained true to the cause of the South."[43]

42. New York *Times*, September 1, 1877.
43. Atlanta *Constitution*, August 24, 1872, and January 21, 1873; Savannah *Daily News and Herald*, July 30, 1866.

The general extended the southern theme to political choices and strategies. For example, in supporting Liberal Republican Horace Greeley for president over Ulysses S. Grant in 1872, Gordon enhanced the credibility of Greeley among southerners by contrasting the attitudes of the two candidates, and stressing Greeley's respect for their sacred cause:

Horace Greeley proposes to shake hands . . . across the bloody chasm. . . . By . . . meeting upon grounds of mutual respect, I am willing to shake hands. But General Grant's mouth piece, Mr. Boutwell, "protests against" this shaking of hands across the chasm and wants "it filled up"—and he tells when it is to be filled up. When we all are so sorry for our sins, that we will not only abide by what had been done . . . but confess the outrages [then we will be accepted]. . . . Well I believe that I would prefer that the chasm shall remain open a while rather than fill it up that way.[44]

To complement his "cause" theme, Gordon included a second argument as part of his sectional strategy: southern principle, a popular teaching applied also in varying forms by Radical Joseph Brown and "Straight Out" obstructionist Robert Toombs. Responding to the appetites of whites for celebrating tradition, Gordon embellished a few safe precepts. He refracted that sacred cause rhetorically into political precepts with which whites could comfortably relate. Because of severe constraints placed upon the political choices of Georgians by Radical Reconstruction, whites were forced to choose from what to them were objectionable alternatives. For example, although in the presidential election of 1872 it was simple for headstrong Robert Toombs to reject Greeley supporters as the "party . . . of the negroes," Gordon, a more moderate spokesman, supported Greeley as the best candidate available. Aware that his delicate position between southern principle and practical politics would be criticized by both Toombs and Brown, Gordon packaged po-

44. Atlanta *Constitution*, August 24, 1872.

litical policy in permanent principle, urging his audiences not to "confuse *ends* with *ways* and *means*—principles with the policy to be pursued in establishing principles." The general assured listeners that "the needle of the Georgia democracy still points to the pole of principle."[45] Gordon taught his friendly audiences the rhetorical form southerners must use in devising a political strategy consistent with southern doctrine:

We may not change our principles, but we may change the methods of securing them. Principle, both moral and political, is eternal and unchangeable. . . . In the case of political principles, the method of setting them up, or what men call policy, is the result of human reason and, therefore, fallible and may be changed according to circumstances. In statesmanship, in politics as in war, results may be attained by strategy, if it is honorable strategy. The changing a line of policy to secure the triumph of a principle is not an abandonment of that principle.[46]

To guide his public communication, Gordon measured political policy by permanent principles of integrity, states' rights, and civil government, translating southern doctrine into political experience: "What are the fundamental principles . . . which we cannot . . . abandon?" he asked. First Gordon insisted on personal honesty, a trait closely tied to southern honor. In supporting Greeley over Grant, Gordon reduced the selection to good versus evil: "Mr. Greeley's platform . . . pledges an honest administration. . . . We prefer honesty as a sentiment. . . . Everybody says Horace Greeley is honest, and Georgians are likely to appreciate that." Gordon also recited the states' rights ritual, a rhetorical requisite for political celebration in the South. Adapting that premise to postwar Georgia, Gordon recommended that citizens concern themselves more with promotion of principle than political consistency: "I love liberty; I hate tyranny. . . . On the one hand is a local self-government—the boon above

45. *Ibid.*, June 14, 1872, August 24, 1872, and January 21, 1873.
46. *Ibid.*, August 24, 1872

all others we crave. On the other is centralization and the Federal clutch at our throats. . . . Let us not stand discussing records of long ago, when the opportunity to recover liberty is presented and passing. We are to deal with a *movement* and not with a *man*."[47]

Gordon sermonized southern principle to believers in metaphoric images of the American Revolution, liberty, and Christian doctrine. He was able to deduce from the southern cause and southern principle practical policy for a particular situation. By omitting controversial details, Gordon focused his audience's attention on valuative symbols with which they were in agreement. Listen as Gordon hallows Horace Greeley in a style characteristic of his restoration rhetoric. Because the speaker shifts so radically from the candidate to premises of principle, even the reader of this speech must remind himself regularly that Gordon is actually favoring Greeley with his flourishes:

We all know that when the original thirteen colonies secured their allegiance to the British crown, they became at once, and of necessity, free, independent, and sovereign States. Mark that proposition. It only then was necessary to unite in new relations. This was done by a written constitution. . . . These ole, time-honored principles, cherished principles of the rights of the States—local government—of the constitutional restraints of the federal power, of the *habeas corpus*, trial by jury, etc., have been familiar to us all from our childhood up.

Equating political philosophy with religious conviction and avoiding needless detail, Gordon condensed regional beliefs into metaphoric premises highly pleasing to white audiences:

Why my country men, these old cherished principles are the very christianity of our politics. They constitute our political Sermon on the Mount, and since the birth of the republic they have been the very decalogue, the very creed of faith of every party of every name that has ever held sway in this country from birth down to these latter days of

47. *Ibid.*, January 21, 1873 and August 24, 1872

58

degeneracy and shame. . . . These principles, I say, are as old as the government itself. . . . When they are lost, Republican government is lost—liberty is lost. Why my country men, they are the very pillars of the temple our fathers built. Let us bury so deep in the soil of our affections these massive pillars that the modern Sampsons of corruption and the storms of political passion never can shake them from their deep foundation![48]

Gordon fortified the white South's stance with a third argument, white superiority. He insisted that the "intelligent and virtuous" whites and not "ignorant and vicious" blacks and Radicals should govern Georgia. Although he was often associated with the Ku Klux Klan, Gordon denied to outsiders knowledge of that group but admitted belonging "to an organization of gentlemen, the nature of which was that of police for the preservation of the peace." Usually more subtle in his racist remarks than Robert Toombs and Benjamin Hill, Gordon disguised his intentions in talk about the "kindliest relations . . . between the races." Gordon pretended publicly to want to "do . . . everything for the elevation of the black race." Disguising the slavery status he and most whites preferred and planned for blacks, Gordon stated: "Let us be kind and forbearing toward him still—remembering that he is beguiled into the commission of outrages." [49] Gordon also veiled his purpose of preserving white power in symbols associated with the southern cause and southern principle. Indeed the southern cause, a way of life conceived in slavery, vivified in battle, and celebrated in reconstruction, was racially based. By connecting causally Radical policy and black politicians with deplorable conditions in Georgia, Gordon pleased the prejudices of whites:

And never, sir, until your carpetbag governments, through the fears and cupidity of the poor deluded negro, had embittered him against

48. *Ibid.*, January 21, 1873.
49. *Ibid.*, June 19, 1868, and May 28, 1872; New York *Times*, April 30, 1878; Atlanta *Constitution*, August 27, 1868.

us, and by his aid and yours had robbed our treasuries, plundered our corporations, blighted our agriculture, blasted our hopes, and hung debt like a millstone about our necks, never until then, and until the administration of law became a mockery, and political subserviency a passport to Executive clemency for crime, was the peace of the South ever broken or ill-will engendered between the races.[50]

Gordon promoted the preservation of white rule in Georgia, a chief motivation of his campaign for home rule. "Give us those [principles of state sovereignty]—give them to all the States in their capacity as States, and we ask no more. We can uphold republican government with nothing less. . . . A people to be free must be self-governed." Believing that the white was "superior in intelligence," and warning of a "war of races," Gordon condemned "atheistic theories of human rights."[51] The general condensed the anger and fear experienced by whites when they observed many former slaves leaving farms, "idling," bargaining for wages, campaigning, and holding office into racial symbols friendly to white prejudices. Applying these powerful appeals to the presidential campaign of 1872, Gordon emphasized in racially potent song symbols the relative attractiveness of Greeley over Grant:

At Baltimore was assembled the great Democratic party of the country. . . . After the nomination the candidate was presented . . . while from horn and pipe and drum came alternately "Yankee Doodle," the "Bonnie Blue Flag," and our soul-stirring "Dixie." At Philadelphia were assembled the Radical party of the North—the party of destruction, the murderers of the Constitution, with the paid renegades and carpet-baggers of the South, while General Grant, the nominee, was presented as on horseback, a panoplied soldier . . . and from horn and pipe and drum, from brazen dusky throats, rolled the mad music of "John Brown's soul is marching on." . . . Like the howling Dervishes shouting to their false Gods, these men bellow their maniac adorations to the soul of the dread criminal, and waking, I can almost fancy,

50. Atlanta *Constitution*, May 28, 1872.
51. New York *Times*, September 1, 1877, and April 30, 1878; Atlanta *Constitution*, August 27, 1868, and June 19, 1868.

with their wild demoniac songs, echoes in the very realms of the damned. Southern Patriot, which picture do you prefer? . . . Is "Yankee Doodle," tempered by Dixie, not better than "John Brown's Soul is Marching on"?[52]

In their public communication after the Civil War, then, Joseph E. Brown and John B. Gordon responded to a turbulent rhetorical situation with contrasting styles and strategies. Motivated primarily by economic concerns, Brown advocated immediate submission as the only practical recourse of Georgians. Refusing to appeal primarily to the pride of whites, Brown explained in businesslike speech the obligations of persons conquered by war. For this unpopular stance Brown was verbally abused and politically reproached. General Gordon preached a popular address of regional purity. In agreement with most whites, Gordon treated seriously what he portrayed as the threat of black voters to white power. In public discourse swollen with military and religious metaphor styled from experiences sacred to southerners, Gordon identified intimately with the regional pride, sacrifice, suffering, and hopes of whites. More rhetorically considerate of the mood of the white people and the period than Brown, Gordon comforted whites through a rhetoric of sectional celebration.

A Common Strategy

After 1872 white spokesmen who had formerly wrangled over doctrine and words united in a new strategy of economic prosperity and conciliation. With the ousting of Radical governor Rufus Bullock, home government was restored to Georgia whites. The Atlanta *Constitution* captured the feeling of most whites when it proclaimed: "Thank God Georgia is redeemed."[53] Joseph Brown, John Gordon, Benjamin Hill, Alfred Colquitt, Henry Grady, and others formed a powerful if fragile

52. Atlanta *Constitution*, August 24, 1872.
53. *Ibid.*, January 13, 1872.

coalition of personalities which ruled Georgia to the end of the century.

How could men, many of whom were so incompatible before, unite so quickly and effectively after 1872? How could a person so unpopular as Brown reestablish his political credibility? When James M. Smith replaced Bullock as governor, home rule was restored to Georgia and a chief cause of dissension was thereby removed. Because whites were once again in power, the perceived threat of black voters was significantly curtailed. Whites believed from long experience that when in authority they could control the public behavior of blacks. With these alleged problems under control, spokesmen focused their attention on other matters. Having served as governor for four terms, Brown had been popular prior to Reconstruction. This native Georgian was respected by many and feared by others because of his positions of power with the Western and Atlantic Rail Road, Southern Railway and Steamship Association, Walker Coal and Iron Company, Dade Coal Company, and the Rising Fawn Iron Works. A skillful politician and keen observer of political trends, Brown took specific steps near the end of Reconstruction to restore his own credibility at home. In 1870 he resigned as chief justice of the Georgia Supreme Court, thereby divorcing himself politically from the despised Radical Bullock. In 1872 Brown united with Gordon, Hill, Colquitt, and many Democrats in supporting Horace Greeley for president and James Smith for governor. Brown still confronted political opposition and was able to achieve public office only because of a "bargain" orchestrated by Henry Grady among the "Bourbon Triumvirate" of Colquitt, Gordon, and Brown. On May 15, 1880, Gordon resigned as United States senator after having only recently been elected to a six-year term. Governor Alfred H. Colquitt consummated the "arrangement" by appointing Brown to replace Gordon in the Senate. Although this infamous covenant was met by many protests, the decision returned

Brown to public office.[54] By 1885, with the help of Grady, Brown was easily reelected to the Senate by a near unanimous vote of the state legislature. In defending his own part in the transaction with Brown and Colquitt, Gordon explained to an Atlanta audience: "Now everyone knows that I am not the champion of Gov. Brown; but I am the friend of Alfred Colquitt and of the democratic party." He had resigned too because, "Your rights were secured, your liberties safe, and the opportunity for congenial and profitable employment for my self presented itself."[55]

With the threat of Radical control diminished, these aggressive and talented salesmen exploited numerous political and business opportunities. While such persons as Brown, Gordon, and Hill were not all personally and politically compatible, they coalesced as a means of governing Georgia and procuring personal profits. This new monopoly agreed that towns and cities should be expanded, mines developed, and factories and railroads built with little interference from government. Although they spoke of "the people's interests," these aggressive spokesmen gave little thought to the equity of their economics and eventually filled their own pockets first from the community purse. They seemed convinced, however, that persons free to exploit the South's resources would be the salvation of Georgians generally.

While talk of principle was more highly prized during Reconstruction than predictions of prosperity, after 1872 that condition changed. The new era brought new demands. Gordon, Hill, and other Democrats southernized the plain discourse that Brown had communicated recklessly earlier. As early as 1869, an editor had asked that citizens "dwell more fully on industrial topics and local natural wealth." After 1872, both nov-

54. *Ibid.*, September 24, 1872; Parks, *Joseph E. Brown of Georgia*, 508–520; Atlanta *Daily Constitution*, September 9, 1880; William Anderson, "Resignation of John B. Gordon from the United States Senate, 1880," *Georgia Historical Quarterly*, LII (1968), 438–42.
55. Atlanta *Daily Constitution*, June 8, 1880.

ice and experienced spokesmen talked in more practical terms about personal and regional wealth. In a speech to the Mechanics' Institute, J. Norcross envisioned for Atlanta "the concomitants of wealth and enjoyment." A Colonel Hardeman inspired that Georgians make "manly efforts to regain and build up their broken fortunes." Meeting the rhetorical standards of the new era, Alfred Colquitt told a Johnstonville audience that he "came to make no oratorical display, but to speak forth the words of truth and soberness." Colquitt encouraged a new kind of "revolution" by which Georgians would control their own "markets."[56] To learn how rhetorical conditions changed after 1872, one need look only at the predicament of Robert Toombs. Prior to 1872 Toombs, though outspoken, identified with the political instincts of white Georgians. After 1872 Toombs's persistent doggedness was viewed by many as an obstacle to the new prosperity: "His violent and extreme sentiments are only calculated to inflame the minds of people in other sections. They will not understand that he has not the following of a corporal's guard and that our people loudly condemn his course."[57]

John Gordon played a key part in the powerful coalition of Bourbon Democrats, serving as United States senator, governor, and leader of the United Confederate Veterans. Never highly successful personally as a businessman, the famous general's name was used to promote coal mining, kindling wood, journalism, lumber, rice farming, southern books, railroads, and life insurance. Somewhat a pawn of the Democrats, Gordon "canvassed" for others "not from choice, but from the call of the political organization of which [he was] a member." Though linked with corruption, not uncommon among Georgia Democrats, he continued to win elections because he "knew how to

56. Atlanta *Constitution*, January 12, 1869, July 12, 1874, and September 13, 1874.

57. Atlanta *Daily Constitution*, September 16, 1874. Toombs continued to ridicule "radicals, scalawags, and negroes"; see also September 16, 1874.

captivate the masses." So effective was the her's speaking that the "Democratic clubs in every county" made "more calls ... for Gen Gordon ... to address them than all the other of our public speakers together." Let us look more closely at how the man formerly perceived as the personification of the Lost Cause could now be applauded as "a practical man, in full sympathy with the practical progress of the age."[58]

While in perfect empathy with southern tradition, Gordon also sensed attractive markets in a region ripe for recovery from war and reconstruction. Gordon preached a new doctrine of dogma *and* dollars. By distinguishing between permanent principle and working policy, Gordon was able to make an alien message salable. What the situation demanded, he insisted, was a new rhetorical form: "Oh! what we want is the patriotism that while it holds fast to the things that are true, will lay aside the old forms of the mere ceremonials of the law. . . . Do this, my countrymen, and your material prosperity is safe, your liberty is safe." Extending this communicative precept, Gordon advised that southern spokesmen follow one rhetorical formula at home and another when away. To be true to themselves, to salve regional wounds, and to convert outsiders to the good life, white Georgians should continue talking ritually of their heritage among themselves. But to influence the East and the West, bargainers would have to act economically independent and master a rhetorical form foreign to their native rhetoric: "But does anyone ask me whether we are to trust only to this practical program, and cease talking, and arguing, and debating? I say no. . . . We must do both. Talk? Oh! Yes. . . . We must proclaim our principles in conventions, on the hustings, through the newspapers, on the house-tops, until the

58. Tankersley, *John B. Gordon*, 254, 299, 316; Felton, *My Memoirs of Georgia Politics*, 114–15, 498–99; Lucian Lamar Knight, *Standard History of Georgia* (6 vols; Chicago: Lewis, 1917), II, 944; Atlanta *Constitution*, January 23, 1873.

very breezes catch the notes and fill the whole land with the sound. . . . Oh! Yes, my countrymen, we must do as Paul commanded Timothy—we must exhort, and appeal, and admonish and rebuke, but we must *act* like Paul too . . . getting hold of all men, that perchance we may save some."[59]

Molding a metaphor from familiar military scenes, Gordon explained to Georgians that to communicate effectively with nonsoutherners they would have to master a new form of salesmanship because outsiders "do not mean to be convinced. They are after power and no argument of ours . . . no pathos . . . can move these leaders. . . . Our batteries of argument, which as I saw were effectual before the war, cannot reach their lines now." As a way of emphasizing the new rhetorical form required of southerners by the new audience, Gordon shifted from figurative language to a plain style of speaking: "To drop all figures you must make it to their interest to listen to you. . . . They are too engrossed in caring for their bloated fortunes and acquiring others to give any time and place to the higher and holier duties of patriotism. . . . Free government is nothing . . . when weighted in the balance with pecuniary interest."

Gordon ended his Atlanta address with an apostrophe to prosperity, an eloquent exhortation of a new rhetorical ideal which obscured the old. In a conformation rare in his former Reconstruction rhetoric, Gordon awakened in southerners a pecuniary motivation which he had attributed primarily to outsiders. After the Civil War, then, Gordon and other conservatives stubbornly resisted Radical intrusions into southern lives by celebrating sacred traditions at home. Ironically, what Radical politics could not permanently perfect down South, Gordon and other Georgia Democrats did. Through their public discourse after 1870 these men corrupted their own regional romanticism by preaching the national prosperity. White Georgians

59. This and subsequent quotations from Georgia General Assembly speech, Atlanta *Constitution*, January 21, 1873.

surrendered voluntarily to a new vision which Gordon and others created in part as a means of influencing capitalists in the East and the West. In the New South the rhetorical form which Gordon had constructed for outsiders became also the pecuniary ideal for white southerners, a vision which would not be seriously threatened until the Fugitive movement during the 1920s and a potential energy crisis in the 1970s. Gordon cast forth the region's new vision in traditional symbols of southern celebration:

When the history of these last few years shall be written, it will contain no brighter pages than those which record your struggles from 1865 to 1872. You are now passing, my countrymen, through your material and political wilderness, but soon, I believe, you shall stand on Pisgah's top and look over into the land of promise! . . . Get wealth —get wealth! Not only as a means of comfort, but of political power. Bring in population, for population is both capital and power. Bring in your immigrants; educate your children to be artisans, and architects, and master mechanics. Build your factories, spin your cotton. The mountain has been going to Mohammed in the East long enough. Let us bring the Mohammed of manufactures to our Southern cotton mountain. . . . Soon the whirl of the spinning jenny shall join you in concert. And then musical spindles and murmuring waterfalls shall raise a hymn of gratitude to God until the very atmosphere around shall revel and thrill and tremble with your triumph. . . . Do this my countrymen and, believe me, you shall in the new epoch, mount on wings of a higher prosperity than ever before. But don't forget your principles. Hold them fast.[60]

Elated that "our people have generally come to their sober senses," Joseph Brown reminded audiences that what he had advocated after the war had become universally accepted. Brown was pleased to work with Gordon, Hill, and other Democrats because he believed they were actually confirming his contentions and adopting his rhetorical ideal. "Let us come together and move forward in a common cause to a common destiny,"

60. *Ibid.*

he advised. "Who was right and who was wrong is not the question," but "what can we best do" to "move forward in a grand and glorious progress to wealth, to power and to greatness."[61] Brown's straight-forward speaking, apparently so out of place to many after a tragic war, was now in more popular usage. Unlike Gordon, however, Brown still did not pretend to model the New South after the Old. Indeed, puffed-up by the self-perception that he had been right all along, Brown rejected the old culture for a new reality:

I may not be a proper representative of certain sentimentality that is in this State. There is a class of people in this State whose fathers a generation or two back possessed either wealth or distinction . . . "the kid-glove aristocracy." . . . I never belonged to that class. . . . I had to work my own way in the world. . . . I have had to deal with the realities of life. . . . If I shall be elected to the Senate I shall go there to represent no sickly sentimentality, I shall go there to represent the interests, the prosperity and the honor of Georgia . . . not . . . as a fossil of the past . . . but as a living man of the present . . . to build up the waste places and restore prosperity and happiness to our people.[62]

At a banquet in Atlanta for President Rutherford B. Hayes— attended also by Gordon, Hill, Colquitt, and Grady—Brown, exaggerating Georgia's resources, warned the president of the new threat posed by a prospering South. Because the state had "the advantages of raw material . . . cheap labor, limitless water power and a mild genial climate," it would "not be a matter of surprise" to Brown "if northern gentlemen interested in manufacturing should in future find it to their interest to remove their machinery to Georgia where these great advantages exist." Georgia had "orange groves," "cotton," "clover," "other

61. Atlanta *Constitution*, September 24, 1872; Atlanta *Daily Constitution*, July 7, 1880. Answering those who still "assailed" his "character" for being "a traitor to the confederacy," Brown reminded critics that he had "lost two brothers in that struggle"; see also November 16, 1880.
62. Fielder, *Life and Times and Speeches of Joseph E. Brown*, 527–31.

grasses," "iron," "gold," "silver," and "copper." Carried away by this time with his own salesmanship, Brown predicted mistakenly that "in three counties we have enough coal to last for centuries to come."[63]

Perhaps Benjamin Hill made the most dramatic shift in his public discourse, stumbling over past promises to share in the new business investments. One editor concluded: "Joe Brown and Ben Hill cheek by jowl politically is a merry piece of humor."[64] Having rivaled Robert Toombs with his violent rhetoric after the war, Hill too was tamed by the new economic temptations: "We will submit to the accomplished facts of the past, whether we approve them or not; we will join our Northern brethren." As early as 1872 this formerly intolerant spokesman asked that an Atlanta audience be more "tolerant." Appropriating Brown's appeals, Hill suggested that "the essence of statesmanship is practicability—the power to take facts as we find them and use them to advantage." Laws must now be "faithfully executed." "We are in the beginning of a new era. Our material prosperity must now begin." Following the new strategical formula precisely, Hill promised his audience that he would "not deal with general principles," but with making cotton and compelling "the negro to quit stealing and go to work." "We must get control of our own labor and regulate our own industry." "I who have written and spoken with more invective perhaps than any other man during our severe trials," he admitted, "desire first of all to declare that . . . I shall . . . find a pleasure in forgetting them. Henceforth he is most my brother who most earnestly gives all his energies to rebuild our State." With his eyes actually fixed on Bourbon profits, this political chameleon told audiences that as he looked "above men and parties" he

63. Atlanta *Daily Constitution*, September 25, 1877.
64. Atlanta *Constitution*, December 29, 1870.

felt "that something glorious and akin to a divine power is now lifting us and our whole country from the slough of despond and putting us on the Mount of Hope."[65]

In summary, the situation in Georgia from 1865 to 1872 suggests that the desire for self-determination was the prevailing concern of whites. Frightened by the new activities of former slaves and a potential loss of their own power, whites turned to persons with pronouncements supportive of the southern cause, southern principle, and white superiority. Under these conditions audiences were more susceptible to emotion and sentiment than they were to realistic appeals.

In this context Joseph Emerson Brown provided a lonely voice for accommodation. In plain language Brown reasoned realistically that a defeated people must abide by the victor's will. Submission, Brown argued, was the best strategy available for achieving economic recovery. Frustrated and hurt, white Georgians responded to their war governor with threats and ostracism. In harsh terms Benjamin Hill declared Brown a "traitor" and his strategy "treachery." But to his credit Brown provided an alternative to the resistance advocated by Gordon, Hill, and Toombs, a reconciliatory attitude which would have been largely absent without his minority stance.

John B. Gordon exploited southern sentiment rather than question it. The former general sanctified himself and southern interests with symbols of resistance. A forceful speaker and a war hero, Gordon publicized the suffering, sacrifice, tradition, and hopes of whites. He achieved fame as a myth maker and a professional spokesman for the southern cause. Reinforcing existing beliefs, Gordon prepared the way for the advent of the New South. But he had little to offer to lessen hate, racism, or economic need.

65. Hill, *Benjamin H. Hill of Georgia*, 428–31; Atlanta *Constitution*, February 24, 1872; Atlanta *Daily Constitution*, August 16, 1873; New York *Times*, September 1, 1877; Atlanta *Daily Constitution*, September 26, 1877.

Only when local government had been restored to white Georgians in 1872 were the citizens willing to accept an attitude of accommodation. Brown, Gordon, Benjamin Hill, Alfred Colquitt, Henry Grady, and other Democrats consolidated their rhetorical strategies, compromised their differences, and took control of Georgia. These articulate spokesmen were more concerned about private arrangements and gain than public well being, about business and political manipulations than ideological differences. With the racial issue nearly resolved to their satisfaction, whites invested their energies in political and business enterprises. In many of his later speeches and letters, Brown, chiding Georgians, reminded them that what he had predicted had come true. Borrowing arguments which Brown had cited all along in support of accommodation and progress, Gordon and Hill changed their emphasis considerably. Although they continued to soothe the voters with a potent romanticism, they also searched for a form of communication suitable for jaunty businessmen. While John B. Gordon, for example, continued his metaphorical flourishes, he also advocated learning a plain speech which Brown had perfected earlier, a second language some speakers experimented with in shifting the public focus from a romantic past to a prosperous future.

BIBLIOGRAPHICAL NOTE

General works include Isaac Wheeler Avery, *History of the State of Georgia from 1850 to 1881* (New York: Brown and Derby, 1881); Mildred C. Thompson, *Reconstruction in Georgia: Economic, Social, Political, 1865–1872* (New York: Columbia University Press, 1915); Olive Hall Shadgett, *Republican Party in Georgia, From Reconstruction Through 1900* (Athens: University of Georgia Press, 1964); and Elizabeth Studley Nathans, *Losing the Peace: Georgia Republicans and Reconstruction, 1865–1871* (Baton Rouge: Louisiana State University Press, 1968). Dissertations of particular interest are Judson

Clements Ward, Jr., "Georgia Under the Bourbon Democrats, 1872–1890" (Ph.D. dissertation, University of North Carolina, 1947); Horace Calvin Wingo, "Race Relations in Georgia, 1872–1908" (Ph.D. dissertation, University of Georgia, 1969); George L. Jones, "William H. Felton and the Independent Democratic Movement in Georgia, 1870–1890" (Ph.D. dissertation, University of Georgia, 1971); and James L. Owens, "Negro in the Reconstruction of Georgia" (Ph.D. dissertation, University of Georgia, 1974). See also William Anderson, "Resignation of John B. Gordon from the United States Senate, 1880," *Georgia Historical Quarterly*, LII (1968), 438–42; Judson C. Ward, "New Departure Democrats in Georgia: An Interpretation," *Georgia Historical Quarterly*, XLI (1957), 227–36; and C. Vann Woodward, "Bourbonism in Georgia," *North Carolina Historical Review*, XVI (1939), 23–35.

For works on Joseph E. Brown see Herbert Fielder, *A Sketch of the Life and Times and Speeches of Joseph E. Brown* (Springfield, Mass.: Springfield Printing, 1883); Louise Biles Hill, *Joseph E. Brown and the Confederacy* (Chapel Hill: University of North Carolina Press, 1939); Darrell C. Roberts, *Joseph E. Brown and the Politics of Reconstruction* (Tuscaloosa: University of Alabama Press, 1973). In his *Joseph E. Brown of Georgia* (Baton Rouge: Louisiana State University Press, 1977), Joseph Howard Parks presents a complete bibliography of manuscript collections, printed papers and documents, newspapers, memoirs, articles, dissertations, biographies, etc. See also Derrell Clayton Roberts, "Joseph E. Brown and the New South" (Ph.D. dissertation, University of Georgia, 1958); and Valgene Littlefield, "An Evaluation of Joseph Emerson Brown's Invention, 1857–1880" (Ph.D. dissertation, University of Oklahoma, 1964).

In his *John B. Gordon: A Study in Gallantry* (Atlanta: Whitehall Press, 1955), Allen P. Tankersley offers a bibliography of manuscripts and private papers, published writings and speeches, newspapers, public archives, state public records, United States public records, publications by contemporaries, articles, and secondary sources. See also John Brown Gordon, *Reminiscences of the Civil War* (New York: Charles Scribner's Sons, 1904); Alice Dunbar, "Political Life of John Brown Gordon" (M.A. thesis, Emory University, 1939). Some of Hill's speeches are in Benjamin H. Hill, Jr., *Senator Benjamin H. Hill of Georgia: His Life, Speeches and Writings* (Atlanta: H. C. Hudgin, 1891). See also Fleeta Cooper, "The Triumvirate of Colquitt, Gordon, and Brown" (M.A. thesis, Emory University, 1931).

Henry Grady as
a Persuasive Strategist

Most treatments of public speaking in the postbellum South
refer to two speeches: Booker T. Washington's address delivered
at the Atlanta Exposition on September 18, 1895, and Henry W.
Grady's speech to the New England Society of New York City
on December 21, 1886. With the latter speech, entitled "The
New South," Grady established himself overnight as an orator
of national stature and as the foremost spokesman of the New
South.

It is regrettable that attention has been limited to the New
York speech to the neglect of Grady's later public utterances as
the basis for much subsequent discussion of his concept of the
New South. Between 1886 and his death in 1889, Grady delivered two major addresses in the South and another important one in the North. On October 26, 1887, he discussed "The
South and Her Problems" at the Dallas State Fair. On November 24, 1887, he spoke to the Augusta Exposition at Augusta,
Georgia, on the topic "The Solid South." Two years later, December 12, 1889, he addressed the annual banquet of the Boston Merchants Association on the subject "The Race Problem in the South." In these three speeches he developed his
New South concept in more detail than in the New York address.

As used in the present essay, the term *New South* refers to a
program that arose in the three decades from the end of the Civil
War until 1900. In years soon after the war many southerners

74

took refuge in the memory of the "Old South," reconstructed out of myth. The mythical Old South, embodying the ideals and principles for which the war was fought, was peopled with chivalrous gentlemen, beautiful, gracious ladies, and happy, singing, contented Negro slaves. However, one group of predominantly young southerners refused to be chained to romantic memories and advocated a program of recovery that called for an economy based on industry and diversified agriculture. They proclaimed that the southern states were now loyal to the Union and that peace and harmony had been established between the white man and the black man. Southern newspapers early assumed the leadership in propagandizing this shift in attitudes. Richard H. Edmonds made the *Manufacturer's Record* an important organ of the movement. Other editors who advanced the new spirit included Francis Dawson of the Charleston *News and Courier* and Henry Watterson of the Louisville *Courier Journal*.[1]

As an advocate of the New South Grady won recognition through his editorials in the Atlanta *Constitution*, a major newspaper and a powerful molder of opinion in the South, but he achieved national acclaim through his New South speech delivered at New York. Henry W. Savage, Jr., concluded that Grady "more than any other . . . attracted nation wide attention to the South's changing attitude toward industry and spread abroad the term 'new South' to emphasize the change."[2] In a similar estimate more recently Paul M. Gaston noted that upon Grady's death "the New York *Times* lauded him as the 'creator of the spirit' that animated the once despondent region. Other

1. C. Vann Woodward, *Origins of the New South, 1877–1913* (Baton Rouge: Louisiana State University Press, 1951), 144–45; E. Culpepper Clark, "Henry Grady's New South: A Rebuttal from Charleston," *Southern Speech Communication Journal*, XLI (1976), 346–58; George Christopher Wharton, "Henry Watterson—A Study of Selected Speeches on Reconciliation in the Post-Bellum Period" (Ph.D. dissertation, Louisiana State University, 1974).
2. Henry W. Savage, Jr., *The Seeds of Time* (New York: Henry Holt and Company, 1959), 206.

contemporaries, in all parts of the country, were similarly impressed by Grady's evangelistic mission and golden words and were extravagant in their praise of him as the first and foremost New South spokesman." After his death Grady's reputation continued to grow. According to Gaston, "Later generations of Southerners, seldom corrected and sometimes abetted by their historians, continued to look upon Grady . . . as the chief apostle of the New South movement."[3]

Since earlier studies[4] have examined in detail Grady's career as an editor and as a speaker, it is not the intent of the present essay to cover again this material. Instead, it will argue the thesis that Grady's success stemmed in large part from his ability as a rhetorical strategist, an adept practitioner of the "rhetoric of accommodation." To make the New South program palatable, he adjusted his ideas to the aspirations of both the northern and southern listeners. To this end this essay considers the nature of the rhetorical challenges presented by those conflicting requirements and how Grady responded to them.

Throughout his New South speeches, Grady developed three basic themes: first, that the South must industrialize and must diversify its agriculture; second, that the citizens were solving the disharmonies between the white man and the Negro; and third, that the southern states had become loyal members of the Union. To win acceptance of these themes, Grady had to overcome two rhetorical problems. First, he had to convince the northerners that the South was "safe" for northern investments, particularly by showing that former confederates were loyal to the Union and by demonstrating that they were promoting racial peace. In this role he functioned as a reconciliation speaker.

3. Paul M. Gaston, *The New South Creed: A Study in Southern Mythmaking* (New York: Alfred A. Knopf, 1970), 17.

4. For example, Raymond B. Nixon, *Henry W. Grady, Spokesman of the New South* (New York: Alfred A. Knopf, 1943) and Marvin G. Bauer, "Henry W. Grady," in William Norwood Brigance (ed.), *A History and Criticism of American Public Address* (2 vols.; McGraw-Hill, 1943), I.

At home he faced the second challenge of generating enthusiasm for the New South concepts without antagonizing southerners over the racial question.

Development of the Industrialization and Agricultural Diversification Theme

As the cornerstone of his New South Grady claimed that southern economic recovery lay in industrialization and agricultural diversification. In his speeches Grady attributed economic ills in the post–Civil War South to continued reliance upon the production of raw cotton. He argued that economic recovery could come only with industrialization, which would make the South more self-sufficient.

Specifically, how did Grady sell this theme to his audiences? In addressing his northern audiences he devoted far less time to this issue than he did when he spoke in the South. In his New York speech, for example, he appeared more concerned with assuring his listeners that the South had already made significant industrial progress, specifically pointing to the southern textile and iron industries. Grady asserted, "We have learned that the $400,000,000 annually received from our cotton crop will make us rich when the supplies that make it are home-raised." He concluded that the South had achieved "a fuller independence . . . than that which our fathers sought to win in the forum by their eloquence or compel in the field by their swords."[5]

In treating the industrialization theme in the Boston speech Grady, equally brief, confined it to a single paragraph in the published text. He spoke of the agricultural diversification and of the richness of the South's mineral and timber reserves. Then, as in the New York speech, Grady praised the developing industry which, he claimed, was already well-established in the

5. New York *Daily Tribune*, December 23, 1886.

South. He boasted that "from this assured and permanent advantage in raw materials, against which artificial conditions cannot much longer prevail, has grown an amazing system of industries. . . . This system of industries is mounting to a splendor that shall dazzle and illumine the world."[6] Thus, in the North, where he was seeking capital and attempting to thwart intervention, he was positive and optimistic and gave assurances of progress. By his selection of evidence and by his own image, he forwarded his mission.

Before southern audiences Grady presented his economic program somewhat differently. While praising southern "progress" Grady devoted his major effort toward indicting the southern emphasis on a cotton economy. With this need he coupled a solution: the South should diversify its agriculture and foster industries to exploit its natural resources. In his Dallas speech Grady gave his most extended discussion of his economic program. Reflecting his knowledge of southerners, he complimented his listeners for the recovery which the South had already made. Praising the role of cotton, he noted that the South enjoyed a virtual monopoly in cotton production at a time when domestic and foreign markets were steadily increasing. However, to temper his praise he warned that neglect of other crops would have disastrous consequences. "Whenever the greed for a money crop unbalances the wisdom of husbandry," Grady observed, "the money crop is a curse." He cited the example of North Carolina, where tobacco, which was the only crop, had caused great poverty. Then applying his analogy to cotton, he warned that dedication to a single crop forced the South into economic servitude to the East and the West. Furthermore, he declared the situation deplorable because it was unnecessary: "To raise cotton and send its princely revenues to the West for supplies and to the East for usury, would be misfortune if soil

6. Atlanta *Constitution*, December 15, 1889.

and climate forced such a curse. When both invite independence, to remain in slavery is a crime."[7]

Interestingly, Grady worked into his speeches a strong un-
dercurrent of sectionalism. He condemned an economy that
forced the South into economic servitude to other regions, that
required the income from cotton to be used to purchase food
and equipment from the West and to borrow operating capital
from eastern bankers. It was as if Grady believed that an economic conflict had replaced the military conflict between North
and South. The implied sectionalism was to appear in other
phases of Grady's New South program.

The second part of Grady's solution rested on the premise
that agriculture alone, no matter how rich or varied, could not
establish or maintain prosperity; no region could become great
simply by producing raw material. In Dallas he drew a telling
analogy between miners who received little of the value of the
Comstock Lode and southerners whose cotton, minerals, and
timbers enriched other sections. Therefore Grady urged southerners to industrialize and take advantage of their almost unlimited iron ore, coal, marble, granite, and lumber. To support
his claim of the financial rewards, Grady offered several contrasting examples of specific northern and southern states and
suggested that northern prosperity came from industrialization.

In addition to insisting that the South possessed great possibilities in its resources, Grady assured his southern audiences
that the removal of the debilitating influence of slavery rendered industrialization possible. In explaining the concentration
of industry in the middle states, Grady in part blamed slavery
for driving enterprising people and capital out of the South. In
his emphasis upon southern industrialization, Grady attempted
to achieve polarization, advocating a southern nationalism in
which the South would be independent of the North. Southern

7. *Ibid.*, October 28, 1886.

cotton and other raw materials would be turned into finished products by southern factories, and then sold to southern markets. He strongly implied that it would be better for Texas to buy from and sell to Georgia than to be dependent upon Massachusetts. To reinforce his views he used the composite term *South* in preference to references to individual states.

But Grady did not limit his proposed solution for southern economic ills to industrialization. Accordingly, he suggested that the farms would always be necessary to supply both food and raw materials and that southerners should move toward diversification: "grains and grasses, the orchard and the vine." He pictured southern self-sufficiency in which each farmer would feed himself and sell his cotton for his surplus income. Before southerners Grady pictured a South which would develop industries to exploit its rich natural resources and which would in turn free itself from dependence on the West and the Northeast. His full-blown treatment of this concept in his southern speeches contrasts with the brief discussion given to it in his New York and Boston addresses. But even more fundamentally in the southern speeches he set forth a detailed program for the future, while to his northern audiences he implied that development was well underway.

Defense of Southern Racial Policies

Grady's second major thrust contended that the racial problem was being solved in the South. That this line was undoubtedly his most important and his most difficult is suggested by the amount of time he devoted to its development, giving it more than half of his Dallas and Augusta speeches and an entire speech in Boston. He knew that his handling of the matter was crucial to his New South strategy because he had to demonstrate that the South was progressing toward a solution acceptable to southerners without offending northern sensibilities.

In the North, Grady confronted a change in attitudes toward

racial problems from those which prevailed immediately following the Civil War. Northern agitation had subsided. Those who pressed for the full rights of the Negro were becoming less and less numerous. Even the federal government was retreating from the hard line taken during Reconstruction. However, Grady looked for a stance on the racial question which would satisfy northerners or at least give them a rationale for believing that the South had arrived at an equitable solution to its racial problems.

In the North Grady chose to emphasize the positive aspects of the southern racial situation, asserting that ties between white man and the Negro originally were "close and cordial." For support he freely called forth the mythology of the Old South. In New York and again in Boston, Grady told his northern listeners that southerners remembered the faithfulness of the Negroes in guarding defenseless women and children for four years while husbands fought against their freedom, and that for this reason the South joined the North in protesting injustices done to "this simple and sincere people." In Boston Grady praised the antebellum bond between slave and master by graphically describing his own rearing by his "old black mammy" and the tenderness of the slaves in protecting the family while the master was away. Grady spoke of a charge from the grave to the living to protect the Negro. In an emotional passage, the kind for which he was famous, he expressed the southern determination to honor that obligation:

Whatever the future may hold for them—whether they plod along in the servitude from which they have never been lifted since the Cyrenian was laid hold upon by the Roman soldiers and made to bear the cross of the fainting Christ; whether they find homes again in Africa, and thus hasten the prophecy of the psalmist who said, "And suddenly Ethiopia shall hold out her hands unto God;" whether, forever dislocated and separated, they remain a weak people beset by stronger, and exist as the Turk, who lives in the jealousy rather than the conscience of Europe; or whether in this miraculous Republic they break through the cast of twenty centuries and belying universal history, reach the full stature of citizenship, and in peace maintain it—we shall give them uttermost justice and abiding friendship.[8]

However, Grady lamented that the old relationship of slave to master had ended. Quoting Benjamin H. Hill, Grady said in New York that "there was a South of slavery and secession—that South is dead." In its place was a South determined to treat the Negro fairly and justly. And, Grady stressed, as early as 1886 the Negro was receiving that kind of treatment. Economically, the Negro was successful, for, as Grady told New Yorkers, "no section shows a more prosperous laboring population than the negroes of the South." Three years later Grady made the same claims in Boston, where he concluded that the Negro's record produced two conclusions: first, it honored the Negro and vindicated his white neighbor, and second, it showed that for every "agitator," there were a thousand Negroes, "happy in their cabin homes, tilling their own land day by day."[9]

Grady further insisted that the southern Negro was progressing in education. He told his New York audience that the Negro shared the school funds, and that schools had been built and made free to white and black children alike.[10] He developed the idea more fully in Boston, citing statistics to prove that whereas southern whites had contributed to education thirty times the amount given by the Negro, the children of Negroes had received one half of the money spent on education.[11]

In legal matters also, according to Grady, the Negro was being given his full rights under the law. He assured his Boston audience that legislation had reduced felonies to misdemeanors to save "this dependent race from their own weakness," that 60 percent of the prosecutors were Negroes, and that Ne-

8. *Ibid.*, December 15, 1889.
9. *Ibid.*
10. New York *Daily Tribune*, December 23, 1888.
11. Atlanta *Constitution*, December 15, 1889.

82

groes preferred white jurors in court cases. In an effort to minimize the reported cases of mistreatment of former slaves by
the courts, Grady asserted that Negroes received better treatment in the South than in the North. To support his case Grady
noted that in the North one Negro in 466 was in jail, whereas
in the South only one in 1,865 was in jail and that in the North
the percentage of Negro prisoners was six times as great as native whites, but in the South it was only four times as great.
Thus Grady concluded: "If prejudice wrongs him in Southern
courts, the record shows it to be deeper in Northern courts."

As to rumors that Negroes had been subjected to disorder
and violence in the South, Grady responded that such charges
would continue to be true to some degree "until there is one
ideal community on earth after which we may pattern." But
having made that concession, he then insisted that the reports of
mistreatment had been grossly exaggerated. Shifting the blame
from the South to the North, Grady argued that two northern
attitudes were responsible for the exaggerations. In the first
place, so Grady claimed, the Negro's status had led people to
magnify his alleged mistreatment. "Inflamed by prejudice and
partisans," this tendency had led to "injustice and delusion."
Secondly, again shifting blame, Grady asserted that some northerners were applying two standards of conduct, one in the North
and another in the South. When "lawless men" assaulted a
county in Iowa, it was an "incident"; if the same activity occurred in the South, northerners would declare it to be "fixed
habit of the community." Pursuing his line of persuasion, Grady
noted that when in Indiana regulators punished vagabonds it
scarcely aroused attention, but "a chance collision in the South
among relatively the same classes" was "evidence that the races
were destroying each other." Further emphasizing the incon-
sistency in the northern position, Grady observed that it would
be as unreasonable to claim that the Union was ungrateful to
its Negro soldier because a Grand Army of the Republic post in

Connecticut refused a Negro veteran as for northern critics to give racial significance to every southern incident or to "accept exceptional grounds as the rule of our society." Explaining such episodes in either North or South as only a sign of human imperfection, Grady presented an effective rationalization: that the men who had made the trip to Boston with him had probably never seen "an outrage committed on a negro," and if they had, no one would be swifter to prevent or punish; these men were typical, so Grady alleged, of southern thinking.

The major negative aspect of southern racial policy to which Grady had to answer in his northern addresses was the charge that the Negro vote was being negated. First, there was the matter of the "solid South" by which, so critics charged, the Negro vote was canceled because the white vote was solidly united. In Boston Grady admitted that southern whites had united their vote, but he rationalized that it was not from prejudice or sectional bias, but from necessity. According to Grady, the South's bitter experience with elections in which the Negro vote had been manipulated by unscrupulous politicians had led the whites to unite—just as Massachusetts would unite if 300,000 black men, the majority illiterate, voted "in a race instinct, holding against you the memory of a century of slavery, taught by your late conquerors to distrust and oppose you, [and] had already travestied legislation from your statehouse, and in every species of folly and villainy had wasted your substance and exhausted your credit."

Continuing his defense, Grady challenged the logic of northern critics who argued that the Negro vote was being illegally suppressed in the South. He resorted to the technique of minimizing through comparison. According to Grady those critics had based their charge on the smallness of the southern vote. Using the same reasoning, Grady argued that northern states would be as open to charges of suppressing Negro votes as the South. For example, he noted that in 1888 Virginia cast 75 percent of her vote, while Massachusetts cast only 60 percent. Grady reasoned that if Virginia was to be condemned for the small percentage of her vote, what conclusion was to be reached about Massachusetts? He reinforced his position with other similar comparisons.

However, not content with minimizing the arguments of the northern critics, Grady offered his Boston audience an alternative explanation for the small Negro vote. He shifted the blame away from the South and onto the shoulders of the northern abolitionists. According to Grady, the real reason Negroes had not voted was disenchantment with suffrage because the abolitionists had promised the Negro much if he exercised his vote, and it had given him little. The southern Negro, Grady suggested, had been promised "forty acres and a mule," and had been warned that Democratic victory at the polls would mean reenslavement; but neither result had come about. What had happened, Grady insisted, was that acceptance of this false advice had cost the Negro the friendship and sympathy of his white neighbors, and politics had brought nothing to compensate for that loss. It was this disillusioning experience, concluded Grady, that had reduced the Negro vote.[12]

Thus Grady portrayed to his northern audiences a South innocent of deliberate mistreatment of the Negro, indeed, a South committed to the protection of the Negro in the exercise of every right guaranteed him by law. His strategy was first to emphasize the positive gains made by the Negro in economics and education, and the efforts of the South to protect legal rights. Second, Grady attempted to blunt northern criticism by denying that the practices of which they accused the South were deliberate policy, born of a desire to refuse the Negro his legal rights. A third element in his strategy was to minimize the problems and to suggest that they had been exaggerated both in

12. All of the quotations from the Boston speech come from *ibid*.

scope and significance. A fourth tactic of Grady was to shift the blame for southern racial troubles to abolitionist influence. And finally, he defended the Solid South as being at worst a necessary evil, forced on the South by the need to protect itself from an incompetent exercise of the franchise by the Negro. All in all, Grady pictured a South where race relations simply were no longer a problem—particularly if outside forces would leave the region alone and permit it to work out its own solutions.

In his southern speeches Grady treated the racial question with quite different tone and content. In New York Grady had quoted Benjamin Hill's remark that "there was a South of slavery and secession—that South is dead"; in Dallas, in beginning his discussion of the racial theme he observed that slavery was over but added that southern slavery had "been administered in the fullest wisdom of man." He took the position that southerners had no reason to apologize for slavery; instead, they should focus on solving the problems resulting from emancipation.

The rhetorical challenge to Grady in discussing the racial theme with his southern audiences resulted from the three relatively distinct southern attitudes toward the Negro. On one hand, the liberal attitude, represented by George Washington Cable, contended that the Negro was now free and entitled to equality with the white man. At the opposite extreme some southerners argued that the only real change in the Negro's status was that he was now *de jure* free. Between these two extremes, moderates were willing within limits to grant the Negro certain rights. Grady had to find a position on the racial question which would please as many southerners as possible. His strategy was to emphasize the continuation of social segregation and to justify the "solid South" as a means of dealing with the Negro vote.

First, Grady made it clear that his attitude toward the Negro did not extend to any compromise of "racial integrity," meaning of course fraternization or social equality. "The races and tribes of earth are of divine origin," Grady insisted; and racial separation is of divine origin. The races stand as "markers of God's will," and no man should attempt to undo God's work by obliterating the distinctions between races. Unity of civilization was no more possible in Grady's view than unity of faith, for "no race has risen, or will rise, above its ordained place." Therefore, attempts to bridge the differences by statutes are doomed to failure in the face of "God's will." Thus, while the South had no desire to deny any legal privileges to the Negro, Grady insisted that God "has ordained that she shall walk in that integrity of race that was created in His wisdom and has been perpetuated in His strength."[13]

But by far Grady directed the greater attention to the second element of his racial philosophy. According to Grady, the only significant source of racial friction in the South grew out of the Negro vote. With this problem in mind he warned the Dallas audience that the "freedman" presented the most important single issue facing the South. Specifically, he raised the specter of political control by Negro voters. Making the problem one of almost paranoid proportions, he spoke of a condition which would parallel the dark times of Radical Reconstruction when Negro voters were used to humiliate and otherwise abuse the white people.

In magnifying the problem Grady suggested that Negro and white voters were nearly equal in number, that the Negro vote was steadily increasing in size, and that the Negro voter had shown himself susceptible to easy manipulation, with the result that unscrupulous men could use the Negro to control the South. Emphasizing the myth of white supremacy, Grady told his Augusta audience that the Negro vote was alien, "being separated by radical differences that are deep and permanent,"

13. *Ibid.*, October 28, 1886.

and that it was ignorant, impulsive, and purchasable. Furthermore, there was no way to eliminate the vote. Such a vote, Grady asserted, would not be dangerous as long as no faction existed to bid for it, but clever politicians could use it to control a community, a state, or the South. Turning to a strong fear appeal, he said that Reconstruction taught the power of the Negro vote. That vote, which Grady termed a "dangerous and alien influence," was one which could not "be won by argument, for it [was] without information, understanding, or tradition hence without conviction." The vote of the Negro could therefore be bought by the promise of race privileges or by money.

Grady suggested two reasons for this problem. Bringing into play the mythology of the Old South, Grady contended that the Negro was by nature unsuited for the exercise of the franchise because he was and always would be racially "inferior." The problem was, Grady frankly asserted to his Dallas audience, "a race issue." However, he further rationalized that the South was not alone in its racial attitudes; white men felt it in Ohio as well as in Georgia. The situation existed wherever the "Anglo-Saxon race" touched an "alien" race, as for example in the case of the Chinese exclusion laws. For his Dallas audience Grady cited several confrontations and asserted that in each one the "Anglo-Saxon blood" had dominated. Invoking the concept of manifest destiny, he concluded that the white man had established the Republic forever as the home of the white man, and therefore "never one foot of it can be surrendered . . . to the domination of an alien and inferior race."

In his second explanation for the South's racial problem Grady again placed the blame for the condition on forces outside the South. Specifically, he challenged the motives of northerners, determined to install the Negro as the dominant voice in southern politics. With a small rhetorical twist, Grady insisted in Augusta that the problem was not of the South's own seeking, but one thrust upon it by the North. He further berated the North for acting "in hot impulse and passion, against the judgment of the world and the lessons of history, and to the peril of popular government, which rests at last on a pure and unsullied suffrage as a building rests on its cornerstone." There was, Grady complained, no precedent for the action of the North in enfranchising the slaves, and he concluded that "posterity will judge on the wisdom and patriotism in which it was ordered, and the order and equity in which it was worked out."[14]

Grady placed particular emphasis on the role of William T. Sherman in sustaining the conflict over the voting issue. In contrast to the complimentary light in which Grady placed Sherman in the New York address, in Dallas he quoted General Sherman as threatening: "The negro must be allowed to vote, and his vote must be counted; otherwise, as sure as there is a God in heaven, you will have another war, more cruel than the last, when the torch and the dagger will take the place of the muskets of well-ordered battalions. Should the negro strike that blow, in seeming justice, there will be millions to assist them."[15] In Augusta Grady carried further his attack on Sherman. Using highly emotional language, Grady drew on bitter memories, reminding his audience of Sherman's "march to the sea" through their own state. Characterizing Sherman, Grady observed that the soldier had "covered the desolation he sowed in city and country through these States with the maxim that 'cruelty in war is mercy'—and no one lifted the cloak. But when he insults the man he conquered, and endangers the renewing growth of the country he wasted, with this unmanly threat, he puts a stain on his name the maxims of philosophy and fable from Socrates all the way cannot cover, and the glory of Marlborough, were it added to his own, could not efface."[16]

14. *Ibid.*, December 2, 1888.
15. *Ibid.*, October 28, 1886.
16. *Ibid.*, December 2, 1888.

Grady condemned the northern press as another source of racial friction. In particular he cited the Chicago *Tribune*, referring to an "inflammatory article" which suggested that the "trouble" was that the Negroes would not shoot and burn for their rights. Grady characterized this statement as an indefensible charge "levelled by a knave at a political condition which he views from afar, and which it is proved does not exist," yet the *Tribune*'s words were applauded in the northern community.

Having blamed the North for creating the problems with the Negro vote, Grady then rationalized that the South had taken the only course available to it to control the Negro vote. Promoting the myth of the Solid South, Grady argued that the South had sought to block Negro domination of the electoral process by having the whites vote as a unit, therefore preventing the Negro vote from being a deciding factor in the elections. Perhaps with the Populists and the Republicans in mind, Grady told his Dallas audience: "The clear and unmistakeable [*sic*] domination of the white race, dominating not through violence, not through party alliance, but through the integrity of its own vote and the largeness of its sympathy and justice through which it shall compel the support of the better classes of the colored race—that is the hope and assurance of the South."[17] In Augusta, turning to a strategy of terror and an appeal to fear, Grady argued from the analogy of Reconstruction that the power of the Negro vote was turned back only when the South became solid again. He warned the audience that the same danger would threaten again if the white vote divided. Then, possibly with northern readers in mind, Grady asserted that the Solid South was not a desirable situation and that the ideal would be for each state to vote without regard to sectional lines, for love of the Union should be uppermost, and reconciliation would

17. *Ibid.*, October 18, 1886.

never be complete "until Iowa and Georgia, Texas and Massachusetts, may stand side by side without surprise." However, this union could not be, for the enfranchisement of the Negro condemned the South "to solidify as surely as self-preservation is the first law of nature." Individual states might drift away, but they would always come back. The duty of the South therefore was "to maintain the political as well as the social integrity of her white race, and to appeal to the world for patience and justice." [18]

Thus in his speeches at Dallas and Augusta Grady argued that the South had always treated the Negro fairly and would continue to do so by granting the Negro every right which he was capable of exercising. Perhaps keeping in mind accommodation, he may well have taken this position with an eye to northern readers. However, in an appeal directed to southerners he insisted that those rights were subject to two major exclusions: no social integration of the races, and no Negro control of the South by mass vote.

When Grady's treatment of the racial question at Dallas and Augusta is compared with his handling of the same theme in New York and Boston, some similarities emerge. In both the North and the South he insisted that the Negro was being treated fairly, and would continue to be so. In Boston Grady also developed in detail the southern position on Negro suffrage and argued that the South must continue to prevent the Negro from exercising political control by the size of his vote. But the differences between Grady's handling of the racial problem in North and South are more striking than the similarities. In the South Grady relied heavily on the anthropological myths of slavery days; the Negro was racially inferior to the white man, and no amount of education or evolution would completely overcome that inferiority. The Negro could be brought

18. *Ibid.*, December 2, 1888.

up to a certain point of development but no farther, and that point would always stand below the level of the white man. Furthermore, while disclaiming sectionalism in both his northern and southern addresses, when he spoke in the South, Grady appealed to sectional feelings in discussing the treatment of the Negro. According to Grady, the South's racial problems were originally caused by northern interference, and the most recent troubles were encouraged by individuals and the press in the North.

But perhaps the most striking difference between the northern and southern speeches is the mood in which Grady discussed the racial situation. Consonant with his desire to present to potential northern investors a South stable and safe for their investments, he conveyed in New York and Boston a mood of optimism. In the first he scarcely gives a hint of any problem, and even in the second, where Grady admits that there was a problem with the Negro suffrage, he suggests by his whole demeanor that the problem will be solved in time, and the Solid South will no longer be a necessity. In direct contrast in the South, however, Grady is less optimistic. In fact, neither at Dallas nor Augusta does he foresee a time when political solidarity of southern whites will be unnecessary. In promoting the cause of the Solid South, Grady warned southerners that they could never let down their guard. His optimism in the North thus contrasts markedly with the pessimism in the South.

Advocacy of Nationalism

In his third major theme Grady again used a strategy of accommodation to develop the claim that the South was a loyal member of the Union. The war had focused attention on the issues which divided North and South and these had become crystallized in the thinking of many northerners into a stereotyped picture of the southerner as possessing characteristics which separated him from the northerner. Most of all there was the war itself, which had signalled for most people in the North the desire of the South to become a separate nation. Grady and his fellow New South spokesmen had the task of convincing any northern doubters that the South had given up its intent to separate from the rest of the nation and was now loyal to the Union. As a means to the greater goal of southern industrialization, the theme was necessary to convey the image that the South was a part of the larger nation. By promoting this nationalistic image of the South, Grady sought to pave the way for northern investments in the region.

In the two northern speeches Grady was concerned with reconciliation. The invitation to speak in New York came because Grady had impressed John H. Inman, a southern-born industrialist then residing in New York. The occasion was the 266th anniversary of the New England Society in New York, and the audience, assembled in Delmonico's, included General William T. Sherman, J. Pierpont Morgan, Lyman Abbot, H. M. Flagler, Jr., Russell Sage, and many of the leading financiers.[19] For his purposes, it was an ideal audience, consisting of several prominent northern capitalists. He realized that his rhetorical problem was to allay remaining fears about the safety of southern investments.

The entire address was constructed as an appeal for reconciliation, and the strategy is worth noting. Using a direct approach, Grady asserted that the South had once again become loyal. He began with the now-famous quotation from Benjamin H. Hill: "There was a South of slavery and secession—that South is dead. There is a South of Union and freedom—that South, thank God is living, breathing, growing every hour."[20] Through the quotation from a prominent southerner he undoubtedly put his listeners at ease, for the reference to a "South of union" was precisely what they wanted to hear. To establish

19. Nixon, *Henry W. Grady: Spokesman of the New South*, 241–44.
20. New York *Daily Tribune*, December 23, 1886.

a cordial relationship he thanked those present for the invitation to speak and pleaded for an indulgent hearing.

Then turning to his first major idea, Grady introduced the Puritan-Cavalier theme, in which the Puritan had symbolized the North and the Cavalier the South. Choosing to destroy the polarization, he noted that Puritan and Cavalier each had now lost their separate identities and merged into the American citizen, "supplanting both and stronger than either." Speaking without a manuscript, he responded to an earlier speaker, Thomas DeWitt Talmadge, and suggested that the ideal American citizen had already come, personified in Abraham Lincoln, the great martyr who was to be emulated and of course the most powerful symbol associated with the late war.

Grady then described the returning Confederate soldier and the devastation to which he returned. However, rather than despairing, the soldier had exhibited distinctive American virtues by putting the war behind him and setting about with enthusiasm to restore the prosperity he had enjoyed before the war. Husbands and wives alike worked with energy and resourcefulness to repair the damages of war "with little bitterness" and "not one ignoble prejudice or memory." These virtues, Grady implied, characterized most southerners. Grady described the growing industrialization and insisted that the South was solving its racial problems on a basis which would be equitable for the black man. In short, Grady concluded that southerners had come to believe that developments were just as satisfactory as before the war, and that the South had achieved a fuller independence than that sought by others in the forum or on the battlefield. In these assertions Grady attributed to the South great American virtues while presenting an argument which was undoubtedly satisfying to his northern listeners.

Up to this point, Grady had honestly faced up to an undeniable fact: the South had rebelled against the Union. His task was now to develop a line of argument which would permit

94

each side to regard the war in a favorable light. A lesser orator might have insulted the South and stirred up the "bloody shirt" image in the North, but Grady pursued a skillful strategy and rationalized the conflict in a vein to preserve the honor of each side.

Consistent with his strategy, Grady presented the South in an admirable perspective; that is, the Confederacy had acted out of conviction and had conducted itself, even in defeat, with honor and dignity. Then to emphasize his lesson Grady asserted that since its defeat the South had become loyal to the Union with nothing to apologize for, for she viewed the struggle as a war between equals, not a rebellion. But accepting her defeat, the South had learned the folly of an economic system saddled by slavery and dominated by agriculture. Furthermore, the South was proud of her new look. Grady concluded the speech with a call for the northern acceptance of the South. Thus Grady turned embarrassing defeat into a positive asset, rationalizing the southern rebellion and successfully minimizing it in the light of his claim of southern loyalty to the Union.

Grady also made an effective plea for reconciliation in the speech delivered to the Boston Merchants Association, December 12, 1889. The inspiration for the address grew out of Henry Cabot Lodge's announced plan to demand federal supervision of polling places in the national elections. After the 1888 election, many moderate Republicans as well as Democrats predicted that such a measure would damage developing peaceful relations between North and South. When on December 3 President Harrison had urged in a message to Congress the adoption of such a bill, Grady was invited to present the point of view of the South.[21]

Grady's purpose was the same as it had been in the New York speech: to remove northern doubts about southern loyalty to the

21. Nixon, *Henry W. Grady: Spokesman of the New South*, 316–19. Lodge's "Force Bill" passed the House by six votes, but failed in the Senate.

Union. However, in Boston he varied his strategy because he had to defend the New South's racial policies in general and the Solid South voting practices in particular. To accomplish this task he chose to minimize the racial problems, shifting the blame to northern interference, and reinterpreting history to show that the South had always been loyal to the Union. As in New York, Grady managed his introduction skillfully, resorting to humor to get the attention and good-will of his audience. Further to enhance his ethos he asserted his intention to "speak in perfect frankness and sincerity" from his "earnest understanding of the vast interests involved" and from "a consecrating sense of what disaster may follow further misunderstanding and estrangement."[22]

Developing his theme, Grady argued that northern agitation over alleged mistreatment of the Negro in the South had produced two undesirable consequences. First, the accusations had seriously impaired southern economic development. Second, the charges of suppression of the Negro vote had become a basis for estrangement between North and South. In replying to the charge of mistreatment, Grady minimized the accusation by asserting that it was not as serious as some northerners had claimed. He further tried to reduce the significance of the problem by insisting that it was being handled satisfactorily. Shifting the blame, he then alleged that the controversy was being intensified by northerners who had little understanding of the circumstances and who were forcing a course of action disastrous to black man and white man alike. Relating the racial problem to his reconciliation theme, Grady appealed for the sympathy and understanding of the North. According to him, what the South needed most was time and patience. Granted that, he pledged that nothing would happen to "disturb the love we bear this Republic, or mitigate our consecration to its

22. Atlanta *Constitution*, December 15, 1889.

service." This love, he insisted, was "no new loyalty." To support this claim, he used two figures who personified the Rebel cause to the North. The first was General Robert E. Lee, commander of the Confederate forces. According to Grady, by his words and actions at Appomattox, Lee had pledged his loyalty to the Union, setting an example for other southerners to follow. The second figure was the Confederate soldier. In a narrative which added strong emotional appeals to his argument, Grady related how a soldier in gray, standing at the base of a Confederate monument, "his empty sleeve tossing in the April wind," urged the young men around him to be loyal and honest citizens of the government against which their fathers fought. Compounding his references to these symbols of the Lost Cause, he clearly intended to emphasize that formerly dissident southerners now joined the North in affirming and supporting the Union.

In concluding, Grady reasserted southern loyalty to the Union. Calling for an end to sectionalism, he urged his listeners to join in "the broad and perfect loyalty that loves and trusts Georgia alike with Massachusetts—that knows no South, no North, no East, no West, but endears with equal and patriotic love every foot of our soil, every state of our Union." Returning to the language of his New York speech, Grady asked his hearers to think in terms of "Americans" and "American" objectives rather than in terms of North or South, thereby reinforcing the point of the whole speech: northerners and southerners were now merged in the common identity of "the American."

Grady did not limit his efforts toward reconciliation to northern audiences but attempted to remove sectional identification in favor of the Union in the South as well. However, at home Grady faced a somewhat different rhetorical problem: for, whereas northern audiences wanted assurance that southerners had given up those regional loyalties that had precipitated the war, southerners revered those memories. Grady was challenged therefore to make the traditions of the Old South compatible with the beliefs of the New South, while suggesting a primary identification as an American rather than as a southerner.

At Dallas and Augusta Grady rejected the thesis that the South was a distinct area set apart from the other states in the Union. In beginning his Dallas speech, Grady stated his purpose as being "to discuss . . . certain problems upon the wise and prompt solution of which depends the glory and prosperity of the South." He then asked rhetorically, why "the South?" In answer he contended that an indivisible union such as the United States would argue against separation into such geographical sections. Furthermore, no local interests or autonomy would account for such a division, and neither sectionalism nor provincialism would form a defensible basis for such a label as "the South." Neither could the South claim distinctiveness on the basis of a governmental theory, for that theory, "having triumphed in every forum, fell at last by the sword." Slavery no longer bound the section into a unit, nor did the war which grew out of slavery. The only basis, Grady concluded, for speaking of "the South" was that the problem, which he was about to discuss, was centralized in the southern states. In concluding the speech Grady called for his listeners to dedicate themselves to the development of the South, but under the deeper dedication to the Union.[23] At Augusta Grady likewise advocated nationalism over sectionalism. Expressing regrets over the necessity of a "solid South" with respect to voting, Grady admitted that the course of action was not the ideal one in which citizens vote without regard to sectional lines. He thought that love for the Union should take precedence over sectional allegiances and that reconciliation would never be complete "until

23. *Ibid.*, October 28, 1888.

Iowa and Georgia, Texas and Massachusetts may stand side by side without surprise."

Clearly, then, Grady told his southern audiences as well as his northern audiences that nationalism must prevail over sectionalism in the South. However, even while deprecating sectionalism he praised the traditions of the Old South, already enshrined in myth. When discussing race relations Grady invoked the plantation myth, picturing happy, trusting, cordial ties between the former slave and his master, the same warm relationship that allegedly existed between them in antebellum days. In another use of the Old South myth, Grady concluded his Dallas speech with an appeal to "the young men of Texas" to carry the transcending Old South traditions "from which none of us can in honor or in reverence depart, unstained and unbroken into the New." Using highly emotional language, Grady continued: "Shall we fail? Shall the blood of the old South —the best strain that ever uplifted human endeavor—that ran like water at duty's call and never stained where it touched— shall this blood that pours into our veins through a century luminous with achievement, for the first time falter and be driven back from irresolute heart, when the old South that left us a better heritage in manliness and courage than in broad and rich acres, calls us to settle problems?"[24]

But perhaps the most remarkable passage involving the Old South myth occurred toward the end of the Augusta speech. Building upon the traditional southern belief in divine Providence, Grady suggested that the Old South traditions might serve a soteriological function for the nation as a whole. Concerning the North, he mentioned that "strange admixtures have brought strange results," suggesting that the anarchist and atheist "walk abroad in the cities" and that "culture has refined it-

24. *Ibid.*

self new and strange religions from the strong old creeds." At
the same time, he thought that "the old-time South is fading
from observance and the mellow church-bells that called the
people to the temples of God are being tabooed and silenced."
It was therefore a time to renew "the straight and simple faith,"
to "give ourselves to the saving of the old-fashioned" by a return to the faith of the Old South."[25] In using this strategy,
Grady achieved two results. First, he demonstrated his reverence for the Old South. Secondly, by suggesting that the South
had a destiny to maintain the morality of the nation, he was rebuilding the southern ego.

But, Grady reasoned that the dangers involved were more
than religious, for the South faced those who would try to divide her from within. Therefore, he insisted that "in working
out our civil, political, and religious salvation, everything depends on the union of our people." The problem that he pictured stemmed from the charge that the New South was promulgated to the detriment of the Old South. Such an indictment
could, of course, seriously damage the New South case in Dixie.
In reply to the critics who mounted the charge, Grady asserted
that the young men of the South (*i.e.*, the New South spokesmen) had not demeaned the Old South. "Where is the young
man in the South," he asked, "who has spoken one word in disparagement of our past, or has worn lightly the sacred traditions of our fathers?" According to Grady, the "undying loyalty"
of the young men of the South to "the memory of our fathers"
was unequaled. Building on that past, they had begun to recon-
struct the fallen fortunes of the South. Grady then turned from
a defense of the New South to an attack on his unnamed opponents. Anyone, he declared, who "enwrapping himself in the
sacred memories of the old South, should prostitute them to

25. *Ibid.*, December 2, 1888.

the hiding of his weakness, or the strengthening of his failing fortune, that man would be unworthy." But on the other hand, "if any man for his own advantage should seek to divide the old South from the new, or the new from the old . . . this man's words are unworthy and are spoken to the injury of his people." In an emotional passage invoking the Old South myth, Grady asserted that the old men of the South were sometimes described as living in a dream-world. It was, Grady concluded, "our duty" to rebuild these dreams for them.[26]

The passage is significant in several respects. The accusation that the New South spokesmen were disloyal to the Old South was a potentially damaging one to the New South advocates. Heard from many sources, it could not be ignored. What is of interest here is the manner in which Grady responded to the accusation. The response had two results: if accepted, Grady suggested that a southerner could be a New South man and hold on to the traditions of the Old South, meaning that he could be a national or "American" in his self-identification without being disloyal to the Old South heritage. But he also introduced an effective rhetorical turn by implying that the real traitors were those who sought to separate the New South from the Old South, for the first was in reality an extension of the goals and aspirations of the second.[27]

When Grady defended southern loyalty to the Union in the North, he sought to account satisfactorily for the South's rebellion and also to explain why the principal cause for that rebellion, *i.e.*, the slavery question, need no longer divide the North and South. He did not apologize for secession but rather sought to present the South as acting from praiseworthy motives be-

26. *Ibid.*
27. Gaston, *The New South Creed*, 153–86, develops in detail the rationalization by which New South spokesmen connected the Old South with the New South.

cause the region was defending honestly held beliefs. In presenting the case for nationalism to the South, he praised directly and indirectly the Old South, stressing that the New South was perfectly compatible with loyalty to the Old South traditions.

Press Reaction

One measure of Grady's success may be seen in the newspaper reports of his speeches. For several days following each of the four addresses, the Atlanta *Constitution* published excerpts from press coverage in both the North and South. Admittedly these reports must be read with an eye to the possibility of editorial bias; the *Constitution*'s staff might be expected to select comments complimentary to Grady, while ignoring negative reactions. The only way to determine with finality the representativeness of the *Constitution*'s sample would be to examine individually the newspapers. Rayford W. Logan examined twelve typical northern newspapers' comments on Grady's New York speech. Nine of those papers commented editorially on the address, with three giving enthusiastic endorsements, two offering more reserved appraisals, one reproducing both favorable and unfavorable comments from other papers, and three offering criticisms.[28] The proportions suggest that a majority of the northern papers responded favorably to the speech, and it is possible that the same conclusion might apply to the coverage of subsequent speeches, though Logan does not provide a similar analysis of those addresses. Also, Logan offers no such examination of southern press coverage. With these limitations in mind, it may be concluded that Grady was enthusiastically received in both North and South. After the New York speech, a correspondent for the Atlanta *Constitution* reported that "the crowd went wild in the effort to reach him. I never saw a

28. Rayford W. Logan, *The Betrayal of the Negro* (London: Collier-Macmillan, 1965), 183–87.

man so crowded with compliments and covered with glory!" The New York *Evening Post* was indeed enthusiastic, as was the Philadelphia *Times*, and other northern papers endorsed the speech.[29]

Neither the Dallas speech nor the Augusta speech produced much comment in the northern press, but the Boston address brought reactions as voluminous as did the one in New York. According to the Boston *Advertiser*, a Republican newspaper, "Mr. Grady . . . spoke uninterruptedly eighty minutes. But during that time not a person took his eyes from him, even to nod to a companion. The effect was marvelous; the impression created profound." Continuing, the *Advertiser* asserted that "the sibilant accent of the musical voice won the room of grayhaired northerners, hundreds with the memory of the war past in their hearts and minds, so that wave after wave of feelings swept over the splendid gathering. He wove together logic and poetry, rhythmic prose and columns of statistics, until the audience was enraptured. Declaring himself so frankly for what he wanted, he won sympathy from the outset." The Boston *Herald* (Independent), the Boston *Post* (Democratic), the Boston *Record* (Independent), and the Boston *Globe* were equally laudatory.[30]

The favorable reactions were not limited to the Boston papers. The New York *World* wrote: "Such a speech as that of Mr. Grady must do good, because the conscience and intelligence of the north are with him." The New York *Herald* was also complimentary.[31] The southern press was also laudatory to Grady's addresses. When Grady spoke in New York, the Albany (Georgia) *News* commented, "He is a fit exponent of the new South," and the Macon *Telegraph* concluded, "He ably

29. Atlanta *Constitution*, December 23, 1886, and December 26, 1886.
30. *Ibid.*, December 15, 1889, and December 16, 1889.
31. *Ibid.*, December 15, 1889, and December 20, 1889.

represented the south on the occasion, the old south and the new south." The Richmond *State* concurred with many other southern papers in its praise of Grady's speaking.[32]

The Dallas and Augusta addresses appear to have received more attention in the southern press than in the northern papers. The Atlanta *Constitution* reported that the two Georgia senators, Joseph E. Brown and John B. Gordon, read advance copies of Grady's Dallas speech and approved his racial views. Concerning the same speech the St. Louis *Republic* concluded, "He said nothing to displease. . . . Grady was a great success. . . . He spoke to an appreciative audience." There appears to have been little press comment in the South on the Augusta speech, but the Augusta *Chronicle and Evening News* endorsed Grady's ideas.[33]

The Boston address, however, provoked substantial press reaction, just as it had done in the North, and the newspaper reports were as favorable in the South as in the North. The Chattanooga *Times* asserted:

His plea was for justice to the south, not mere toleration. . . . It was a brave speech, an unanswerable array of sound premises and logical deductions, and if it fails to do good then the truth need no further be told. . . . Mr. Grady is entitled to a unanimous vote of thanks from the solid south. His sledge-hammer blows were delivered when they must have the greatest effect. Let this speech be made a model for those delivered by southern men before northern audiences, and the south will at least compel respect if it does not secure confidence, justice and sympathy in the herculean task its situation imposes on its people of the white race.[34]

Similar appraisals appeared in the Augusta (Georgia) *Evening News and Chronicle*, the Charleston (South Carolina) *News and Courier*, the Thomasville (Georgia) *Times-Enterprise*, the Macon (Georgia) *Evening News*, the Jonesboro (Georgia) *News*,

32. *Ibid.*, December 27, 1886.
33. *Ibid.*, October 28, 1886, November 1889, and December 2, 1888.
34. *Ibid.*, December 15, 1889.

the Rome (Georgia) *Tribune*, the Memphis (Tennessee) *Commercial*, the New Orleans *Times-Democrat*, and two Baltimore papers, the *Herald* and the *Sun*.[35]

When related to Grady's three major themes, the press reaction is even more revealing because it suggests the importance attached to each of the themes. Grady's contention that the southern hopes of economic prosperity lay in industrialization and agricultural diversification was ignored in the press notices, although at the time of Grady's New England Society speech the northern newspapers carried numerous stories related to growing business ties between North and South.[36] His insistence that the South was loyal to the Union and that sectionalism had been displaced by nationalism received only little more attention, apparently because the northern press considered the matter settled. The San Francisco *Examiner*, which made no reference to Grady's speech until its issue of December 23, suggested that "the forces that have been silently working for the rehabilitation of the Southern States are now manifest. . . . Just now the 'late rebel states' are attracting their full share of attention from capitalists, politicians and men of letters. . . . The days of sectional lines are past and can never be revived again."[37] The Philadelphia *Times* concluded that "Mr. Grady's assertions taken in connection with the statement of northern men like Charles Dudley Warner and Judge William Darrah Kelly that the South of today is in fact a new south, should be accepted as final, and the bitter partisan prejudices which are kept alive only for partisan advantage should be buried out of sight and forever." Then the *Times* added: "The south today is as loyal to the union as the north and just as glad that slavery was abolished and cannot be restored. If the prejudices of war can die out of the hearts of the conquered certainly

35. *Ibid.*, December 16, 1889, and December 21, 1889.
36. Logan, *The Betrayal of the Negro*, 188–91.
37. Quoted *ibid.*, 191.

it should die out of the hearts of the conquerors, as it undoubtedly has out of the hearts of the men in blue who did the real fighting against those in gray." Grady's success in reaching the South with the theme is reflected in the comment by the Albany (Georgia) *News* that "he is a fit exponent of the new south, holding fast to the sacred memories of the old," and also in the conclusion of the Macon (Georgia) *Telegraph*: "He ably represented the south on the occasion, the old south and the new south."[38]

By far the largest portion of the newspaper reports in the North and the South dealt with how Grady treated the race question. As observed earlier in this essay, an examination of the speeches indicates that Grady himself obviously considered this theme his most important, and the newspaper space devoted to it indicates that the press agreed. The substance of the coverage suggests with equal clarity that both the northern and southern newspapers found his racial position persuasive.

The most extended comments about his handling of the racial theme occurred in connection with the Boston address. Northern newspapers praised both his qualification to speak on the topic and his analysis. The Boston *Post* suggested that Grady knew the problem better than most northerners, and the paper also questioned whether Negro rights could be assisted by federal legislation. "The time when the federal government did interpose at the south is not very far distant," noted the *Post*, "and we may well ask our partisan friends whether that interposition produced such happy results as to incline us toward trying the experience again." The paper also suggested that "the strength of Mr. Grady's oration, as a contribution to the discussion of the question, lies in its emphasis—unconscious as well as intention—of that fact. To a fair-minded person it must also show, not only the maintenance of the old

38. Atlanta *Constitution*, December 26, 1886, and December 27, 1886.

spirit of kindliness between the two races, but the growth in the whites of the feeling most of all to be desired—a sense of their responsibilities and of the meaning and gravity of the problem which they have to face. They best understand its elements, and are most interested in its solution, and it is not to be denied that they have already made substantial progress toward that solution, and are daily growing in that clearness of vision and temperateness of spirit which shall hasten the work." The *Post* also commended the speech as essential reading for everyone who wanted to be informed about the race problem in the South. The Boston *Globe* and the *Herald* similarly agreed with Grady's views on the race question.[39]

New York newspapers also approved Grady's position. The New York *World* wrote:

Such a speech as that of Mr. Grady must do good, because the conscience and intelligence of the north are with him. The majority of northern men are not deceived by appeals to passion. The south asks for a patient waiting until she can work out the problem which the country has imposed upon her. Federal interference in behalf of negro supremacy must keep the south solid, and the races politically divided. The true union between the sections and the natural divisions between the parties, will come with the adoption of the patriotic view of Mr. Grady, and the rejection of the sordid and traitorous policy of needy partisans whose greed of power is not deterred by the good of the country. Southerners have a knowledge of and liking for the negro much greater than his self-appointed friends can possibly have.[40]

The most extended treatment of the speech in New York occurred in the New York *Herald*, which suggested that the Negro leadership in the South should carefully study the warm reception received by Grady's ideas in the North:

A remarkable phenomenon demands the attention of the leaders of colored public opinion in the south and north. They cannot prudently shut their eyes—or the eyes of their constituency—the colored people

39. *Ibid.*, December 20, 1889, December 15, 1889, and December 16, 1889.
40. *Ibid.*, December 15, 1889.

of the union—to the sympathy and applause given by all New England and a great part of the north to the recent address of Mr. Grady, of Georgia, at a Boston banquet. . . . What they are bound to notice and to call to the attention of colored men of influence everywhere in the south, is that all New England applauded Mr. Grady; that in the ancient stronghold of abolition, in the region where the negro has been accustomed to count upon finding his most zealous friends and defenders—there, at least, he has apparently worn out friendship.[41]

A few northern newspapers did raise questions about Grady's pronouncements on the race question. The Detroit *Tribune* insisted on waiting until the South had proved by its deeds the truth of Grady's claim of "honor and equity" before accepting his assertions. In particular the *Tribune* referred to the treatment of the Negro at the polls and suggested that only when the South corrected abuses of the Negro vote could Grady's word be taken at face value. The Chicago *Tribune* expressed similar reservations, citing the mistreatment of Negroes in Louisiana, Mississippi, Virginia, and the Carolinas, which had resulted in a mass exodus of Negroes from those states.[42] But on the whole, those who praised Grady's racial position by far outweighed his detractors, and persons in the North clearly commended his assertions.

Newspaper reaction in the South was equally favorable. The Chattanooga *Times* called the speech "brave, an unaswerable array of sound premises and logical deductions," and the Augusta (Georgia) *Chronicle* noted that Grady's "statement of the negro problem in Boston Thursday night was a straightforward and eloquent plea for white supremacy of the south."[43]

It seems evident, then, that a majority of the newspapers, both North and South, commended Grady for his presentation of the New South. It is equally evident that they endorsed his

41. *Ibid.*, December 20, 1889.
42. Logan, *The Betrayal of the Negro*, 186.
43. Atlanta *Constitution*, December 15, 1889.

handling of the crucial racial issue. To the extent that the newspapers mirrored public opinion, the coverage of Grady's speeches indicates that the North was willing to accept Grady's assurances that the Negro was being fairly treated and the pledge that what inequities existed would be corrected. The newspapers did reflect public opinion,[44] and so Grady's strategy was successful.

Final Appraisal

Grady's speeches succeeded primarily because his strategy rationalized for his audiences beliefs that they wanted to hold. From our perspective it is obvious that Grady's claims for his New South were extravagant, and that there was a gap between those claims and reality. In the first place, although Grady implied that industry was already making great strides in the South, southern industrialization from 1860 to 1900 was not impressive. To be sure, Chattanooga and Knoxville became industrial centers, and Birmingham became a "southern Pittsburgh." But the primary industrial achievement was the cotton textile mills, and the growth illustrates graphically the failure in general to solve the economic ills of the South. Hailed as a means of correcting the economic plight of the sharecropper and tenant farmer, the cotton mills instead created a new class of underpaid, poorly fed and poorly housed "mill-hands" who were little better off than in their previous role. According to William H. Nicholls, "the social and economic organization of these mill villages represented the bodily transfer of the plantation system from cotton field to textile factory—a fact which did little to make industrialization a very attractive, democratic, or self-sustaining process."[45]

44. Logan, *The Betrayal of the Negro,* provides a detailed examination of the evidence for this conclusion.
45. William H. Nicholls, *Southern Tradition and Regional Progress* (Chapel Hill: University of North Carolina Press, 1960), 24; W. J. Cash, *The Mind of the South* (New York: Random House, 1941), 202–205.

Thus the movement for which Grady claimed so much produced relatively little visible improvement in the standard of living of the average southerner. Furthermore, the southern approach to industrialization carried inherent problems which would have made equality with northern industry impossible. The South became basically a colonial economy, with railroads, iron, and steel coming under northern control in the 1880s. The pride of southern industrial accomplishment, the cotton mills, produced mainly unfinished cloth which was sent North for final processing, and in spite of the fact that many cotton mills were built by local subscription, the owners relied on northern capital in order to operate. Even the natural resources of which Grady boasted so extravagantly soon came under the control of men outside the South.[46] Southern industry was thus firmly in the control of and operating for the benefit of northern capitalists. There is irony in the fact that the industrialization which Grady had touted as a means of southern escape from northern economic domination had resulted in increased southern dependence on northern economic interests.

Similarly, there was a disparity between Grady's picture of the Negro's status in the South and the reality. It was true, as Grady suggested, that some Negroes had become landowners and businessmen and, indeed, a few had acquired wealth. However, the price of land was too high for most of them, who worked for cash wages or as tenant farmers or sharecroppers. According to the census of 1880, approximately 90 percent of southern Negro workers were either farmers or servants; not even a fifth of them owned the land they worked, and in some districts this figure dropped to one in a hundred. In Georgia, where Negroes formed almost half of the population, they owned less than 2 percent of the land, 8 percent of the cattle and farm animals, and 5 percent of the farm tools.[47]

46. Woodward, *Origins of the New South*, Chap. 11.
47. Thomas D. Clark and Albert Kirwan, *The South Since Appomattox, A*

In the Boston speech Grady described the mobility of Negroes within occupations. In reality the employment for the Negro in the postwar period steadily worsened. Negroes of the antebellum South had functioned as common laborers and as highly skilled craftsmen, protected in the latter occupations by the wealthy landowners who found free slave labor preferable to white craftsmen who charged for their services. After emancipation, with no wealthy and powerful landowners to protect them, Negroes were driven from skilled into unskilled work. By 1900 they were all but eliminated from the skilled trades.[48] Thus from a position of virtual dominance in the skilled crafts in 1865, Negroes reached the point in 1890 when they composed only 16.1 percent of the carpenters, 28.2 percent of the masons, 19.8 percent of the painters, 33.2 percent of the plasterers, and 2.5 percent of the machinists. The black man found little work in the textile industry except in the most menial jobs. He was employed mainly in unskilled and poorly paid occupations: railroad building, brickmaking, quarrying, street cleaning, sewer cleaning, sewer digging, and scavenging.[49]

Grady also boasted of the educational progress of the Negro. Actually southern attitudes toward the education of the black man varied widely. Some white southerners accepted the Negro as free and urged that he be assisted in developing a school system separate from the whites. In 1866 the Texas Teacher's Convention declared: "In every neighborhood, on every plantation, and at all suitable places, let the negro, with the aid of the Southern white people, build up schools. The negroes will contribute from their own labor and small resources. But white people must also help. In every way let the negro see that the Southern whites are his best friends. We must rise above the prejudices

Century of Regional Change (New York: Oxford University Press, 1967), 309–310.

48. *Ibid.*

49. Francis Butler Simkins, *The South Old and New* (New York: Alfred A. Knopf, 1947), 407.

and avarices growing out of our past relations to the negro and recent political events and be just and magnamious [sic]." However, many poor whites objected to any form of Negro education on the premise that it would "obliterate distinctions between them and the blacks." In this attitude the poor whites were not alone, for the majority of southerners of all classes encouraged barriers to the education of the Negro. At the beginning of the New South period, many southerners rationalized the belief that the greatest benefit to Negroes came through their day-to-day contact with whites, in which they could observe and learn from the white man. These attitudes were based on the premise of the superiority of the white race. Upon this myth southern whites developed a policy of begrudgingly providing black children with a kind of education distinct from that offered white children. It was aimed at perpetuating segregation by controlling Negro thought.[50]

Grady's picture of Negro suffrage conformed in part to reality. White leaders in the South had manipulated Negro votes to redeem state governments from carpetbagger and scalawag control, and the Bourbons continued to solicit Negro votes as long as they could. Once the majority of southern states were redeemed and the need for Negro voting support diminished, white leaders turned to the threat of a return to Radical Reconstruction as a means to establish the "solid South" referred to by Grady; all white men were urged to vote as a block regardless of their political leanings in order that political control would remain in the hands of the white man. Thus Grady was correct in asserting that the southern whites were using the Solid South idea to negate the effects of the Negro vote.

However, the movement to disfranchise the Negro was already underway when Grady spoke; it began as early as 1874,

50. Claude H. Nolen, *The Negro's Image in the South: The Anatomy of White Supremacy* (Lexington: University of Kentucky Press, 1967), 106–108, 120–31.

and during the 1870s and 1880s de facto disfranchisement was carried out by a variety of methods, including stuffing the ballot box, "losing" Negro ballots, and moving polling places unexpectedly. By 1890, one year after Grady's death, legal disfranchisement had begun as southern states incorporated the "Mississippi plan" into their new state constitutions.

Close study of the speeches suggests that Grady was not a reformer or a radical, but basically a conservative who shared many of the beliefs of the Bourbons. Richard Weaver supports that generalization, arguing that Grady was in many ways similar in his beliefs to Jefferson Davis. Weaver documents two examples to support his claim, noting first that Grady viewed with alarm, particularly in his southern speeches, some of the very movements which made the New South movement possible. Secondly, Weaver saw Grady's conservatism reflected in the orator's claim that the strong religious faith which had characterized the Old South would be replaced by unbelief or, even worse, heresies brought in by the outsiders. Most notable in Grady's conservatism was his stand on the racial question. While pleading for the North's patience with southern racial policies, Grady at the same time preached a racial attitude which continued in most essential respects the conservative southern view of the Negro. Traditional throughout in all except his nationalism, Grady stands, as Weaver observes, "much nearer the apologists than to the liberals and reformers.[51]

However, through his skill as a strategist, Grady submerged the harsh realities in the attractive New South myth. His task was made easier because both his northern and southern audiences were ready for the myth he had to offer. Northern investors were greedy to tap the industrial potential of the South and needed only the kind of assurances Grady offered that the South

51. Richard M. Weaver, *The Southern Tradition at Bay: A History of Postbellum Thought*, ed. by George Core and M. E. Bradford (New Rochelle, N.Y.: Arlington House, 1968), 343–45.

was a safe and stable place for their investments. The most substantial obstacle to northern acceptance of the South as a loyal part of the Union was the alleged southern mistreatment of the Negro, and Grady was successful in his plea for sympathy and patience, coupled with his assurances that the South had already made significant progress. In his handling of the racial question Grady was also aided by the growing weariness of the North over continuing agitation about the Negro's status, and the orator's analysis provided a convenient rationalization for the North to rid itself of the problem.

In the South Grady and his New South myth appeared at an opportune time. The myths of the Old South, the Lost Cause, the Solid South, and others had been a potent force in southern attempts to recover self-esteem and to account for why the Confederacy had lost the war. In promoting the New South myth, Grady added to the mythology an image of a dynamic, progressive South based upon hope and optimism. Grady succeeded, then, because he was able to fit his ideas to his audience. By skillful strategy, he rationalized the cherished beliefs and desires of North and South alike and thereby became one of the most effective promoters of the New South myth.

BIBLIOGRAPHICAL NOTE

Among the numerous secondary works about Grady, four merit special mention. Raymond B. Nixon's *Henry W. Grady, Spokesman of the New South* (New York: Alfred A. Knopf, Inc., 1943) is a valuable and detailed source of basic biographical material. More specifically oriented to Grady's speaking, Marvin G. Bauer surveyed the Georgian's oratory in "Henry W. Grady" in William Norwood Brigance (ed.), *A History and Criticism of American Public Address* (New York: Russell & Russell, 1960), Volume I. Written in the aura of public adulation of Grady, Bauer's monograph develops the thesis that Grady faced audiences still committed to the enmity between regions engendered by the Civil War. The revisionist historians have raised serious doubts about that thesis. A more balanced view of Grady's New South advocacy, and one which gives full weight to the revisionists, is Mills Lane's excellent "Introduction" in *The New South* (Savannah, Georgia: The Beehive Press, 1971), a collection of five Grady speeches and a group of his essays related to the New South theme. The fourth book is Edwin Dubois Shurter, *The Complete Orations and Speeches of Henry W. Grady* (New York: Hinds, Noble and Eldredge, 1910). A collection of eight of Grady's more important speeches, the Shurter volume is useful in the absence of access to the Atlanta *Constitution*, though as Bauer points out (p. 405) the book has some errors in details.

Theses and dissertations analyzing Grady's speaking include: John W. Ackley, "The Elements of Persuasion in the Oratory of Henry W. Grady" (M.A. thesis, University of Southern California, 1933); Marvin Bauer, "Henry Grady Spokesman of the New South" (Ph.D. dissertation, University of Wisconsin, 1936); E. C. Bryan, "Henry W. Grady as an Occasional Orator" (M.A. thesis, University of Iowa, 1931); Richard L. Fleisher, "Henry W. Grady: Toward a Revaluation" (M.A. thesis, University of Illinois, 1968); Earline Grizzle, "Style in the Public Address of Henry W. Grady" (M.A. thesis, University of Houston, 1967); Dorothy Siedenburg Hadley, "Contemporary Estimate of Henry W. Grady as a Public Speaker" (M.A. thesis, Northwestern University, 1930); Ethel J. Keeney, "The Sources of Persuasive Power in the Speeches of Henry W. Grady" (M.A. thesis, Northwestern University, 1930); and Eleanor A. Urban, "A Comparison of the Rhetorical Approach Used in 'The New South' and Other Selected Speeches of Henry Woodfin Grady" (M.A. thesis, Northern Illinois State University, 1966).

The Atlanta *Constitution* provides much useful information

about Grady's speaking career. In addition to complete texts of Grady's major addresses, the *Constitution* describes the speech settings and reproduces press reaction to the Grady speeches in both the North and the South. Scrapbooks and manuscripts of unpublished speeches may be found in the Grady Collection at Emory University.

Ceremonial Orators and National Reconciliation

"So while we love our dead and revere our trampled
principles, we must not forget that we have yet a
life to live, a part to play in our nation's history."[1]

John Temple Graves, April 26, 1876

Rhetorical and literary critics, historians, and journalists have
for years dismissed the ceremonial oratory of the South as superficial and ephemeral, full of sound and fury, but with little
significance. What they have neglected to understand, however, is that in this kind of public address there are important
reflections of the southern mind. Carefully attuned to moods
of their time, the ceremonial orators, speaking on the theme of
reunion, gave impetus and support to the postwar reconciliation movement. Ceremonial speaking provided much-needed
social fellowship in the bedraggled South and served to uplift
audiences in need of succor and inspiration.

The Confederate soldier, weary of struggle and defeat, came
back home in 1865 with his dreams of an aristocratic, romantic South long forgotten and with bleak prospects before him.
The war had destroyed much more than the southern economy
and the "peculiar institution"; it had almost crushed the southern spirit—that is, the southerner's view of himself and his
world. Ceremony and ritual served to help him forget and pro-

1. John Temple Graves, "Memorial Address," delivered at West Point, Georgia, April 26, 1876 (text from an undated newspaper clipping in John Temple
Graves Scrapbook, South Caroliniana Library, University of South Carolina).

vided him with a way to tolerate his bleak present and his questionable future. This essay discusses the part that ceremonial speakers played in bringing reconciliation closer to reality within the South.[2] It considers orators, their common rhetorical strategies, and the major symbols and values they often utilized in speeches.

I

In the postwar years, four ceremonial occasions were frequently observed: Memorial Day, or as it was often called, Confederate Decoration Day; dedication of Confederate Monuments; veterans' reunions; and academic ceremonies.

Memorial Day, seen as a tribute to the nation's war dead, began in the spring of 1865 when women and veterans in both North and South decorated graves with freshly cut spring flowers. Mrs. Mary Williams of Columbus, Georgia, is generally credited with the southern impetus toward setting aside a formal day to pay tribute to the "gallant Confederate dead." In March, 1866, Mrs. Williams described her proposal in a letter to the *Columbus Times*: "We feel it is an unfinished work unless a day be set apart annually for its special attention. . . . We can keep alive the memory of the debt we owe them, by dedicating at least one day in each year to embellishing their humble graves with flowers . . . and we propose the 26th day of April as the day."[3] In less than a decade this custom had spread throughout the South, and although some localities adopted Mrs. Williams' April 26 holiday, the date varied from town to

2. The southern speaker exploring the reconciliation theme before northern audiences has been dealt with elsewhere by Huber W. Ellingsworth, "Southern Reconciliation Orators in the North, 1866–1900" (Ph.D. dissertation, Florida State University, 1955) and Ellingsworth, "The Confederate Invasion of Boston," *Southern Speech Journal*, XXXV (Fall, 1969), 54–60.

3. I. W. Avery, *The History of the State of Georgia from 1850 to 1881* (New York: Brown and Derby, 1881), 715.

town. In contrast to the Confederates, the Unionists in 1868 legalized May 30 as "Memorial Day" and commemorated it under the direction of local posts of the Grand Army of the Republic.[4]

An editorial in the Atlanta *Constitution* of April 22, 1887, explained the significance of the Confederate memorial day: "For the past twenty years the people of the South have been accustomed to gather about the graves of the heroes of the 'lost cause' on the 26th of April to pay their tribute. . . . The 26th of April was chosen because it is the anniversary of the surrender of the last organized army of the confederacy. . . . The women of the South instituted it, and they have constantly maintained it with loving pride and heroic devotion."[5] A typical southern Decoration Day included many ceremonial rituals. It opened with a parade composed of the veterans, women, and school children who marched from the center of town to the cemetery, where a band and assembled church choir presented "appropriate" musical selections. The formal program, consisting of prayers, hymns, short messages by various notables, and the "oration of the day" was presented from a platform usually decorated with black sashes and drapes, evergreen boughs and flowers, and pictures of Confederate heroes.

This annual observance served to give the "Lost Cause" mythic proportions and almost a religious character.[6] In an 1887 editorial the Raleigh, North Carolina, *News and Observer* clearly expressed in typical language the prevailing sentiment throughout the South: "Again the 10th of May rolls around and we repair to the last resting places of those who wore the grey . . . to recall once more the heroic value of the sleeping army

4. Paul H. Buck, *The Road to Reunion, 1865–1900* (New York: Vintage Books, 1937), 121.
5. Atlanta *Constitution*, April 22, 1887.
6. Thomas D. Clark and Albert D. Kirwan, *The South Since Appomattox, A Century of Regional Change* (New York: Oxford University Press, 1967), 51.

and the virtues of those who gave up all that made life sweet to go cheerily to war because it was for home and country."[7]

In a memorial address (1879) at New Bern, North Carolina, Alfred Moore Waddell aptly described the function of speakers "on these occasions," suggesting that it was their duty "to paint, as best they may, that picture of the past on which Southern eyes will always gaze with admiration, and before which, Southern hearts will always throb with mingled pride and sorrow." Waddell was at pains to make clear the nature of the speaker's challenge:

They try to portray in vivid colors the heroism, the splendid courage, the patient toil and suffering, the unselfish patriotism and the sublime devotion of our countrymen who died in an unequal struggle for the preservation of what they believed to be the sacred inheritance of constitutional liberty bequeathed to them by their fathers. . . . Not beneath withered branches swaying in the winter wind, and amidst dead leaves strewed upon the naked earth shall such services be held; but in the tender spring-time, when the music of soft winds, odorous with the breath of flowers and gladdened by the songs of birds, transfigured nature makes manifest the miracle of the resurrection.[8]

The newspaper account called Waddell's speech "a most scholarly, beautiful and appropriate address," which "for good taste and ability, has been rarely equaled and never surpassed by any similar oration in this city."[9] As Waddell makes clear, Memorial Day served an important social role in the postwar South for the orators who wished to promote intersectional reunion.

Another important speech event in the postwar South was the monument dedication. Practically all communities of the old Confederacy purchased a statue of some sort to commemorate their war dead, even though the destitute southern towns

7. Raleigh (N.C.) *News and Observer*, May 10, 1887.
8. Alfred Moore Waddell, "Memorial Day Address," delivered at New Bern, North Carolina, May 9, 1879 (text from an undated, unknown newspaper clipping in Waddell Papers, Southern Historical Collection, University of North Carolina Library, Chapel Hill).
9. New Bern (N.C.) *Newbernian*, May 17, 1879.

often had real struggles trying to raise the money needed for these projects of remembrance.[10] If a local area did not have a hero of its own to honor, the statue was dedicated to the "Confederacy," or the "Boys in Grey," or the "Private Soldier." Each dedication ceremony involved the same essential ingredients: a parade through the city streets, several brief welcoming addresses, musical selections "appropriate to the occasion," a poem or two read by the local town-laureate, and the ever-present oration. At the close of the ceremonies, the cover was lifted from the monument to present a granite symbol of the Lost Cause.

When in 1875 Richmond dedicated Thomas J. "Stonewall" Jackson's statue, Moses Drury Hoge, the famous Richmond minister, delivered the oration of the day; it was later to be called the "noblest oration of his later life." According to newspaper accounts the ceremony was the "most imposing pageant ever seen" in the capital of Virginia. It attracted an estimate crowd of 40,000 who watched the procession and the fireworks in the evening. A reception was held for Mrs. Jackson at the governor's mansion.[11]

Further south in the old Confederacy, Augusta, Georgia, also dedicated a monument to the "Boys in Grey." On April 13, 1875, the officers of the Ladies Memorial Association symbolically laid the first bricks of the foundation "with delicate, ungloved hands." A reporter thought it "was a holy duty they performed . . . that of rearing a shaft of marble in memory of the brave men who fought and died for a cause they considered just." A

10. For example, in order to raise money for the Pensacola monument, the Ladies Monument Association sponsored lectures, dinners, recitation programs, musical productions, and accepted the proceeds from horse races held by the Pensacola Driving Association. The total cost of the monument was approximately $5,000. *Pensacola Daily News*, March–June, 1891.

11. Edwin A. Alderman and Joel Chandler Harris (eds.), *Library of Southern Literature* (17 vols.; Atlanta: Martin and Hoyt, 1910), VI, 2439; *Charleston News and Courier*, October 27, 1875; Allen W. Moger, *Virginia: Bourbonism to Byrd, 1870–1925* (Charlottesville: University Press of Virginia, 1968), 26.

few days later, on Confederate Memorial Day, the same group dedicated the cornerstone with the usual procession, ceremony, and oration. The city merchants closed their shops at one o'clock and the streets were "thronged with volunteers in uniform, members of societies, with badges, and citizens generally." An observer noted that "every window and housetop, from pavement to roof, contained as many as it could hold." The cornerstone was lowered into position after a prayer, an anthem by the choir, a selection by Mozart played by the Eighteenth United States Army Band stationed in Columbia, South Carolina, and a Masonic ceremony. The ritual included depositing in the cornerstone certain memorable items, including the rolls of local officers, lists of church members, rosters of the Georgia Society for Prevention of Cruelty to Animals and the Hebrew Benevolent Society, the names of local school children, as well as Confederate memorabilia such as postage stamps, money, a flag, lists of Confederate dead, and musters of various Georgia military units.[12] After hearing Clement A. Evans' oration, the procession reformed and marched to the cemetery to place flowers on the graves.

These were not unique events, as the practice of raising monuments to war heroes continued for several decades to be characteristic of southern culture. As the dedicatory orators pointed out, men since time immemorial have praised in earthwork, stone, song, and words the deeds of their forebears. The South, fully aware of its past, steeped in tradition, and passionately devoted to family and locality, continued this tradition. Recognizing the rhetorical significance of these symbols and signs, one editorial described the Augusta monument as "a witness to the valor of Southern men and the devotion of Southern women. . . . This memorial shaft bears testimony in their be-

12. Augusta (Ga.) *Daily Chronicle and Sentinel*, April 27, 1875.

half—it is a protest to God and man of the righteousness of their cause and the purity of their motives." [13]

Not only did the South recall its heroes and memorialize them in stone, it also kept alive their traditions through military unit reunions. Much ceremonial oratory occurred at these gatherings. The living survivors of the conflict assembled early to share their memories and recount their exploits as veterans have done for ages. These meetings were at first informal and unstructured, but as the years passed, members of the Confederate military units began to organize, elect officers, and hold regularly scheduled annual conventions. As on other occasions they made parades and pageantry the order of the day, including business meetings, election of officers, campfires, barbeques, reminiscences, and an oration by a prominent southern military hero. These assemblies gained national attention in the last two decades of the century and became a major means for the expression of conciliatory sentiment. The orators frequently declared in extended passages that old soldiers were willing to let bygones be bygones. In his thorough study of the reconciliation process Paul Buck wrote that the "spirit of good will which permeated every aspect of American life during the eighties received its deepest and sincerest expression from the aging veterans who once had borne the heat of battle." [14]

As an example of the significance of these groups, the charter of the Robert E. Lee Camp of Confederate Veterans (Alexandria, Virginia) sets forth the purpose and scope of these various veteran's organizations: "to perpetuate the memories of their fallen comrades, and to minister, as far as practicable, to the wants of those who were permanently disabled in the service, to preserve and maintain that sentiment of fraternity born of hardships and dangers shared in the march, the bivouac and the

13. Augusta *Daily Chronicle and Sentinel*, April 27, 1875.
14. Buck, *Road to Reunion*, 245.

battlefield." It proposed "not to prolong the animosities engendered by the war, but to extend to their late adversaries . . . courtesies which are always proper between soldiers, and which in their case a common citizenship demand at their hands."[15] This was a large order for a voluntary association. Near the final years of the century death claimed more members than they could replace by recruitment; consequently the membership began to drop.

The academic ceremony was yet another speaking opportunity for reconciliation oratory. College and academy cornerstone laying, building dedications, literary society meetings, alumni reunions, and general convocations all had their orators who often admonished the students, graduates, and alumni on the rights and duties of citizenship. Part of their charge were frequent pleas for intersectional peace and harmony. Typical of these collegiate affairs was the cornerstone-laying ceremony held at Emory College on June 8, 1881, when George I. Seney, a New York financier and railroad magnate, donated $50,000 for the construction of a new building. In the college chapel, "an appreciative audience" enjoyed an anthem composed for the event, two hymns, a "full, strong, eloquent" prayer, a reading of "appropriate selections" from the Bible, and finally, the dedication speech by President Atticus G. Haygood.[16]

These ceremonial moments made deep impressions on the citizens and students. An example which clearly demonstrates their impact is the reunion of the Confederate Survivors' Association, held in Augusta, Georgia, on Memorial Day, 1887. Governor John B. Gordon, a leading reconciliation orator, Chautauqua lecturer, railroad magnate, and military hero, was the featured speaker. The railroads reduced their rates, bringing

15. *Ceremonies and Speeches at the Dedication of the Monument to the Confederate Dead* (Alexandria, Virginia: n.p., 1889), 3.
16. Atlanta *Daily Constitution*, June 10, 1881.

"thousands" to Augusta for the event. A newspaper editorial supported a committee request that the stores close for the day: "It is but right that our businessmen should accede, for April 26th is now really the only holiday into which the city enters with any extent."[17] In sum, the ceremonial occasions served as focal points for fellowship and as such were a key factor in reinforcing community values. Indeed, the oration of the day, often printed, reached a wider and often more influential segment of the population.

II

All of these ceremonial events required a major oration presented by an esteemed guest speaker. These men were invited to speak because they were considered outstanding orators and community leaders as well. It will help us see more clearly the pattern of reconciliation speaking if we examine closely four of these leading models and their specific orations. John Temple Graves, a Georgia journalist and orator, gave two noteworthy Memorial Day addresses. One was presented at West Point, Georgia, on April 26, 1876, and the other delivered to a Union "Decoration Day" ceremony in Jacksonville, Florida, nine years later. Graves was considered a major speaker and was in wide demand for ceremonial events. At the opening of the 1890 Piedmont Exposition in Atlanta, he was introduced as the "orator of Georgia."[18] His speaking career had begun early, as this West Point speech was presented less than a year after he graduated from the University of Georgia.

In the West Point speech Graves made national reconciliation one of his main themes. He argued that southerners would play a part in the nation's future and reminded his listeners

17. Augusta *Chronicle*, April 22, 1887.
18. Atlanta *Constitution*, October 16, 1890. (Clipping in John Temple Graves Scrapbook.)

that Georgia was one of the original thirteen states. As such, "we still claim, and justly, the heritage and honor of American citizens." He urged his listeners to "tear aside this veil of prejudice and personal feeling" and to "speak peace to the troubled tides of passion and revenge that sweep upon the surface of our sectional heart." Graves asserted that northern "dastardly and designing politicians" have "fostered and fed the flame of sectional hatred," but that the South's "Northern brethren" have hearts "that beat true and pure." By blaming northern politicians for waving the "bloody shirt," Graves gave his southern audience a scapegoat, making it easier for them to rationalize their reentry into the Union: the problem lies with the politicians, not with their fellow citizens. Their northern brothers are forgiving, so Graves's listeners should be no less understanding.

Advancing his theme of promoting true peace between the sections, Graves urged southerners of his generation to "come as brothers with the clasped hand of brothers, knowing around the common altar of our common country, no North, no South, no East, no West." His call to meet at the "common altar of our common country" reflects the religious nature of his appeal for unity and the intensity with which he argued for reunion. He explained that both sides fought for what they believed and that had the "political renegades" left them alone, "they would have clasped hands above the red stream of their comrades [sic] blood, and settled there forever the issues of the war." He called for "a sorrowing, regretful sigh about the last home of the soldier in blue, who fought and died for his belief." The young orator thus invoked the Lost Cause mythology to reinforce his plea for reunion.

Nine years later, Graves, by this time a successful Jacksonville, Florida, journalist and editor of the *Daily Florida Union*, spoke in a Decoration Day celebration in that city, sponsored by the Grand Army of the Republic. Graves penned across the bottom of the scrapbook copy of his address a revealing note: "This speech was one of the most successful of my life."[19] Graves assessed the event as "a grand affair" in which he spoke to "an immense concourse of people."

Graves's entire address focused on the theme of reconciliation. Early in the speech, to set the tone, he described the scene: "The Grand Army of the Republic locking arms with the remnant of Confederate Veterans leads a great host of citizens who sing: 'My country 'tis of thee.'" Graves depicts the nation as once again whole: "the bloody chasm is bridged by Northern heartiness and Southern warmth and mutual generosity, and the heart of Florida beats at last in loyal unison with the heart of Maine." Graves cited a number of examples of northern reconciliatory efforts and implied, as he had done in the earlier speech, that if the North can be reconciliatory, the South must be no less willing to become reunited. In concluding, Graves appealed to the whole nation to "chant the praises of our dead together" and "honor these men simply as soldiers who fought like lions, who endured like martyrs, and bore the separate flags of the cause they loved with a heroic faith, a matchless patience, a splendid patriotism that will live as long as the name of Jackson and the name of Grant." Again, the semireligious intensity of his reference to martyrdom and "heroic faith" serves to strengthen his appeal by recalling the chivalrous glory of the Confederacy and invoking the commonly held images of the Lost Cause.

In these two speeches, one presented by an untested young man, the other delivered by a respected citizen who had earned

19. John Temple Graves, "Union Decoration Day Speech," delivered at Jacksonville, Florida, May 30, 1885 (text from an undated newspaper clipping in John Temple Graves Scrapbook, South Caroliniana Library, University of South Carolina).

a good name for himself, Graves appeals to the traditional southern value of honor[20] and paints an optimistic, positive verbal
picture of the reunited nation and its future. By urging his audience to remember and respect their past, he relates clearly to
his listeners' family and regional heritage, thus gaining credibility through identification. From that base he turns to the future and advocates a reunited nation.

Yet another ceremonial speaker of prominence was Tennessee's David M. Key, the postmaster general in President Hayes's
administration. His opportunity for a reconciliation address
was occasioned by the death of the victorious Union general
Ulysses S. Grant. Twenty years after Appomattox, the bitter
memories had been numbed a bit by time, and Grant's death
was mourned by many southerners. In Atlanta, Savannah,
Charleston, Knoxville, and in many other southern cities and
towns, businesses closed, flags were displaced at half-mast, and
bells tolled. In many cities, the Negro churches and Negro mi-
litia units held special services and parades. In the capital of
the Confederacy, the Richmond howitzers fired their cannon
on the half hour from sunrise to sunset. City offices, banks,
and a few businesses were closed in Lynchburg, Virginia; and
at Pensacola, Florida, bells tolled from noon until 2:00 P.M. on
August 8.[21]

One of the most impressive services was held at the Methodist church in Chattanooga, Tennessee, on Saturday, August 8.
The ceremony was dominated by the reconciliation theme, beginning with the opening parade into the church. Each member of the host Grand Army of the Republic was accompanied

20. As both Clement Eaton and Richard Weaver have illustrated, the southerner, both common man and planter, developed a sense of honor which served
as one of the major bases for his life-style. Eaton, *The Waning of the Old South
Civilization, 1860's–1880's* (Athens: University of Georgia Press, 1968), 3–4,
30, 50–51, 53, and Weaver, *The Southern Tradition at Bay: A History of Postbellum Thought*, ed. George Core and M. E. Bradford (New Rochelle, N.Y.: Arlington House, 1968), 47, 59–72.
21. Columbia (S.C.) *Daily Register*, August 9, 1885.

by a Confederate soldier as a sign of brotherhood and reunion. Every seat and all standing room in the church was filled, and "hundreds" stood outside the doors. Key delivered a brief "eloquent" address which "was listened to with marked attention throughout." [22]

In his address Key says that although this particular service cannot escape the "sight and presence" of "our late struggle," he trusts "the time has come when we can offer . . . our prejudices and animosities as an unclean sacrifice . . . upon the altars of patriotism and religion." [23] In a passage reminiscent of Graves's theme, Key then develops the idea that the differences between the sections would have been resolved had the soldiers who fought the war been left alone to solve them in their own way. According to Key—and indeed many other southern orators of this period—if one finds a person "who wallows and revels in the bitterness and hates of the past" it will be seen that his name "was upon no muster roll, or if it was, that roll tells of no deeds of valor he performed or wounds he endured." But, contended Key, those who enlisted and fought for "great principles" on either side were "prepared to stand by the decisions" of arms.

Key used General Grant as a model for reconciliation and magnanimity, observing that the victorious general allowed southern soldiers to keep their horses so they could be used for spring plowing that April of 1865. Additionally, and perhaps more important for the hero worship of General Robert E. Lee, Grant had prevented Lee's arrest as a traitor and rebel at war's end. The southern speaker later made the ultimate expression of reconciliation when he admitted that "it was best for us, for the South, that General Grant and his cause triumphed, and there are many, very many thousands of as gallant men as periled their lives to the southern cause who are of the same opin-

22. *Ibid.*; Chattanooga *Sunday Times*, August 9, 1885.
23. Chattanooga *Sunday Times*, August 9, 1885.

ion." Key told two stories about his personal experience with Grant which reflect the dead general's kind feelings toward southerners, his compassion for others, and his modesty. By presenting these instances, Key effectively supplemented his personal approach and amplified the tone of reconciliation and intersectional harmony which he was so careful to create and sustain in his message.

The Tennessee orator skillfully adapted this speech to a difficult rhetorical situation. As a former Confederate soldier and a southerner speaking at the memorial service for the Union commander sponsored by the Grand Army of the Republic, Key was in an awkward position as he acknowledged early in the address; and in his words, he was "anxious not to wound or offend." He knew that he must not irritate the southerners present nor show disrespect to his northern hosts. He placed the blame for Reconstruction and disharmony on politicians and not on the general citizen on each side who had "risked his honor and his life." By showing specific examples of Grant's magnanimity, Key led the southerners in his audience to see virtue in a northern hero. He recalled that in all of Grant's military and civil dealings with the South he was "kindly and generous to his Southern opponents when he had the opportunity." Therefore, the South could have little reason to dislike him or fail to honor him. If the South could respect the general who defeated the Confederacy, argued Key, progress toward reconciliation could be made. Key devoted his entire speech to a single strategy, viz., to show the South how commendable the conqueror really was. Surely, his address helped to bridge the chasm between the northerners and southerners present in his audience by instilling in them respect for the late president and victorious Union commander.

The third reconciliation orator to be considered is John Warwick Daniel, the "Lame Lion of Lynchburg." Daniel was a lifelong resident of Lynchburg, Virginia, where he was born in 1842.

He studied at Gessner Harrison's classical school, enlisted as a private soldier in the Confederate Army, and rose to the rank of major before being wounded in the Wilderness Campaign. As a result of this injury he was forced onto crutches for the rest of his life. Daniel came to be revered for "his fidelity to the Lost Cause."[24] Consequently, he was elected to the United States House of Representatives in 1884 and to the Senate the following year.

Although Grant's army had won the Civil War, the great southern folk hero was Robert E. Lee. Throughout the states of the Confederacy, many monuments were dedicated to Lee. The university where he served as president changed its name to honor him and furnished a mausoleum for his body. At the unveiling of this tomb, in June, 1883, Daniel delivered the oration of the day to an audience of some 8,000 to 10,000.[25] In this three-hour address at Lee's tomb, Daniel returned time and again to the theme of reconciliation. His chief tactic was to focus on the great military hero as a model of reconciliation for all southerners to follow. First, he showed how Lee was a loyal and patriotic American who descended from a line of notable forebears. He was, Daniel observed, "the son of the renowned 'Light Horse Harry Lee,' who was the devoted friend and compatriot of Washington in the revolutionary struggle . . . [and was] descended indeed from a long line of illustrious progenitors."

Daniel recalled that Lee had served with distinction in the Mexican War, and he related how Lee anguished over the decision to follow Virginia out of the Union. In order to show the

24. "John Warwick Daniel," *Dictionary of American Biography*, V, 68; Alderman and Harris, *Library of Southern Literature*, I, 108.
25. John W. Daniel, *Oration at the Inauguration of the Mausoleum and the Unveiling of the Recumbent Figure of General Robert Edward Lee at Washington and Lee University* (Richmond: West, Johnston and Co., 1883); W. Allan, *Historical Sketch of the Lee Memorial Association* (Richmond: West, Johnston and Co., 1883), 17.

great southern hero's love of the Union, Daniel quoted from a letter written by Lee to one of his sons in January, 1861: "As an American citizen, I take great pride in my country, her prosperity and institutions, and would defend any State if her rights were invaded. But I can anticipate no greater calamity for the country than a dissolution of the Union." Reading further from Lee's letter, Daniel revealed a basic feeling southerners had about the war, and perhaps the major reason why so many were willing to settle the intersectional dispute by the last resort of war: "I would be willing to sacrifice everything but honor for its [the Union's] preservation." Thus, "honor" was a central value for the Confederacy—one which played a significant role in their decision making.

Daniel pictured Lee as a perfect model for his theme of national reconciliation, urging his listeners to follow the example that Lee had set during the postwar years. In a typical passage Daniel described Lee's stance:

Lee thoroughly understood and thoroughly accepted the situation. He realized fully that the war had settled, settled forever, the peculiar issues which had embroiled it; but he knew also that only time could dissipate its rankling passions and restore freedom; and hence it was he taught that 'silence and patience on the part of the South was the true course'—silence, because it was vain to speak when prejudice ran too high for our late enemies to listen—patience, because it was the duty of the hour to labor for recuperation and wait for reconciliation. . . . Thus was he reviled and harrassed, yet never a word of bitterness escaped him; but on the contrary, only counsels of forebearance, patience and diligent attention to works of restoration.

Daniel then quoted many of Lee's own reconciliatory statements in order to suggest the Virginian's forgiving spirit. He also included several stories about the general's postwar years to illustrate how Lee was a symbol and leading spokesman for reconciliation.

Another typical reconciliation speaker was the South's youngest general, Thomas M. Logan. After the war Logan moved from

South Carolina to Richmond, where he became a wealthy and influential lawyer and railroad executive.[26] At a veterans' reunion in Columbia, South Carolina, in 1875, Logan suggested that the South had now "accepted the result, and there is now nothing surer in the political world, than that this country will continue in the future a united nation."[27] In this speech Logan created a feeling of hope and optimism about the future and about striving to sustain an image of the nation truly reunited. He appealed to the Hampton Legion to honor the past, but, at the same time, to look confidently to the future and to prepare for it as a part of a reunited country. Logan asserted that the American nation had grown by inevitable natural laws into a "vast social organism."[28] No longer was the country a mere aggregation of states. Rather, it was "so far advanced in its growth as a national body politic . . . that unity is a necessity of its further development." Logan showed how this "social organism's" network of veins, arteries, and nerves (the American railroad and telegraph systems) led to more efficient, effective government and, therefore, inevitably to a reunited nation. He asserted: "The future is not for State, but for national development, and we [the South] recognize the fact."

III

We turn now to a consideration of the major rhetorical strategies adopted by the southern ceremonial speakers of the period. The examples studied here attempted to reinforce the idea of reconciliation through five such strategies. The most common approach was to make the blunt assertion that the nation was

26. "Thomas Muldrup Logan," *Dictionary of American Biography*, XI, 367–68.
27. Columbia (S.C.) *Daily Phoenix*, July 22, 1875 and July 23, 1875.
28. In his study of "Science and Symbol in the Turner Frontier Hypothesis," William Coleman states that in the nineteenth century "no metaphor was so striking or so compelling as the image of the social organism." *American Historical Review*, LXXII (October, 1966), 25.

once again a reunited, reconciled country after the fire-and-sword experiences of war. The South had chosen this final arbiter and had lost, and there was no further court of appeals; now the former Confederacy was back in the Union, a permanent part of a reunited people. Over and over again, one finds this assertion made, with little or no concrete support for it. The ceremonial orators seemed to believe the contention self-evident, and by their urging southerners to accept the verdict of the sword, the door to reunion and mediation was opened.

A second common strategy of the postwar ceremonial orators was to illustrate how the South had made significant contributions to the nation and then to suggest that, as part of the reunited nation, the section would continue to do so. The South's gallery of great public figures were cited as examples: Jefferson, Washington, Marshall, Madison, Henry, Monroe, the Lees, the Rutledges, the Masons, and the Randolphs. If southerners had made this kind of contribution to the founding and building of a nation, the argument ran, was it not reasonable to assume that southerners would participate in the rebuilding of a country? The ceremonial orators argued that the South would be rejecting much of its past if southerners did not continue to contribute to the nation's well-being; they would be proclaiming that what Washington, Jefferson, and Lee had created and sustained was of little worth. Few southerners could or would take that position.

In the advocacy of reconciliation, speakers developed the strategy of presenting reconciliatory models, urging their audiences to promote national harmony and forgiveness in a manner similar to that of Robert E. Lee, Benjamin H. Hill, Ulysses S. Grant, James A. Garfield, or Abraham Lincoln, as well as the typical soldiers of the Union and the Confederacy who counseled reunion and practiced forgiveness. These men were shown to be worthy of emulation; and since they were heroes—even the private soldiers were seen in that light—it was an easy matter for the orators to appeal to their listeners to follow their examples.

Another common strategy of the ceremonial speakers was the age-old one of "scapegoating." The reunion orators were eager to find scapegoats for barriers to reconciliation, and they often found them in the "scheming politicians" who prevented reunion for their own selfish and opportunistic reasons. When developing this strategy, speakers would characteristically assert that the common folk and the former soldier all longed for the intersectional peace that the politicians were keeping from them.

A fifth rhetorical strategy was to proclaim strongly the bright future of the nation and of the South within that nation. Senator Matthew C. Butler asserted before the literary societies at Wofford College: "We shall develop a civilization greater than any that has ever blessed the human race."[29] Henry Grady, the renowned Georgia orator, echoed these sentiments in an address he delivered at the University of Virginia in 1889, when he proclaimed the "manifest destiny" of America.[30] "This government carries the hopes of the human race. Blot out the beacon that lights the portals of this Republic and the world is adrift again." But if we [the South], "save the Republic; establish the light of its beacon over the troubled waters, [then] one by one the nations of the earth shall drop anchor and be at rest in the harbor of universal liberty." Later in the speech, Grady invoked the time-honored American belief that God supports America's national destiny. When "the hour of her trial has come," said Grady, "He will lift up His everlasting gates and bend down above her in mercy and in love." Finally, in his in-

29. Matthew C. Butler, *The Constitution: Address Delivered at Wofford College, Spartanburg, South Carolina, June 15, 1886* (Washington, D.C.: R. O. Polkinhorn, 1886), 14.

30. Henry W. Grady, "Against Centralization," address delivered before the Literary Societies of the University of Virginia, June 15, 1889 (text in Emory University Library, Atlanta, Georgia).

imitable style, Grady looked to a future when "under one language, one liberty, and one God, all the nations of the world harkening to the American drum-beat and girding up their loins shall march amid the breaking of the millennial dawn into the paths of righteousness and of peace!" Grady argued that there was an unlimited future for the American nation and that the South was to play a role in it. By comparing this vision of future greatness to the bleak desolation of recent southern life, the audiences were stirred to imagine that it would be in their best interest to become reconciled and to cooperate in the drive for national ascendance. The patriot's reward for helping bring about reconciliation would be the glorious national future which Grady proclaimed.

IV

Pursuing these five reconciliation strategies, the typical ceremonial speakers frequently drew upon certain symbols and values to achieve their argumentative goals. The speeches studied here are replete with symbols which served to vivify the abstraction of reconciliation. Time and time again speakers referred to national symbols such as the flag, the Constitution, the Declaration of Independence, the presidency, heroes of the Revolutionary War and the early national period. These references all served to remind the southern audiences of their historical roots, hence giving support to the reunion message by way of credible evidence of the nation's heritage, ideals, and values.

Often more overt and tangible symbolic actions were integrated into the ceremonies surrounding these reunion speeches. The demonstrations of solidarity usually called for audience participation and involvement. Combined grave decoration events and "arm-in-arm" parades participated in by both blue-clad and gray-clad veterans were often seen as visible evidence that the nation was one. "Burying-the-hatchet" ceremonies or situations where cannons were spiked to prevent their future employment were used by reconciliation promoters as tangible actions reflecting national peace and reunion.

Of the several values that these ceremonial speakers could have used to reinforce their reunion message, five were most frequently employed. All of these orators relied heavily on the values of *duty* or *honor, patriotism, forgiveness, friendship*, and *cooperation* as they sought to make their reconciliation strategies meaningful for their listeners. Indeed it was these values which supported their leading arguments for reconciliation.

Honor, traditionally a powerful concept in the South,[31] was the leading value stressed by these speakers. In his oration at the Benjamin Hill statue in Atlanta, James C. C. Black described the duty of southerners after the war in typical phrases: "Our Southern soldiers returned to their desolated homes like true cavaliers, willing to acknowledge their defeat, abide in good faith the terms of the surrender, accept all the legitimate results of the issue, respect the prowess of those who had conquered, and resume their relations to the government with all the duties those relations imposed."[32] Honor-bound to follow his duty, the chivalrous southern soldier was called to accept his defeat.

The second-most-used value was the appeal of *patriotism*, or national loyalty. In his Memorial Day address at West Point, Georgia, John Temple Graves reminded his listeners: "We cannot fail to know that we are and ought to be numbered among the Union of original States. We still claim, and justly, the heritage and honor of American citizens."

31. See, for example, Ralph T. Eubanks' essay "The Rhetoric of the Nullifiers," in Waldo W. Braden (ed.), *Oratory in the Old South* (Baton Rouge: Louisiana State University Press, 1970), especially 31–32.

32. James C. C. Black, "Address at the Unveiling of the Hill Statue," delivered at Atlanta, Georgia, May 1, 1886 (text in University of North Carolina Library, Chapel Hill).

Speaking to the reunion of the Hampton Legion in 1875, General Thomas M. Logan pointed out that "it requires neither prophet to foretell, nor oracle to pronounce, that there is a great future for the United States. . . . Truly, a vast empire is in process of formation."[33] For the southerner who had only recently been charged with the ultimate crime against the state—treason—this assurance of national love and loyalty was vital and comforting.

A third important value to which these speakers appealed was that of *forgiveness*. John W. Daniel's oration on Lee provides a good example. Because he had such a subject as Lee, who tried after the war to be as forgiving as possible, Daniel built much of his address around this particular value. With great frequency he used Lee's own words and actions to suggest a model of the forgiving spirit: "It should be the object of all to avoid controversy, to allay passion, and give scope to every kindly feeling." Late in the address Daniel devoted an entire section to discussing the concept of forgiveness. He began by saying: "Lee had nothing in common with the little minds that know not how to forgive. His was the land that had been invaded; his the people who were cut down . . . his was the cause that perished. He was the General discrowned of his mighty place and he was the citizen disfranchised. Yet Lee forgave and counseled all to forgive and forget."[34] Not only did Daniel appeal to the strong Christian virtue of forgiveness, he also touched on the Lost Cause mythology which was so potent for southern audiences.

Again, these reconciliation speakers often expressed in their speeches the value of *friendship*. For example, in his eulogy on President Garfield, Atticus Haygood advocated that the American citizen "should cultivate a true spirit of national brotherhood. To say and to do things simply to irritate or injure an op-

33. Columbia (S.C.) *Daily Phoenix*, July 22, 1875 and July 23, 1875.
34. Daniel, *Oration at Figure of Lee*.

ponent is mean, and unworthy [of] a civilized, to say nothing of a Christian man."[35] One senses a deeply felt longing for reunion in Thomas Logan's assertion that, "our feelings, as well as our interest, already incline us to strengthen and cement the bonds of real union, by cultivating feelings of good will and friendship."[36]

Finally, some of these reconciliation orators extolled the value of *cooperation*. In one of his addresses, James W. Throckmorton pointed to a specific example of cooperation: "The graves of Southern soldiers that died from wounds and disease in Northern prisons and hospitals are strewn with flowers by the wives and daughters of brave men who fell upon the battlefields of the South, and the graves of Northern soldiers who lie buried in the South are tenderly cared for by the fair women whose homes they invaded."[37] This illustration became an even more potent appeal since it touched on the "cult of Southern Womanhood," so central in southern life.[38]

In the dedication speech for a new building at Emory College Atticus Haygood illustrated cooperation with an actual example of George Seney, who had donated the money for the building: "He lives a thousand miles away; he belongs to a people with whom we have had conflicts long and bitter. . . . And yet, on his own motion and unsolicited, he has sent you, Methodists and people of Georgia, these gifts, because he wanted to help you, and because he loves you."[39] Haygood hoped that such cooperation would serve as an example that would enhance the feeling for reconciliation.

35. Atticus G. Haygood, "Garfield's Memory," delivered at Emory College, Oxford, Georgia, October 5, 1881 (text at Emory University Library).
36. Logan, "Address to Hampton Legion."
37. James W. Throckmorton, "Speech Delivered at Re-Union of Hood's Soldiers," delivered at Waco, Texas, June 27, 1889 (test in University of Texas Library, Austin).
38. See Eaton, *Waning of Old South*, 167–68.
39. Atticus G. Haygood, *Seney Hall*, (Macon, Georgia: J. W. Burke, 1881). This speech was delivered at Emory College, Oxford, Georgia, June 8, 1881.

W. STUART TOWNS

V

The messages of these ceremonial speakers attest to the spirit of reconciliation present among southerners, and there can be little doubt that many southerners after the war longed for national harmony—latent though it might have been, and mixed often with feelings of bitterness and despair. C. Vann Woodward affirms a deep-seated southern feeling of Americanism when he writes, "The South was American a long time before it was Southern in any self-conscious or distinctive way."[40] One simply need only recall in this connection the statement Patrick Henry made a century before in the Virginia Ratifying Convention of 1788. In a speech opposing the Constitution Henry cried, "I am a lover of the American Union. . . . The dissolution of the Union is most abhorrent to my mind. The first thing I have at heart is American liberty; the second thing is American Union; and I hope the people of Virginia will endeavor to preserve that Union."[41] Henry's strong American sentiment was still present in many southerners in the immediate pre–Civil War years. An example is Robert E. Lee's searching decision to leave the Union with his native state, and to offer his sword to the Confederacy. Countless southerners of less prominence also had to make that difficult decision.

The South, it will be remembered, was hardly unified in support of secession. As James L. Golden had demonstrated, there were quite a few southerners who, on the very eve of the civil conflict, deplored and fought against the dissolution of the Union. Sam Houston, the hero of Texas independence, remarked ten years before Sumter: "If I am of the South, can I not recollect the North? What is our country? It is a nation

40. C. Vann Woodward, *The Burden of Southern History* (Baton Rouge: Louisiana State University Press, 1960), 25.
41. Patrick Henry, "Against the Federal Constitution," in Ernest J. Wrage and Barnet Baskerville (eds.), *American Forum* (Seattle: University of Washington Press, 1960), 16. This speech was delivered to Virginia Ratifying Convention, Richmond, June 5, 1788.

140

composed of parts, East and West, South and North. It is an entirety. There are no fractions in it. It is a unit, and I trust it will so remain."[42] Houston still held these views in 1861 when war came; as governor of Texas he argued strongly against the fatal step of disunion in his state's secession convention.

Again, Benjamin F. Perry of South Carolina delivered a speech to the 1860 National Democratic Convention in which he said he came as "a Democrat and a Union man," who was "determined to do all that I could to preserve the Democratic party and the Union of the States."[43] David M. Potter expresses it well when he writes that "one of the truly diagnostic, perennial features in the life of the South has been the obsessive impulse of its people" to be both "Southerners and *Americans*." Potter demonstrates that "Southern loyalties to the Union were never really obliterated but rather were eclipsed by other loyalties, with which, for a time, they conflicted."[44] These ceremonial addresses examined here were designed to intensify deep-rooted loyalties to the Union. By reinforcing this sentiment effectively through public utterance, these speeches constituted an enormous force in the process that Paul H. Buck called "the Road to Reunion."[45]

BIBLIOGRAPHICAL NOTE

Much of the research for this paper was done in connection with a Ph.D. dissertation, "Ceremonial Speaking and the Reinforcing of American Nationalism in the South, 1875–1890" (University of Florida, 1972). Newspapers, especially the *Atlanta Constitution*; Augusta, Georgia, *Daily Chronicle and Sentinel*; Charleston, South Carolina, *News and Courier*; and

42. James L. Golden, "The Southern Unionists, 1850–1860," in Braden, *Oratory in the Old South*, 260.
43. *Ibid.*, 273.
44. David M. Potter, *The South and the Sectional Conflict* (Baton Rouge: Louisiana State University Press, 1968), 30–31, 78.
45. Buck, *Road to Reunion*.

Columbia, South Carolina, *Daily Phoenix*, were most helpful. Partial or complete texts of the speeches were often found in these and other southern newspapers.

Often the speeches were published in pamphlet form by a local printer and were distributed locally. Many were later deposited in southern collections at the University of South Carolina, University of Georgia, Louisiana State University, University of Virginia, University of North Carolina at Chapel Hill, and Duke University.

Almost none of the speakers mentioned in this essay have been studied in depth, with the exception of Atticus G. Haygood (see Harold W. Mann's *Atticus G. Haygood*, University of Georgia Press, 1965). Several of these men warrant fuller treatment, especially Alfred Moore Waddell, whose papers are in the Southern Historical Collection, University of North Carolina library, Chapel Hill, and John Temple Graves, whose *Scrapbooks* and other memorabilia are in the South Caroliniana Collection, University of South Carolina, Columbia.

Rhetoric of the United Confederate Veterans: A Lost Cause Mythology in the Making

Confederate veterans were slow to form themselves into a region-wide association representing all of the old "rebels." In fact, it was not until 1889 that the South produced a counterpart to the Grand Army of the Republic.[1] Paul H. Buck speculated that this lateness was due, in part, to northern hostility that usually confronted the formation of "rebel societies." However, Buck also suggested that the southern veteran, humiliated by defeat, was inclined "to withdraw from public gaze."[2] Therefore, it took time for this old soldier to muster that self-confidence and pride requisite to his return to the public eye. He needed to reassess humiliating defeats, turning them eventually into individual and regional triumphs.

Many societies of former Confederate soldiers and sailors had been formed between 1865 and 1889, but only with local or otherwise restricted memberships. During the 1880s, however, a phenomenon occurred which was of considerable import to Confederate veterans. New South apostles began to use Old South and Lost Cause themes, symbols, and heroes as aids in promoting political causes and New South doctrines.[3] There-

1. The Grand Army of the Republic was founded April 1, 1866. See Mary R. Dearing, *Veterans in Politics: The Story of the G.A.R.* (Baton Rouge: Louisiana State University Press, 1952), 86.
2. Paul H. Buck, *The Road to Reunion* (Boston: Little, Brown, 1947), 241.
3. C. Vann Woodward, *Origins of the New South, 1877–1913* (Baton Rouge: Louisiana State University Press, 1951), 155–58, Vol. IX of ten volumes in Wendell Holmes Stephenson and E. Merton Coulter (eds.), *A History of the South*.

fore, interest in the Civil War and in the old veterans them-selves began to grow. One result of this new Lost Cause enthu-siasm was that by 1889 sufficient interest was generated for the establishment of a region-wide association, the United Con-federate Veterans.

Apparently the idea for the UCV was born in New Orleans, Louisiana, sometime early in 1889. A committee representing the Louisiana Division of the Army of Tennessee and the Vet-eran Confederate States' Cavalry Association distributed a cir-cular letter to Confederate veteran societies, calling an organi-zational meeting for June 10, 1889. On that date sixty veterans, delegates from ten organizations, met in New Orleans to adopt a constitution and to extend an invitation to John B. Gordon, then serving as governor of Georgia, to become their first com-mander in chief.[4]

The United Confederate Veterans held their first annual re-union July 3–4, 1890, in Chattanooga, Tennessee, and much of what occurred in this city became, on a small scale, a model for reunions that were to follow. The festivities included a parade, a visit to a famous battlefield (Chicamauga), an entertainment which dramatized a significant Civil War battle (Gettysburg), a special edition of the city's newspaper devoting numerous pages to biographical sketches of Confederate leaders, much display of bunting, and an equally bountiful display of regional elo-quence.

This first reunion, however, was small in comparison to those yet to come: just nineteen camps sent delegations; the festivi-ties and ceremonies attracted only 4,000 visitors; an estimated 80,000 spectators viewed the parade; and official business of the convention occupied less than a day.[5] By contrast, when

4. *Proceedings of the Convention for Organization and Adoption of the Constitution of the United Confederate Veterans . . . New Orleans, La., June 10, 1889* (New Orleans: Hopkins' Printing Office, 1891), 1–7.

5. *Minutes of the First Annual Meeting and Reunion of the United Con-federate Veterans . . . Chattanooga, Tenn, July 3rd, 1890* (New Orleans: Hop-

the UCV convened in Richmond six years later 150,000 spectators viewed the parade, and the entertainments attracted an estimated 65,000 visitors to the city, among whom were over
10,000 veterans. In addition, delegations came from 850 camps,
and official activities covered three days, with unofficial activities occurring several days before and after the reunion.[6]

During the 1890s the UCV held other annual reunions in
Jackson, Mississippi; New Orleans, Louisiana; Birmingham,
Alabama; Houston, Texas; Nashville, Tennessee; Atlanta, Georgia; Charleston, South Carolina; and Louisville, Kentucky.
Throughout these years enthusiasm for the Lost Cause continued to grow, so much so that the number of old Confederate
soldiers attracted to these gatherings increased from 5,000 at
Chattanooga to a high of perhaps 16,000 at Nashville.[7] In fact,
after the Birmingham meeting, UCV conveners were always
estimated at between 10,000 and 12,000. Furthermore, the total influx of visitors into convention cities ranged from 50,000
to 75,000, and crowd estimates for some individual events ran
to over 100,000.[8]

In addition to large crowds, UCV reunions were also marked
by much color and excitement. Bunting, martial displays, fireworks, parades, and Confederate paraphernalia added to the
festivities, but the behavior of old veterans themselves pro-

---

kins' Printing Office, 1891), 6–7; New Orleans *Daily Picayune*, July 5, 1890;
and Chattanooga *Daily Times*, July 5, 1890. The minutes of the United Confederate Veterans have been bound in six volumes and may be found among
the United Confederate Veteran papers housed in the Louisiana State University Archives, Baton Rouge. For each set of annual minutes pagination begins
with 1; therefore, subsequent citations of these minutes will contain only the
number of the annual convention and the respective page or pages.

6. Richmond *Dispatch*, July 3, 1896; Richmond *Times*, July 3, 1896; *Minutes of the Sixth Annual Meeting and Reunion of the United Confederate
Veterans*, 6.

7. New Orleans *Daily Picayune*, July 5, 1890; Nashville *Banner*, June 23,
1897.

8. Atlanta *Constitution*, July 23, 1898; Nashville *Banner*, June 23, 1897;
Louisville *Courier-Journal*, June 1, 1900.

vided the most excitement. For example, the former Confederates staged impromptu marches, practiced their Rebel yells, and expressed unbridled enthusiasm for those who supported the Lost Cause. However, they reserved their greatest demonstrations for former military leaders, for the family of Jefferson Davis, and for such traditional symbols of the Confederacy as "Dixie" and the Stars and Bars. General John B. Gordon, for fifteen years commander in chief of the UCV, seldom entered a reunion hall without receiving at least a five-minute ovation, and similar receptions were given Generals Wade Hampton, Joseph "Fightin' Joe" Wheeler, Edmund Kirby-Smith, James Longstreet, and P. G. T. Beauregard, and former postmaster general of the Confederacy, John H. Reagan.[9] Similarly, the widow of Jefferson Davis and her two daughters, Winnie and Margaret, could not make entrances without causing at least temporary cessations of official activity.[10]

Perhaps the most prominent feature of these convocations, however, was oratory, and the platforms at UCV occasions were at one time or another occupied by some of the most noted southern speakers of the period: John B. Gordon, John H. Reagan, Benjamin Morgan Palmer, J. L. M. Curry, John Warwick Daniel, William B. Bate, Basil Duke, Bennett H. Young, Robert Love Taylor, Stephen D. Lee, Gordon McCabe, Edward C. Walthall. Several of these men spoke as "orator of the day," while others delivered addresses at one of the many peripheral events, such as monument dedications or special memorial services.

These speakers were usually venerated by the old soldiers, but they received even greater reverence if they had served actively and courageously in the real fighting. In fact, speakers were lavished with special affection if they had been severely wounded. A visible battle scar or war-won disability converted

9. New Orleans *Daily Picayune*, April 9, 1892; Houston *Daily Post*, May 23, 1895; Nashville *Banner*, June 22, 1897; Atlanta *Constitution*, July 21, 1898; Charleston *News and Courier*, May 12, 1899.
10. Houston *Daily Post*, May 22, 1895.

any old soldier into a powerful Confederate symbol and in turn made him more attractive on a UCV platform. John W. Daniel, United States senator from Virginia, obtained benefits from a wound which had placed him on crutches for life; Charles E. Hooker, United States congressman from Mississippi, proudly stood before the veterans with only one arm, the other lost at Vicksburg; and James H. Berry, United States senator from Arkansas, addressed the old soldiers with one leg missing, lost in the fighting at Corinth, Mississippi.[11] Other UCV orators who could claim lesser battle scars were Gordon, Bate, Walthall, Clement A. Evans, Charles T. O'Ferrall, and Joseph Wheeler. Nothing brought louder cheers than some mention of a physical sacrifice endured for the Confederacy, and nothing inspired greater sympathy than sight of a fellow comrade badly crippled by his struggle for the Lost Cause.[12]

Speakers for UCV reunions and for other Confederate memorial events were usually chosen from the ranks of former CSA military leaders. In fact, of the thirty-four orators who were perhaps most prominent in this movement, thirteen had been Confederate generals, and fourteen had served as lower ranking officers.[13] However, some had simply been enlisted men,[14] and

11. New Orleans *Times-Democrat*, April 9, 1892; *Minutes of the Eighth Annual Meeting and Reunion of the United Confederate Veterans*, 227.

12. Atlanta *Constitution*, July 21, 1898.

13. Lieutenant Generals Wade Hampton and Stephen D. Lee; Major Generals William B. Bate, Samuel G. French, John B. Gordon, Edward C. Walthall, and Joseph Wheeler; Brigadier Generals William L. Cabell, Basil Duke, Clement Evans, William L. Jackson, Bradley T. Johnson, and Evander McIver Law; Colonels William C. P. Breckinridge, Robert H. M. Davidson, Charles E. Hooker, Richard Henry Lee, and Bennett H. Young; Majors Joseph B. Cumming, John Warwick Daniel, Thomas G. Jones, and Charles T. O'Ferrall; Captains Pope Barrow, George Clark, Gordon McCabe, and George Moorman; and Lieutenant James H. Berry. The terminal rank of several Confederate generals, including Gordon and Wheeler, is in dispute. I have accepted the ranks given by Ezra J. Warner, *Generals in Gray* (Baton Rouge: Louisiana State University Press, 1959).

14. Thomas C. Catchings and Thomas B. Turley apparently were not officers.

others were former chaplains.[15] In addition, two of the more
important speakers served the Confederacy primarily in civilian capacities.[16]

After the war most of these men entered politics and held offices either at the state or national level. In fact, twelve of the
thirty-four served in either the United States House or Senate,[17] and three became state governors.[18] Furthermore, three
were prominent educators[19] and at least four won fame for their
historical writings.[20]

When these orators addressed gatherings at Confederate memorial events they usually discussed one or more of three
themes: (1) the causes of the war, (2) the Confederate soldier,
leader, and woman during the war, and (3) the meanings of defeat. Therefore, this paper will examine UCV rhetoric in these
three areas and relate that rhetoric to the building of a regional
myth.

I

In 1894 John H. Reagan was the featured speaker for the reunion of the Texas division of UCV, and in his speech he demonstrated the typical concern for the question of causes: "Of
late we occasionally hear the inquiry as to what caused the
great war. . . . A struggle which cost hundreds of thousands of

15. Three are quoted in this study: J. William Jones, J. H. McNeilly, and
Benjamin Morgan Palmer. However, Palmer apparently served only as an unofficial chaplain-at-large.
16. John H. Reagan, postmaster general of the Confederacy, and J. L. M.
Curry, who served in the Confederate Congress. Toward the end of the war,
however, Curry did serve as a lieutenant-colonel of cavalry.
17. Pope Barrow, William B. Bate, James G. Berry, William C. P. Breckinridge, Thomas C. Catchings, John W. Daniel, Robert H. M. Davidson, John B.
Gordon, Charles E. Hooker, John H. Reagan, Thomas B. Turley, and Edward C.
Walthall.
18. John B. Gordon, Thomas G. Jones, and Charles T. O'Ferrall.
19. J. L. M. Curry, E. M. Law, and Stephen D. Lee.
20. Basil Duke, J. L. M. Curry, Clement A. Evans, and Bradley T. Johnson.

valuable lives, and by which many billions of money was spent and property sacrificed, could hardly have been engaged in without a sufficient cause." [21] What then was the "sufficient cause" that Reagan and other Confederate speakers wanted to discuss?

Any answer to this question should first note that few of these orators spoke of slavery as being that cause. Indeed, one persistent contention was that "the South did not make war in defense of slavery." [22] Consequently, abolition was described as merely an "incident to the war," while the institution itself was referred to as "the occasion for the separation" and as "the point attacked," but never as the "cause." [23] In fact, Lincoln's public declaration of intent to save the Union, but not necessarily to free the slaves, was frequently cited as support for this argument. [24]

Nevertheless, to soften criticism of the antebellum South, speakers depicted slavery as an institution which civilized the Negro. "Our race found the black man a wanderer in the wilderness," declared Daniel, "and gave him a home; it found him naked and clothed him; it found him a savage, a cannibal, and a heathen and made him a Christian; it found him muttering gibberish and gave him a language; it found him empty-minded and it filled him with instruction." So rich had been this influence, claimed Richard Henry Lee, that the Negro had been declared fit, "in the judgment of the conquerors of the South," to

21. John H. Reagan, "Causes of the War," *Confederate Veteran*, IV (March, 1896), 75.

22. Bradley T. Johnson, "Placing Principle Above Policy," *Confederate Veteran*, V (October, 1897), 509.

23. Charles E. Hooker in *Minutes of the Eighth Annual Meeting and Reunion of the United Confederate Veterans*, 30; Richard Henry Lee, "The Causes of the War," *Confederate Veteran*, I (July, 1893), 201; Johnson, "Placing Principle Above Policy," 509.

24. Thomas G. Jones, "To the Confederacy's Soldiers and Sailors," *Southern Historical Society Papers* (Richmond: Southern Historical Society, 1889–1900), XXVI, 191; E. M. Law, "The Confederate Revolution," *Southern Historical Society Papers*, XVII, 96.

function as a franchised citizen in the most democratic nation in the world.[25]

If, however, additional arguments were needed to free the Old South from condemnation, other orators were ready. Jabez Lamar Monroe Curry charged that several southern states had actually enacted legislation to curtail the early slave trade,[26] and Thomas C. Catchings argued that it had been the Yankee trader who had promoted slavery and that the North abandoned the institution "only when they [the slaves] had ceased to be a profitable investment." John W. Daniel concluded that the South merely continued a system which she had earlier received "from the imposition of tyranny."[27] Therefore, Daniel, Catchings, and Curry, as well as William C. P. Breckinridge, Thomas G. Jones, and Reagan, suggested that the South had actually been victimized by this institution, that antebellum plantation owners had inherited a system which they could not long continue or easily discontinue.[28]

The most basic contention, however, remained that the South had not fought to preserve slavery but that she had fought to preserve constitutional freedoms:

The principle of defense of which the South accepted battle, after peacefully seceding from the Union, was found in the Constitution.—William B. Bate[29]

25. John W. Daniel in *Minutes of the Third Annual Meeting and Reunion of the United Confederate Veterans*, 27; Lee "The Causes of the War," 205.

26. For a more accurate interpretation of this legislation see Ulrich Bonnell Phillips, *American Negro Slavery* (Baton Rouge: Louisiana State University Press, 1966), 133–34.

27. Thomas C. Catchings, "Memorial Exercises at Vicksburg," *Confederate Veteran*, VIII (July, 1900), 316; Daniel, in *Minutes of Third Annual Meeting*, 30.

28. See William C. P. Breckinridge, "The Ex-Confederate, and What He Has Done in Peace," *Southern Historical Society Papers*, XX, 231; John H. Reagan in *Minutes of the Ninth Annual Meeting and Reunion of the United Confederate Veterans, Division of Texas*, 14–17. These minutes also may be found in the United Confederate Veterans collection housed in the Louisiana State University Archives, Baton Rouge.

29. William B. Bate, "Words for the South," *Confederate Veteran*, III (November, 1895), 343.

The war . . . did not originate in ambition, nor did we fight for spoils, for conquest or for fame. . . . We went to war . . . to save the Constitution as we read it.—Edward C. Walthall[30]

We fought for the Constitution as our fathers taught it to us.—James H. Berry[31]

It was argued that constitutional freedoms had been threatened by aggressive northern interests, and that Confederates had seceded only after they "despaired of maintaining the original principles of the Union which they had helped to form."[32] "The men of the South," proclaimed Robert H. M. Davidson, "believed in the doctrine of absolute sovereignty of the states, in the right of secession and in the doctrine that the consent of the governed was the only correct foundation of government, and . . . the consent meant was that of a state, and not the whole or entire number of the states." Speakers declared, therefore, that in 1861 this sovereignty of the states—and particularly the southern states—had been in jeopardy. "The South," asserted Bate, "claimed . . . nothing more than equal protection —not of persons only, but of states."[33] But the North, argued J. H. McNeilly, denied this claim, and southerners finally realized that reverence for the Union was being used "to destroy their liberty under the Constitution," that their states were being "degraded to a subordinate place in the great sisterhood."[34] Southern agrarian interests, it was claimed, were sacrificed to northern industrial interests, and the North seemed determined to drive her sister South even deeper into a minority status.[35]

30. Edward C. Walthall, "The Confederate Dead of Mississippi," *Southern Historical Society Papers*, XVIII, 300.

31. James H. Berry in *Minutes of the Tenth Annual Meeting and Reunion of the United Confederate Veterans*, 64.

32. Clement A. Evans, "Contributions of the South to the Greatness of the American Union," *Southern Historical Society Papers*, XXIII, 17.

33. Robert H. M. Davidson, "Confederate Dead of Florida," *Southern Historical Society Papers*, XXVII, 119; Bate, "Words for the South," 343.

34. J. H. McNeilly, "By Graves of Confederate Dead," *Confederate Veteran*, II (September, 1894), 264.

35. Law, "The Confederate Revolution," 94; Charles T. O'Ferrall in *Min-*

Faced with these circumstances, asserted the orators, southerners exercised their constitutional right to withdraw from the
Union. It was over this action, they declared, that war erupted,
not slavery.

Confederate ceremonial speakers such as Reagan, Curry,
Catchings, and Evander McIver Law expounded elaborate arguments to prove that at every step the South stood on constitutional grounds. Southern positions relative to slavery, nullifi-
cation, and secession had all, it was charged, been advocated
earlier by northern states.[36] Confederates, therefore, had followed no radical course. Instead, it had been the North's decision to compel dissident states back into the Union that had
been radical and unconstitutional. By this unprecedented procedure, reasoned Bradley T. Johnson, the North demonstrated
her belief that the Constitution could be "altered by force . . .
amended by the bayonet."[37]

The speakers emphasized yet another cause for the war, one
which lay, they argued, in the basic differences existing between the two regions. These differences, it was charged, had
developed during the earliest days of the nation. "There were,"
said Bate, "two great divisions of the Anglo-Saxon race domi-
ciled in the colonies with distinct economies arising from the
operations of climate, soil and occupation. They were trading
and planting people—where agriculture and commerce had created a difference in every feature of domestic life. Their systems
of labor, their habits of life, their thoughts and their aspirations

utes of the Sixth Annual Meeting and Reunion of the United Confederate Veterans, 12.

36. Reagan, "The Causes of the War," 75–79; J. L. M. Curry in Minutes of
the Sixth Annual Meeting and Reunion of the United Confederate Veterans,
57–63; Law, "The Confederate Revolution," 85–110; and Catchings, "Memorial Exercises at Vicksburg," 313–19.

37. Bradley T. Johnson, "Monument to the Confederate Dead at Fredericksburg," Southern Historical Society Papers, XVIII, 403.

divided and separated along diverging lines, until apprehensions, jealousies and distrusts existed, no less distinct than the climatic differences which surrounded them."[38]

In advancing this argument orators pointed to alleged variances in social structure, in basic human values, in commercial interests, and even in religion. And an important corollary to this reasoning was that the South had emerged as the superior section and that the North had responded with envy. The rhetoric of Bradley T. Johnson best exemplifies this rationalization. "By race characteristics and geographical environment," asserted Johnson, "the civilizations of the North and the South had developed on different lines." The North, he declared, had "adopted the philosophy of materialism, and had come to believe that the highest duty of man was to accumulate power; and as money . . . had come to be a source of all material power the pursuit of wealth had got to be the . . . highest aim of human effort." The result, he felt, had been that "supreme selfishness had become the all-pervading sentiment and directing force of the [northern] society." On the other hand, Johnson claimed that the antebellum South, "with a more generous climate, had developed a more sentimental society." Here values had been considerably different from those of the North: "In this sparsely settled country the ties of blood kept their hold. Husband and wife, parent and child, all the ramified relations of kinship, retained their binding force. Devotion to veracity and honor in man, chastity and fidelity in women, were the ideals that formed character." All these factors, reasoned Johnson, permitted the growth of "a society which for intelligence, culture, chivalry, justice, honor and truth" had never been excelled. Therefore, the South accepted war not merely in "an attempt to preserve political institutions, but to perpetuate a social organization . . . the sanctity of marriage, the inviolability of

38. Bate, "Words for the South," 342.

the family, the faith in truth, honor, virtue, the protection of home."[39]

In general, then, these orators explained the war as a phenomenon which had resulted in part from a South-North cultural dichotomy. The South was agricultural; the North was a land of Yankee traders. The South possessed the blood of the courageous, dashing, and generous Cavalier; the North, the blood of the stern Puritan and the ill-bred foreign immigrant.[40] The South preferred a national government structured as a confedration of sovereign states; the North believed in federalism. The South was superior in the production of statesmen and thinkers; the North was superior only in the devious negotiations of trade. The South was religious and found her values in the church, home, family, and community; the North believed only in commerce.[41] In short, orators proclaimed the two regions to have been so distinctly different that antagonisms had been inevitable. Civil conflict developed, therefore, from this basic disparity in natures, ideologies, and values, fanned into open hostility by the jealousies of the less endowed North. Thus these orator-apologists proclaimed that the war had been fought for practically everything but slavery. More profound and fundamental principles had been at stake. Rights of the individual, rights of the states, rights of geographical regions, rights of economic subgroups, rights of political minorities—these, said the speakers, had been the real issues of the war.

Such arguments pulled attention away from the one issue in

39. Johnson, "Monument to the Confederate Dead at Fredericksburg," 400–401; Johnson, "Placing Principle Above Policy," 509.

40. Reagan in *Minutes of the Ninth Annual Meeting and Reunion of the United Confederate Veterans, Division of Texas*, 10. For an example of the use of this Cavalier myth see Joseph B. Cumming, "New Ideas, New Departures, N_ South," *Confederate Veteran*, II (December, 1894), 362.

41. Reagan in *Minutes of the Ninth Annual Meeting and Reunion of the United Confederate Veterans, Division of Texas*, 11; Johnson, "Placing Principle Above Policy," 507; Daniel, "Oration of Senator Daniel." 27; Thomas G. Jones, "To the Confederacy's Soldiers and Sailors," 200–201.

which Old South and Confederacy causes were the most vulnerable to criticism. Focus subsequently fell on arguments of constitutionality, an issue in which, conversely, the Old South had felt the most secure. This shift was immensely helpful to the apologists. They could defend abstract principles without a close examination of actual societal practices protected by these principles. By the same token, they could claim victory for these abstract principles while acknowledging defeat in "less important" areas. In addition, principles, as opposed to practices, assume more of an aura of religiosity. A war waged in defense of a principle may be depicted as "holy"; a war waged to defend a practice is rooted, for its justification, in less sacred terms.

Furthermore, an image of a Lost Cause tied to slavery could not long endure. Advancements in social morality had rendered that institution an ugly embarrassment. Add to this reality the fact that slavery was the one issue in which Confederate defeat was most obvious, and the reasons for this shifting of ground become clear. However, as a consequence of this shift, a great myth was fostered: the war was fought not for slavery, but for rights so elusive that they seldom became grounded in specific regional behavior. The Lost Cause, so defined, could live forever, for it rested on no foundation made vulnerable merely by the explicitness of its character.

II

Relieved of the difficult problem of causes, these orator-apologists turned their attention to two other questions: How did southern people conduct themselves during the war, and was Confederate defeat due to any imperfect performance of soldiers, leaders, or private citizens? In answering these questions speakers devoted considerable rhetoric to accounts of regional courage and sacrifice, and the resulting images took on the aura of heroic legend. In general, this rhetoric spoke of a people wholly unified for a cause; of soldiers who worshiped their flag and their leaders; of leaders who stood ready to die with their men; of women who shouldered unbelievable burdens in the home and community while still sustaining the spirit of their men; of an entire region that remained true to God and to principle.

It was the Confederate soldier, however, who usually received the largest share of praise. Motivated by the immediate presence of many former Rebels, speakers poured forth a flood of superlatives in their honor:

What mind can contemplate, what tongue can speak without emotion of the gallant volunteer army which came forth at the great call of nature, of honor, and of their country? It is impossible for their countryme to recollect them but with tenderness, with affection, with tears. —Thomas B. Turley[42]

I rejoice that we raise this monument to the memory of such heroes. . . . It is to perpetuate their stainless name and untarnished honor. It is that our children may thrill with the thought that they are descended from such a race.—Stephen D. Lee[43]

I yield to no one in love for the Confederate soldier and admiration for his deeds. I never see his halting gait or empty sleeve, or honorable scars, that I do not involuntarily take off my hat in profound respect for the man.—J. William Jones[44]

Sir, if I had the power I would erect to the [Confederate] private soldier the most splendid memorial that gratitude could suggest, genius could plan or money build.—John B. Gordon[45]

The image that emerged from these superlatives depicted this soldier as a loving husband, father, son, or brother who "would as soon have brought disgrace on his home . . . as to sully his own name." Completely dedicated to Confederate

42. Thomas B. Turley, "Confederate Monument, Shelbyville, Tenn.," *Confederate Veteran*, VII (November, 1899), 498.

43. Stephen D. Lee in *Minutes of the Fourth Annual Meeting and Reunion of the United Confederate Veterans*, 20.

44. J. William Jones in *Minutes of the Tenth Annual Meeting and Reunion of the United Confederate Veterans*, 108.

45. John B. Gordon in *Minutes of the Seventh Annual Meeting and Reunion of the United Confederate Veterans*, 55.

causes and leaders, he daily demonstrated his "chivalry," his "strength of character," his "firmness of purpose," his "hardihood of nature," and his "noble manhood." As a man of God, he carried his religion into camp and field and distinguished himself as a true "Christian soldier." As an American patriot, he demonstrated the same passion for freedom which had immortalized his Anglo-Saxon forefathers. As a skillful, courageous, and determined "knight" of battle, he stood for four long years against "overwhelming odds," "counted not the cost," and "remembered only that a great issue was involved, a great cause was at stake." His figure would "stand out in history as the most resplendent illustration the world has ever known of duty eagerly performed, of unrequited sacrifice without complaint, and of spirit proof against despair." His countrymen would recall him as "a man valiant as Rupert, as chivalrous as Saladin, as true to love of liberty as Bruce, who gave his heart for Scotland, and Warren, the propatriot who fell at Bunker Hill for freedom." And, finally, he would be remembered as a man who "returned home from the fields of his disaster, vanquished but not destroyed; sorrowful, but not without hope." With indestructible spirit and indefatigable patience he would lay down his arms and rebuild his society, even while the forces of an alien government labored against his efforts.[46]

Such, therefore, was the image of the Confederate soldier as fostered by this rhetoric. Except in less meaningful matters such as salutes and formal drill, he was painted as the epitome of what a soldier ought to be. His deficiencies in these areas, suggested Thomas G. Jones, only served to make him colorful.

46. Thomas G. Jones, "To the Confederacy's Soldiers and Sailors," 200; McNeilly, "By Graves of Confederate Dead," 265; J. William Jones in *Minutes of Tenth Annual Meeting*, 104–105; Hooker in *Minutes of Eighth Annual Meeting*, 34–35; Turley, "Confederate Monument, Shelbyville, Tenn.," 498; Walthall, "The Confederate Dead of Mississippi," 303; Clement A. Evans, "Honoring Our Dead at Macon," *Confederate Veteran*, III (May, 1895), 147; Bate, "Words for the South," 357; and Evans, "Contributions of the South to the Greatness of the American Union," 20–21.

No mention, however, was made of his desertions, of his lack of discipline, and of the artful methods by which his chieftains had to flatter him into taking commands.[47] Such criticisms probably would have been inconsistent with the demands of these ceremonial occasions.

The soldier's image, however, did not exceed in superlatives the image of the southern woman. This "goddess of virtue" was frequently a topic for discussion, and orators spared no degree of eloquence in proclaiming her greatness:

Of all the examples of that heroic time . . . the one that stands in the foreground, the one that will be glorified with the halo of the martyr-heroine, is the woman—mother, sister, lover—who gave her life and heart to the cause.—Bradley T. Johnson[48]

No pages of history will be brighter and more resplendent than those which shall record the marvelous deeds and terrible trials of the women of the South.—Robert H. M. Davidson[49]

"The women of the South!" These words convey a eulogy in themselves, and are so interwoven with our Southern history as to give to it its brightest page and sweetest charm.—William B. Bate[50]

From such extremes of praise there emerged a highly romanticized portrait of the Confederate woman. She had been a creature of delicate breeding, accustomed to the quiet gentilities of southern plantation life. She had belonged to a social class "whose mothers and grandmothers had decorated the most brilliant courts of modern Europe and formed the highest social organization of America." But even though she had been "brought up like a princess, tenderly shielded from all save the sweet

47. Thomas G. Jones, "To the Confederacy's Soldiers and Sailors," 203. For a more balanced view of the Confederate soldier see David Donald, "The Southerner as a Fighting Man," *The Southerner As American*, ed. Charles G. Sellers, Jr. (Chapel Hill: University of North Carolina Press, 1960), 72–88; also Wilbur J. Cash, *The Mind of the South* (New York: Vintage-Knopf, 1941), 45–46.
48. Johnson, "Placing Principle Above Policy," 508.
49. Davidson, "Confederate Dead of Florida," 121.
50. Bate, "Words for the South," 359.

and beautiful side of life," she still became "foremost and bravest in the struggle."[51] She suffered the "drudgery of the farm and shop," "worked in the fields," operated looms to "furnish clothing to loved ones in the army," and like an angel of mercy "visited and attended the hospitals with lint and bandages for the wounded, and medicine for the sick." But most important, she willingly "gave up father, husband, son to the defense of country and home," and provided that moral, spiritual, and patriotic encouragement necessary to keeping her men "firm and straight." Finally, she often endured the ultimate horror of seeing her own house and community destroyed, of being "driven from home by a brutal soldiery," of viewing the "lambent flames of the incendiary," of hearing "the sound of crackling rafters as they crumbled into ashes."[52] Then, when women of weaker character would have been reduced to emotional and spiritual ruin, she stood proud and welcomed home the returning soldier with words such as "All is not lost. I have you, our daughter, and our God." In this spirit she directed her courage and strength to rebuilding. But she never forgot the cause, and "in tender appreciation of the brave deeds wrought in the name of truth and freedom" she "dignified this land with soldiers' monuments, gathered the sacred dust, guarded unmarked graves, and canonized those who suffered martyrdom during this eventful epoch."[53] In every way—or so the image proclaimed—she

51. Reagan, "Causes of the War," 78; Johnson, "Monument to the Confederate Dead at Fredericksburg," 399; Joseph Wheeler in Minutes of the Ninth Annual Meeting and Reunion of the United Confederate Veterans, 122.

52. John H. Reagan in Minutes of the Seventh Annual Meeting and Reunion of the United Confederate Veterans, 35; Hooker in Minutes of the Eighth Annual Meeting, 39; Johnson, "Monument to the Confederate Dead at Fredericksburg," 399; Hooker in Minutes of the Eighth Annual Meeting, 39.

53. Andrew Booth, "Decoration Day Address," New Orleans Daily Picayune, April 7, 1899; Charles C. Jones, Georgians During the War Between the States, An Address Delivered Before the Confederate Survivors' Association in Augusta, Georgia (Augusta, Ga.: Confederate Survivors' Association, 1889), 32.

had been a full partner in the Confederate struggle and was now as much a symbol of the Lost Cause as was the Confederate soldier.

The image of CSA leaders was also highly romanticized. Confederate generals such as Robert E. Lee, Stonewall Jackson, Albert Sidney Johnston, "Jeb" Stuart, and John B. Gordon were praised as men who possessed "nobility of character" and "purity of soul," as "heroic leaders" who would "go into history illuminated by a halo of courage and skill and purity of life and patriotism unsurpassed by any other names in history," as military men who outstripped their northern counterparts in generalship, as "Christian" gentlemen of "humble, devout piety," as Cavaliers "fit to measure with the knightliest," and as men who were simply "the greatest of God's creation."[54]

But among all the recipients of this praise, Robert E. Lee was the most glorified. Curry spoke of the "stainless character" of this "great hero"; McNeilly argued that the Old South had been "splendidly vindicated" by this "manliest of men, 'pure as light, and stainless as a star'"; and Stephen D. Lee asserted that Lee, Davis, and Jackson were "men who wore the white flower of a blameless life—men of clean lips and spotless names." Lee was also described as "the greatest American since the days of Washington," as "greater than Napoleon and Wellington," as "verily the greatest captain in history," and as "the highest type of Southern manhood."[55]

Confederate leaders had, it was suggested, inspired love and

54. Johnson, "Placing Principle Above Policy," 508; Reagan in *Minutes of the Seventh Annual Meeting,* 34; Daniel in *Minutes of Third Annual Meeting,* 36 and 39; J. William Jones in *Minutes of Tenth Annual Meeting,* 106; and Stephen D. Lee in *Minutes of the Sixth Annual Meeting and Reunion of the United Confederate Veterans,* 166.

55. J. L. M. Curry in *Minutes of the Ninth Annual Meeting and Reunion of the United Confederate Veterans,* 156; McNeilly, "By Graves of Confederate Dead," 265; and Stephen D. Lee in *Minutes of the Sixth Annual Meeting,* 158; Turley, "Confederate Monument, Shelbyville, Tenn.," 499; and Walthall, "The Confederate Dead of Mississippi," 303–304.

respect by frequently demonstrating a willingness to suffer the same privations and to face the same dangers required of their men.[56] Furthermore, they had remained true to the strict codes of conduct demanded by their Cavalier heritage, and after Appomattox they had, in the true spirit of noble gentlemen, quietly yielded to the arbitrament of war without losing the love and dedicated following of southern people. Ever true to Confederate principles, these former military leaders then suffered through the madnesses of Reconstruction and finally threw off the incubus of alien rule to reemerge as indigenous leaders of the South. Subsequently they returned their state and local governments to systems of constitutional order, rebuilding their region into a modern, progressive, industrialized society.[57]

Such, therefore, was the image of the Confederate military leader as promoted in this oratory. By contrast, his civilian partner did not receive much praise. In fact, of all the Confederate civilian leaders, only Davis was given any significant attention. There are two possible explanations for this inequity. First, these ceremonies were distinctly military in emphasis, and, second, there may have been some lingering dissatisfaction with that civilian leadership. During the war the military had not always been pleased with activities in Richmond and in the statehouses,[58] and in an earlier postwar period than the one this essay treats military commanders occasionally found opportunity to enunciate their dissatisfactions. In 1872, for example, General John B. Hood addressed the Survivors' Association of South Carolina and spoke of the "grave misfortunes"

56. See the story by J. William Jones concerning Lee's willingness to lead a charge, in *Minutes of Tenth Annual Meeting*, 102–103.

57. S. G. French, "Gave Their Lives for Home and Country," *Confederate Veteran*, II (July, 1894), 210; Reagan in *Minutes of the Seventh Annual Meeting*, 32; and McNeilly, "By Graves of Confederate Dead," 265; Daniel in *Minutes of Third Annual Meeting*, 44; and Reagan in *Minutes of the Seventh Annual Meeting*, 34.

58. See David M. Potter, *The South and the Sectional Conflict* (Baton Rouge: Louisiana State University Press, 1968), 263–86.

which the Confederacy had suffered at the hands of its civilian congress and the state governors. "From this congress," argued Hood, "The poison of dissension and demoralization . . . found its way to every quarter of our beautiful land. Governors, in some instances, stubbornly refused to cooperate with the administration, thus gnawing at our very vitals. Rarely did they visit Richmond save for the purpose of fault finding, and complaining that they had been required to furnish more men or money than another state."[59] If such feelings remained in the hearts of Confederate military men during the 1890s, they were not given utterance. This was the era when the myth of Confederate unity was being promulgated, and speakers may have remained silent on the topic of civilian leadership because they felt incapable of discussing it in the spirit of the time.

Speakers did not, however, remain silent on Jefferson Davis. The former Confederate chieftain was praised to such a degree that the resulting image approached deification. For example, Davis was described as "the greatest statesman this country ever produced," as a "stainless gentleman," a "gallant soldier," and a "devoted patriot," as a "savant, Christian hero and stainless citizen," and, in short, as a "God-like character." He was spoken of as a martyr to the Confederate cause and drawn as a Christ figure who took "upon himself the sins of a whole people," who "vicariously suffered for all with sublime abnegation of self," who "was selected as our victim to suffer in our place," and who "carried on his great heart the sufferings of the people." And throughout this "misfortune and suffering," Davis had endured "with a dignity, a courage and a patience that commanded the respect and admiration of his enemies, and endeared him for all time to the people of the South."[60] In truth,

59. John B. Hood in *Proceedings of the 1872 Annual Meeting, Confederate Survivors' Association of South Carolina* (Charleston: Walker, Evans, and Cogswell, 1873), 12.

60. J. William Jones in *Minutes of the Tenth Annual Meeting*, Stephen D. Lee in *Minutes of the Sixth Annual Meeting*, 155; and George Moorman in

this panegyrical image of Jefferson Davis may have been the one Confederate myth least rooted in reality. As president of the Confederacy, Davis had not been particularly popular, and David M. Potter has suggested that the ineptness of his administration may well have been one factor causing Confederate defeat.[61] Such negative thoughts, however, were not expressed at UCV ceremonial occasions. The myth had become more important than the man. For the man had aroused controversy and not just a little ridicule; the myth was unimpeachable.

Another image emerging from this rhetoric is that of a totally unified, wholly dedicated, long-suffering, and courageous Confederate people. But since much has already been said about the private soldier, the Confederate leader, and the southern woman, and since attributes credited to these constituent units were in turn credited to the entire southern society, there seems to be little reason to reexamine the numerous passages in which speakers praised southerners as being patriotic, aristocratic, chivalrous, loyal, religious, home-centered, courageous, moral, honorable, and completely dedicated to Confederate principles. However, if some final example is needed, one might turn to a summary statement made by Edward Walthall: "There is some priceless element in Southern character that I cannot define, which makes our people at once practical and sentimental— makes them good soldiers and good citizens, sustains them in every trial, adapts them to every changed condition and anchors them upon their honor as a rock; something that makes the men knightly in their deference for women, and makes the gentle woman strong when trouble comes. I know not what it

---

Minutes of the Ninth Annual Meeting and Reunion of the United Confederate Veterans, 62; Hooker in Minutes of the Eighth Annual Meeting, 32–35; Breckinridge, "The Ex-Confederate, and What He Has Done in Peace," 232; Stephen D. Lee in Minutes of the Sixth Annual Meeting, 162; Berry in Minutes of the Tenth Annual Meeting, 63.
61. Potter, The South and the Sectional Conflict, 284.

is, but . . . it is real, it is Southern, and it is worth preserving."[62]

Orators did make one additional claim worthy of discussion, the contention that southern people had exhibited extraordinary ingenuity in establishing a government and fighting a war at the same time. Confederates, noted Reagan, "entered the contest without a general government, without an army, without a navy, and without a treasury; they organized all these during the existence of the war."[63] "The exigency," observed McNeilly, "demanded not only wise statesmanship and military ability, but also the discovery and utilization of all material resources, the creation of new industries, and the invention of new appliances." But the South, McNeilly charged, rose to this challenge. Her "planters and farmers" left their "pastoral peace or rustic toil" and became "artizans, builders, manufacturers, financiers, and seamen." Southern men proved adaptive and creative, inventing "new devices, building ships . . . forging arms, sailing the seas, digging into the depths of the earth." Necessity compelled the people to develop latent powers, to spring forth "not by slow process of growth, but by sudden answer to the call of Providence to a full realization of the splendid possibilities of achievement in their reach." Thus, McNeilly's reasoning led him to conclude that the New South was not new at all, that it was born of indigenous but sleeping forces and talents. The New South, therefore, was "not the result of an infusion of foreign life"; it was merely the natural outcome of "efforts to carry on the war."[64]

Additional claims for indigenous powers were advanced in yet another way. Orators such as Daniel, Johnson, and Evans praised the postwar South for throwing off the alien forces of Reconstruction and for reestablishing "social prosperity and

62. Walthall, "The Confederate Dead of Mississippi," 311–12.
63. Reagan, "Causes of the War," 75.
64. McNeilly, "By Graves of Confederate Dead," 265.

political liberty." For this accomplishment northerners were given some credit, since it had been "their war, their reconstruction, their effort to subvert society" which welded the South into "a solid mass and aroused energies unknown." Therefore, the South of the 1890s was "not a New South . . . formed with regravitated fragments which lately wandered into the skies." Instead, it was "truly the greater South, flowing forth under new conditions from the stem of the old plant and out of the rich original soil."[65]

In drawing this image of a totally unified, courageous, and ingenious Confederate people, orators said nothing of the pettiness exhibited by the Confederate congress and state governors, nothing of controversies between Richmond and the military commanders, nothing of complaints over conscription and the system of impressment to obtain military supplies, nothing of charges of profiteering leveled against southern merchants, and nothing of the large number of "hiders" who fled to mountains and forests to avoid military service. Such, no doubt, have been the circumstances in every war, but UCV orators argued that this war and these people had been different.

III

Speakers, therefore, found no fault with either the Confederate people or the Confederate cause. Such circumstances, however, placed a heavy burden on apologists to justify defeat in other ways. Furthermore, it was unsatisfactory to argue simply that fate allowed a just cause to be defeated even though it was skillfully and courageously defended by a virtuous people. Such reasoning depicted Providence as being extremely indifferent to the cause of justice. In addition, the orators were always quick

65. Daniel in *Minutes of the Third Annual Meeting*, 25; Johnson, "Monument to the Confederate Dead at Fredericksburg," 414; Evans, "Contributions of the South to the Greatness of the American Union," 21.

to argue that Confederate principles had not been proved wrong by the mere accident of defeat. "The old wager of battle in which he who fell was adjudged to be the guilty party" was a "rule of a rude and barbarous age" and had been "long ago abandoned . . . because of its shocking injustice." Therefore, "the failure of a right cause does not make it wrong any more than does the success of a wrong cause make it right," and "right and wrong before God are not settled by success or defeat of arms."[66]

Southern people, however, had always placed great faith in the ever-present hand of Providence; therefore, this defeat needed to be explained in terms of a worthy goal which Providence could bless. That goal, as might be guessed, was a return to constitutionally guaranteed freedoms and a general reacceptance of governmental principles defended by the American Founding Fathers and by the Confederates. If it could be shown that the nation was making such a return and that such was due in part to the Confederate struggle, then the Lost Cause had not been lost at all.

As is indicated by the following quotations, orators certainly declared their cause to be still viable:

The cause for which so many Confederate soldiers perished *is not lost*. It still lives in the *autonomy of the states*.—Samuel G. French[67]

It is sometimes said that our cause is lost. Some causes are never lost. They may be crushed in defeat, they may go down in seeming ignominy, but in the end, like truth crushed to earth, they rise again.—George Clark[68]

Who says the cause is lost? I deny it in behalf of dead Confederates and living Confederates. I deny it in behalf of Southern women. . . . I

66. Pope Barrow, "Memorial Day at Savannah, Ga." *Confederate Veteran*, III (May, 1895), 130; Davidson, "Confederate Dead of Florida," 119; McNeilly, "By Graves of Confederate Dead," 264.
67. French, "Gave Their Lives for Home and Country," 210.
68. George Clark, "Reunion of Texas Veterans at Waco," *Confederate Veteran*, II (April, 1894), 122.

deny it emphatically in behalf of the immutable and intellectual God.
—S. T. Wilson[69]

Did these speakers believe, then, that the Confederate struggle
had been lost, but that with the end of Reconstruction—and
particularly during the 1890s—the tide had turned in favor of
Confederate principles? "The world is surely coming to the
conclusion," declared Bradley Johnson, "that the cause of the
Confederacy was right. Every lover of Constitutional liberty
. . . begins to understand that the war was not waged . . . in defense of slavery, but . . . to protect liberty won and bequeathed
by free ancestors." "In the gloom of Appomattox," asserted
Thomas Turley, the cause did seem lost. But this gloomy appearance had only been temporary, and now "the grand principles upon which that cause was based—love of liberty, devotion to constitutional freedom, and adherence to the right of
local self-government—live on and will live as long as our system of government lasts." "Southern People," added S. F. Wilson, "fought for the cause of self-government, and because of
that fight Constitutional liberty exists in America today." The
Confederate protest, declared McNeilly, "was against the destruction of the states, and against the omnipotence of the Federal government." Because of that protest, "each state will be
henceforth more secure in her inalienable right to her local
government and her individual development."[70]

Johnson, Turley, Wilson, and McNeilly argued simply that
Confederate ideology was experiencing a rebirth, that the tide
of centralism had turned, and that the entire nation was beginning to accept values for which southerners had fought. In truth,
a phenomenon did occur during the late 1880s and throughout

69. S. F. Wilson in *Proceedings, Seventh Annual Meeting and Reunion, Association of Confederate Soldiers, Tennessee Division* (Nashville: Foster and
Webb, 1894), 8.

70. Johnson, "Placing Principle Above Policy," 507; Turley, "Confederate
Monument, Shelbyville, Tenn." 499; Wilson in *Preceedings, Seventh Annual
Meeting*, 8; McNeilly, "By Graves of Confederate Dead," 266.

the 1890s which no doubt supplied these speakers with evidence for their beliefs. C. Vann Woodward indicates that during this period northern attitudes toward the South began to shift. He observes, for example, that when the South began enacting Jim Crow laws and Negro disfranchisement legislation the North acquiescently turned her back. Woodward also notes that the 1880s and 1890s saw Confederate themes, characters, settings, and social values become fadishly popular in northern circles, particularly in literary works. Wilbur J. Cash observes that southern literary themes "grew constantly in popularity, until in the 1890's they were near to dominating all others." By this method, argues Woodward, "Yankeedom took to heart the Lost Cause."[71] Bradley T. Johnson may have had these factors in mind when, in 1896, he declared: "Success is worshipped, failure is forgotten. That is the universal experience and the unvarying law of nature. Therefore, it would seem that the fall of the Confederacy was in some way a success and a triumph, for it cannot be that universal law has been set aside for this sole exception, the glorification of the lost Confederacy."[72]

But if the South was now winning, and if Providence had been on her side from the beginning, why could not her victory have been more direct? Evans seems to have had an answer to this question. "The Confederacy," he said, "gave to the world a principle. . . . Perhaps it is required that a nation must die that the world may be lifted up and a principle established."[73] Thus it was conjectured that the Confederacy became a martyr for ideals it upheld. Such reasoning was by no means alien to the rhetoric of these veterans. For example, it was often suggested that Confederate soldiers died to benefit the entire nation, that

71. C. Vann Woodward, *The Strange Career of Jim Crow* (New York: Oxford University Press, 1955), 54–56; Woodward, *Origins of the New South*, 155; Cash, *The Mind of the South*, 128.

72. Johnson, "Placing Principle Above Policy," 507.

73. Clement A. Evans, "Oration at the Fourth Annual Reunion," Birmingham *Daily News*, April 26, 1894.

they placed themselves upon their country's altar for sacrifice. And here the word *country* should be emphasized, for the orators did not choose to say "their region's altar" or "the Confederacy's altar." George Clark, for example, charged that the Confederate soldier "put all on his country's altar, and went forth and gave his heart and his life to the cause." Stephen D. Lee referred to the Birmingham monument as "an irresistible impulse of homage" to the Confederates' "immolation on the altar of their country." And Charles E. Hooker spoke of Confederate dead as "those dear departed comrades, who, while, they lived, lived for us and their country, and when they perished poured out their rich young lifeblood, a generous libation on the country's altar."[74]

There is also evidence that speakers saw this sacrifice as an act of divine will. The reasoning involved is best exemplified by an argument advanced by Richard Henry Lee. The Confederate cause had not been defeated because it was unjust, declared Lee, nor because its leaders lacked skill and its soldiers lacked bravery, "but because he who rules above deemed it best it should fail." In saying this Lee drew a distinction between justice and God's will, thereby suggesting that the deity might have thwarted immediate justice in order to achieve a greater good. The greater good, he then implied, was an eventual dominance of Confederate principles throughout the nation: "Although the final result was not according to our desires and hopes . . . who knows but that the devotion of the South to the true principles of the Constitution may not in the future cause the fructification of those principles and their growth throughout the land."[75] Therefore, if Confederates had won in 1865 they would have won only for themselves; in defeat they achieved

74. Clark, "Reunion of Texas Veterans at Waco," 122; Stephen D. Lee in *Minutes of the Sixth Annual Meeting*, 20; Hooker, *Minutes of the Eighth Annual Meeting*, 40.
75. Richard Henry Lee, "The Causes of the War," 205.

a victory for the entire nation. Furthermore, it was suggested that the North would eventually recognize this fact. "It may come to pass," observed Hooker, "that all the states will unite in thanking the Confederate states . . . for preserving what Mr. Calhoun declared was 'the breath of the nostrils of the government, the states.'" But even if this recognition did not occur, "state sovereignty, the cardinal principle of the Confederate revolution," would still live "to sustain and vitalize the grandest system of government which human wisdom . . . ever evolved." And "the cause which went down in defeat at Appomattox" would become "a precious heritage to a reunited people."[76]

For those apologists who were convinced that Providence was at work in all history, these arguments structured a comforting rationale: God allowed a just regional cause to be defeated, so that it might receive greater recognition, thereby precipitating an eventual nationwide acceptance of that cause. For those who viewed history with less assurance of its being directed from above, however, the arguments meant simply that man's own innate wisdom finally prevailed. The nation had wandered temporarily from a correct ideological path, but the Confederate struggle showed the error of these ways. The Constitution would now be preserved, and Confederate dead would go down in history as heroic martyrs "who poured out their blood like festal wine, a libation to liberty."[77]

IV

George B. Tindall tells us that "there are few areas of the modern world that have bred a regional mythology so potent, so profuse and diverse, even so paradoxical, as the American South."[78] During the 1890s, ceremonial oratory of Confederate veterans

76. Hooker in *Minutes of the Eighth Annual Meeting*, 38; Law, "The Confederate Revolution," 87; Turley, "Confederate Monument,' Shelbyville, Tenn.," 499.
77. McNeilly, "By Graves of Confederate Dead," 264.
78. George B. Tindall, "Mythology: A New Frontier in Southern History,"

contributed significantly to this mythology. After the war, one of the most difficult tasks confronting Confederate apologists had been to build acceptable bridges between what the antebellum South had expected and what the postbellum South knew to be reality. Defeat had to be softened or changed into victory; causes had to be purified; Confederate fighting men, leaders, and women had to be vindicated; and southern values in general had to be exonerated. Such steps were necessary before the South could turn an era of humiliation into an era of triumph, and from there into a source of regional pride.

Early apologists such as Robert Taylor Bledsoe, Edward Albert Pollard, and Jefferson Davis laid down much of the groundwork for this Confederate myth,[79] but it remained for post-Reconstruction speakers and writers to make these ideas come alive. In an era when New South advocates were calling for a rebirth of regional spirit, when southerners were being told they could compete with the North on her own terms, it was important that the South be provided with a heroic tradition from which pride could be extracted. The Confederate myth, along with the legend of the Old South, provided such a heroic tradition, and consequently was welcomed both by spokesmen of the old order and by those of the new. In fact, as Woodward notes, the New South advocate John B. Gordon became "the living embodiment of the legend," and no "awkward rationalizations" were demanded.[80] Furthermore, as was noted earlier, one factor in the rising popularity of Lost Cause themes was

---

in *The Idea of the South*, ed. Frank E. Vandiver (Chicago: University of Chicago Press, 1964), 1.

79. Robert Taylor Bledsoe, *Is Davis a Traitor?* (Baltimore: Innes, 1866); Edward Albert Pollard, *The Lost Cause* (New York: E. B. Treat, 1866); and Jefferson Davis, *A Constitutional View of the Late War Between the States* (2 vols.; New York: D. Appleton, 1881). These apologetic works and others have been thoroughly reviewed by Richard M. Weaver, *The Southern Tradition at Bay: A History of Postbellum Thought*, ed. George Core and M. E. Bradford (New Rochelle, N.Y.: Arlington House, 1968).

80. Woodward, *Origins of the New South*, 158.

that these themes and shibboleths were employed in promoting the New South.

Myths have been described by Mark Schorer as "instruments by which we struggle to make our experience intelligible to ourselves."[81] By explaining Confederate defeat in acceptable terms, these myths gave intelligibility to the southern experience of 1861–1865. In addition, however, they provided southerners with a basis for regional pride. As Mircea Eliade has observed, mythology is used as "a constant reminder that grandiose events took place on Earth and that this 'glorious past' is partly recoverable. . . . Directly or indirectly, myth 'elevates' man."[82]

BIBLIOGRAPHICAL NOTE

The official papers of the United Confederate Veterans are housed with the Department of Archives, Louisiana State University, Baton Rouge. Included in this collection are the *Minutes of the UCV*, 6 vols.; *Orders of the UCV*, 2 vols.; letter boxes; account books; packets of miscellaneous documents; and the published minutes of several affiliate groups such as the Association of Confederate Soldiers, Tennessee Division, and the United Confederate Veterans, Division of Texas.

A second collection of UCV materials is preserved among the Papers of the Louisiana Historical Association, Special Collections Division, Tulane University Library. The minutes of numerous veterans' associations and memorial societies, along with letters and some unpublished manuscripts of speeches, are in this collection. Additional materials are located in the Confederate Collection II, Emory University, Atlanta, and in

81. Mark Schorer, "The Necessity of Myth," in *Myth and Mythmaking*, ed. Henry A. Murray (New York: George Braziller, 1960), 354.
82. Mircea Eliade, *Myth and Reality* (London: George Allen and Unwin, 1964), 145.

the Papers of the United Confederate Veterans, Tennessee Division, Tennessee State Library and Archives, Nashville.

A major source of Confederate veteran oratory is the *Confederate Veteran*, a magazine which served as the unofficial organ of all Confederate veteran groups. This periodical contains numerous descriptions of ceremonial events which served as the background for this oratory. Confederate veteran speeches may also be found in the *Southern Historical Society Papers*, R. A. Brock (ed.), published by the society in Richmond, Virginia, and in the various newspaper accounts of the UCV conventions.

Several secondary sources should prove useful to the student of UCV rhetoric: *History of the Confederate Memorial Association of the South* (New Orleans: Graham Press, 1904); W. W. Garber (ed.), *In Memoriam Sempiternam* (Richmond: The Confederate Memorial Society, 1896); and William W. White, *The Confederate Veteran*, No. 22, Confederate Centennial Studies (Tuscaloosa, Alabama: Confederate Publishing Company, 1962).

Booker T. Washington Versus
W. E. B. Du Bois: A Study
in Rhetorical Contrasts

During the waning years of the nineteenth century and the early years of the twentieth century one of the major controversies in the New South was the question of the nature and extent of Negro education. Championship of the cause of education for Negroes was never popular because it violated strongly held attitudes of southerners, who believed that the Negro was inferior and therefore incapable of receiving much benefit from education and that when, by some means, he did become educated he created problems and ill will by becoming "arrogant." Thus, given white reluctance to speak for Negro education and the difficulty the Negro faced in gaining opportunities to speak, the accomplishments of two Negroes, Booker T. Washington and W. E. B. Du Bois, hold significance as contributions of remarkable leaders and at the same time offer a telling contrast in philosophies and strategies concerning Negro civil rights. Underneath their differences, Washington and Du Bois agreed upon the basic need to improve the condition of the American Negro, to lift him from poverty and oppression, and to help him become a respectable citizen with equal rights and privileges, but they disagreed over the means of achieving their goals. Washington favored acquiescence and industrial training; Du Bois supported militancy and higher education.[1]

1. Booker T. Washington, *Up from Slavery* (Garden City, N.Y.: Doubleday, 1900), 217–37; W. E. B. Du Bois, *The Souls of Black Folk: Essays and Sketches* (Chicago: McClurg, 1903), 41–47, 45–59.

174

Booker Taliaferro Washington was born in a slave cabin on a Virginia tobacco plantation in either 1858 or 1859 and moved to West Virginia with his family after the signing of the Emancipation Proclamation. While employed in the salt and coal mines during the day, he went to school at night. When he was fifteen he worked for a Mrs. Ruffner, who apparently instilled pride in the young boy. Later when referring to that experience he said that his "mind was awakened and strengthened." He further observed that he got "rid of the idea . . . that the head meant everything and the hands little in working endeavor, and that only to labour with the mind was honourable while to toil with the hands was unworthy and even disgraceful." Young Washington continued his studies at Hampton Institute in Virginia where he learned about agricultural and industrial education as moral forces and as ways of earning a livelihood. Following three years of teaching in West Virginia, he studied for one year at Wayland Seminary in Washington, D.C. He admired some of the faculty there, but was distressed by the lack of moral fiber in the students. He concluded that their purely academic training in liberal arts was not practical enough.[2]

While at Wayland Seminary, Washington was invited to join the faculty of Hampton Institute to direct a new program of industrial education for Indians. After two years there he accepted the position of principal of a new Normal School for Negroes in Tuskegee, Alabama. In keeping with his recent experiences Washington instituted a system of industrial education to which he devoted the remainder of his life. From that base he exercised influence on politicians, Negro leaders, educators, and philantropists throughout the country.

William Burghardt Du Bois was born in Great Barrington,

2. Washington, *Up from Slavery*; Booker T. Washington, *Working with the Hands* (New York: Doubleday, Page, 1904), 9–10; August Meier, *Negro Thought in America, 1800–1915* (Ann Arbor: University of Michigan Press, 1963), 88–89; Samuel R. Spencer, Jr., *Booker T. Washington and the Negro's Place in American Life* (Boston: Little, Brown, 1955), 39–41.

Massachusetts, three years after the Civil War. According to his own words, as the only Negro in the school, he experienced virtually no racial discrimination. "In the ordinary social affairs of the village . . . I took part with no thought of discrimination on the part of my fellows, for that I would have been the first to notice."[3] His childhood was similar to that of other children in Massachusetts, and unlike that of Booker T. Washington. Perhaps the only similarity between the childhood and youth of Du Bois and Washington was that they both never knew their fathers and were raised by fairly strong and encouraging mothers.

In 1884 Du Bois graduated from high school with honors at the age of sixteen and entered Fisk University in Nashville, Tennessee, from which he was graduated in 1888. At Fisk he began his writing and public speaking career. His editorship of the *Fisk Herald* and his development into an articulate speaker provided him two effective means by which to express his developing belligerent attitudes toward racial discrimination. In 1888 Du Bois entered Harvard as a junior. Although he only rarely participated in activities outside the classroom, on one occasion he did surface to use his oratorical skill to obtain funds. In 1890 he was graduated *cum laude* in a Harvard class of 300, was selected one of six commencement speakers, and attracted national attention with his address entitled "Jefferson Davis: Representative of Civilization." Bishop Potter of New York wrote in the Boston *Herald* the following comment which is representative of what others said: "When at the last commencement of Harvard University, I saw a young colored man appear . . . and heard his brilliant and eloquent address, I said to myself: 'Here is what an historic race can do if they have a clear field, a high purpose, and a resolute will.'"[4]

3. W. E. B. Du Bois, *Dusk of Dawn: An Essay Toward an Autobiography of a Race Concept* (New York: Harcourt, Brace, 1940), 14.
4. W. E. B. Du Bois, *The Autobiography of W. E. B. Du Bois* (New York: International Publishers, 1968), 125, 139, 438, 147.

Despite the fact that at age twenty-two Du Bois had more education than most young men, he still felt the need to continue his formal studies. With the aid of a Slater Fund Fellowship for Graduate Study Abroad he studied history and economics at the University of Berlin from 1892 to 1894 and traveled extensively in Europe. In June of 1894 he sailed for New York, "a caricature of what Booker T. Washington despised; a highly educated but penniless man, indulging in the affectation of gloves and cane while traveling in the steerage."[5] Now twenty-six, Du Bois had come home to find a job. He sent applications to several colleges and received favorable responses from three within a period of eight days. He accepted the first offer, which came from Wilberforce College in Ohio, although he later pondered what direction his life would have taken had he accepted an offer from Booker T. Washington at Tuskegee in Alabama.[6] At Wilberforce he taught Latin, Greek, German, English, and modern history. In 1896 he left, after only two years, because he was disturbed by the orthodoxy and appalled by church-college politics.[7]

Du Bois spent the academic year of 1896–1897 as an assistant instructor at the University of Pennsylvania, but his name was not included in the faculty list because he devoted his full time to a detailed study of the black ghetto in Pennsylvania, particularly in Philadelphia. In 1897 he accepted a professorship of economics and history at Atlanta University, where he took charge of the work in sociology and directed conferences on the problems of the Negro. Later in life he explained that "the main significance of his work at Atlanta University . . . was the development of a program of study on the problems affecting the American Negroes, covering a progressively widen-

5. *Ibid.*, 438; Spencer, *Booker T. Washington,* 146.
6. Du Bois, *Autobiography,* 185.
7. Herbert Aptheker (ed.), *The Correspondence of W. E. B. Du Bois, 1877– 1934* (3 vols.; Amherst: University of Massachusetts Press, 1973), I, 38.

ing and deepening effort designed to stretch over the span of a century."[8]

Du Bois placed great emphasis on research from 1896 to 1910, studying the problems of the Negro. His conviction was that "the sole aim of any society is to settle its problems in accordance with its highest ideals, and the only rational method of accomplishing this is to study those problems in the light of the best scientific research."[9] He reported his findings in numerous articles and speeches and in the publication of a book each year; consequently, he won acceptance in scholarly circles throughout the world. During this period he developed an increasing concern over the plight of the southern Negro, and he gradually moved from polite agreement with Booker T. Washington to an open break and an active public debate over how to improve life for the Negro.

In 1910 Du Bois, one of the founders of the National Association for the Advancement of Colored People, became the NAACP's director of publicity and research and editor of the NAACP periodical, *The Crisis*, a position he held until 1934.[10] Through teaching, writing, and speaking, he advocated a militant approach to education and improvement of Negro life. Whereas Washington gained recognition as a diplomat, politician, tactician, and an approachable, friendly person who possessed the ability to communicate with rich and poor from both races, Du Bois has been described as reticent and "aloof." His contribution was as a college professor who wrote papers, gave lectures, and urged his students to propagate his ideas.[11]

8. Du Bois, *Dusk of Dawn*, 57–59; Du Bois, *Autobiography*, 209, 438.

9. W. E. B. Du Bois, "The Study of Negro Problems," *Annals of the American Academy of Political and Social Science*, XI (January, 1898), 10.

10. William M. Tuttle (ed.), *W. E. B. Du Bois* (Englewood Cliffs, N.J.: Prentice-Hall, 1973), 27.

11. Elliott M. Rudwick, *W. E. B. Du Bois: A Study in Minority Group Leadership* (Philadelphia: University of Pennsylvania Press, 1960), 118–19.

At the turn of the century the aspirations fostered by emancipation and Reconstruction were still not realized and various legal and extralegal devices were utilized to deny their fulfillment. By 1895 disfranchisement of the Negro had been largely completed in the southern states. By 1900 most had passed Jim Crow railway laws, and by 1908 they had enacted streetcar segregation laws. Violence against the Negro in the form of beatings and lynchings occurred frequently in the South. Thirty-five years of emancipation had not raised the level of Negro rights, and race prejudice was becoming more intense. Negroes were considered an inferior race which existed primarily for the benefit of the white race. Both law and custom increased segregation.[12]

Negro education also reflected discrimination. A great disparity existed between Negro and white students in per capita educational expenditures. In an address before the Young People's Christian Union in Indianapolis, Indiana, on August 28, 1897, Washington related the following statistics: "In this county in Alabama each colored child had received only 31 cents for his education for one year. Think of it, 31 cents in that county for the education for one year of a black child, and compare it with the $20 a year which each child receives for his education in this part of the North."[13] In Madison Square Garden in 1904 Washington again emphasized the discrepancy in educational expenditures between black and white children: "In the year 1877–78 the total expenditure for education in the ex-slave states was a beggarly $2.61 per capita for whites and only $1.09 for blacks; on the same basis the United States

12. Meier, *Negro Thought in America*, 161–67; C. Vann Woodward, *Origins of the New South, 1877–1913* (Baton Rouge: Louisiana State University Press, 1951), 355–58, Vol. IX of ten volumes in Wendell Holmes Stephenson and E. Merton Coulter (eds.), *A History of the South.*
13. Louis R. Harlan (ed.), *The Booker T. Washington Papers, 1895–1898* (7 vols. to date; Urbana: University of Illinois Press, 1975), IV, 322–23.

Commissioner of Education reasons that for the year 1900–01, $35,400,000 was spent for the education of both races in the South, of which $6,000,000 went to Negroes, or $4.92 per capita for whites and $2.21 for blacks."[14] In the last speech before his death, delivered before the American Missionary Association and National Council of Congregational Churches, New Haven, Connecticut, on October 25, 1915, Washington returned to the inequity of educational expenditures: "The Negroes constitute about 11 per cent of the total population of the country. A little less than 2 per cent of the expenditures of over $700,000,000 expended annually for education is spent upon them. Of the $600,000,000 spent on public schools the Negroes receive about 1½ per cent."[15] Statistics such as these revealed that the Negro received only the crumbs from the white man's table. Against this hostile background Washington believed that black people were unwise to press for educational, social, and political equality. In violent disagreement Du Bois declared that this philosophy of patience was unacceptable.

During the 1890s similarities existed in the ideas of Washington and Du Bois. Although some black leaders criticized Washington's speech at the Atlanta Exposition in 1895, Du Bois initially reacted favorably. In a letter to Washington, he said: "Let me heartily congratulate you upon your phenomenal success at Atlanta—it was a word fitly spoken."[16] Following the address, Du Bois defended Washington's position in the New York Age, "suggesting that here might be the basis of a real settlement between whites and blacks in the South, if the South opened to the Negroes the doors of economic opportunity and the Negroes cooperated with the white South in polit-

14. E. Davidson Washington (ed.), Selected Speeches of Booker T. Washington (Garden City, N.Y.: Doubleday, Doran, 1932), 121–22.

15. Ibid., 280.

16. Aptheker (ed.), Correspondence of W. E. B. Du Bois, I, 39. Letter dated September 24, 1895.

ical sympathy."[17] Both men "placed economic advancement before universal manhood suffrage and both were willing to accept franchise restrictions based not on race but on education and/or property qualifications equitably applied. Both stressed racial solidarity and economic cooperation."[18] The major difference between the two men rested not on the ultimate goals for the Negro, but on the timetable and manner of reaching those objectives.

When Washington's first teacher in West Virginia said that the purpose of education was to enable one to speak and write the English language correctly, Washington had not completely agreed. Unable to see how that alone could relieve the poverty and misery of his mother and other people, he made his foremost aim in school to learn ways and means by which to make life more endurable and attractive. At Tuskegee, Washington found that his immediate task was to sell both white and black people on the desirability of industrial education. Many whites felt that any type of training made Negroes "uppity" and had little practical use. Washington was particularly exasperated with whites or blacks who could quote great writers upon any question but could not act upon actual problems in their lives.[19] Therefore, he viewed industrial training as a practical means of equipping the student for a particular job that would make him more acceptable to the community.

Although Washington had some previous platform speaking experience, he felt that his public speaking career really began with a speech to the National Education Association, delivered in Madison, Wisconsin, July 16, 1884, to an audience of four thousand delegates. A tense atmosphere developed because the

---

17. Du Bois, *Dusk of Dawn*, 55.

18. Meier, *Negro Thought in America, 1880–1915*, 196.

19. Washington, *Up from Slavery*, 199–200; Booker T. Washington, "Chapters from My Experience," *World's Work*, XXI (November, 1910), 13637–40.

president of the association, Thomas W. Bicknell, had included program topics on Negro and Indian education and had invited black speakers to participate. Many of the black teachers who came were denied their rooms at the hotel and the NEA had to threaten to sue to gain housing for them.[20] In his speech, which included an outline of his educational program for racial improvement, Washington argued that the Negro should remain in the South and fit himself "to live friendly and peaceably with his white neighbors both socially and politically." He continued:

In spite of all talks of exodus, the Negro's home is permanently in the South: for coming to the bread-and-meat side of the question, the white man needs the Negro, and the Negro needs the white man. His home being permanently in the South, it is our duty to help him prepare himself to live there an independent, educated citizen. . . . Any movement for the elevation of the Southern Negro, in order to be successful, must have to a certain extent the cooperation of the Southern whites. They control government and own the property—whatever benefits the black man benefits the white man. The proper education of all whites will benefit the Negro as much as the education of the Negro will benefit the whites.[21]

Washington believed that racial progress must be moral and economic rather than political; and in the speech he expressed a lack of confidence in political remedies:

As to morals, the Negro is slowly but surely improving. In this he has had no standard by which to shape his character. The masses in too many cases have been judged by their so-called leaders, who are as a rule ignorant, immoral preachers or selfish politicians.
Poverty and ignorance have affected the black man just as they affect the white man. They have made him untruthful, intemperate, selfish, caused him to steal, to be cheated, and made the outcast of society, and he has aspired to positions which he was not mentally and

20. Washington, *Up from Slavery*, 199–200; Harlan (ed.), *Booker T. Washington Papers*, II, 262. Interview of Thomas W. Bicknell which first appeared in the Boston *Advertiser*, July 7, 1903.
21. Harlan (ed.), *Booker T. Washington Papers*, II, 255–62.

morally capable of filling. But the day is breaking, and education will bring the complete light. The scales of prejudice are beginning to drop from the eyes of the dominant classes South, and through their clearer and more intelligent vision they are beginning to see and recognize the mighty truth that wealth, happiness, and permanent prosperity will only come in proportion as the hand, head, and heart of both races are educated and Christianized.[22]

Because of the history of the Negro people in América, Washington acknowledged that the black man was inferior socially, culturally, and economically, but he insisted that the race was not innately inferior. He suggested that the Negro had to prove tangibly and concretely that he was worthy of the blessings of liberty and that this demand required a new set of values which could not be acquired through traditional education:

There should be no unmanly cowering or stooping to satisfy unreasonable whims of southern white men, but it is charity and wisdom to keep in mind the two hundred years' schooling in prejudice against the Negro which ex-slaveholders are called upon to conquer. A certain class of whites South object to the general education of the colored man on the ground that when he is educated he ceases to do manual labor, and there is no evading the fact that much aid is withheld from Negro education in the South on these grounds. Just here the great mission of industrial education coupled with the mental comes in. It kills "two birds with one stone," viz.: secures the cooperation of the whites, and does the best possible thing for the black man. . . . Harmony will come in proportion as the black man gets something that the white man wants, whether it be of brains or of material.[23]

This stance did not imply that Washington was accepting a subordinate role for the Negro as a permanent condition: "I explained that my theory of education for the Negro would not, for example, confine him for all time to farm life . . . but that, if he succeeded in this line of industry, he could lay the foundations upon which his children and grandchildren could grow to

22. *Ibid.*
23. *Ibid.*

higher and more important things in life."[24] Suggesting his view was not racial, he insisted that similar training was needed to help the poor of both races out of their plight. Washington described his program of racial improvement and industrial education in this fashion: "First, to give the student the best mental training; secondly, to furnish him with labor that will be valuable to the school, and that will enable the student to learn something from the labor per se; thirdly, to teach the dignity of labor. A chance to help himself is what we want to give to every student."[25] It should be noted that these goals of industrial education as outlined in this early speech remained constant throughout Washington's career. He included the following statement in his autobiography *Up From Slavery*:

> In our industrial teaching we keep three things in mind; first, that the student shall be so educated that he shall be enabled to meet conditions as they exist now, in the part of the South where he lives—in a word, to be able to do the thing which the world wants done; second, that every student who graduates from the school shall have enough skill, coupled with intelligence and moral character, to enable him to make a living for himself and others; third, to send every graduate out feeling and knowing that labour is dignified and beautiful—to make each one love labour instead of trying to escape it.[26]

In essence Washington's program attempted to do as much as possible under the circumstances. The myths held by both black and white concerning the nature of education and the role of the Negro in society made any bolder approach impracticable. One of his contemporaries suggested that Washington's philosophy was that "it is better to build even upon the shifting sands of expediency than not to build at all, because you cannot secure a granite foundation."[27]

24. Washington, *Up from Slavery*, 203.
25. Harlan (ed.), *Booker T. Washington Papers*, II, 255–62.
26. Washington, *Up from Slavery*, 312.
27. Kelly Miller, "Washington's Policy," Boston *Evening Transcript*, September 18–19, 1903, in Hugh Hawkins (ed.), *Booker T. Washington and His Critics: The Problem of Negro Leadership* (Boston: D. C. Heath, 1962), 51.

Washington did not ignore the value of the liberal arts, but he insisted that the academic and religious instruction must be accompanied by industrial training. He emphasized this position in many of his speeches. The following is one example:

As to the kinds of education, I believe in all kinds of education—college, university, and industrial education—but I am most interested in industrial, combined with public school education for the great masses of our people; that is our salvation. There is a place, an important one, in our life for the college man, the university man, as well as the man with a trade or with skill in his fingers. To indicate what I think of college education, I would add that the Tuskegee Institute employs more colored graduates of colleges than any single institution in the world.[28]

When a student entered Tuskegee he was encouraged to study academic subjects as well as to learn and work at a trade. Each complemented the other. Roscoe C. Bruce, director of the academic department at Tuskegee, wrote the following account of student schedules: "The student-body is fundamentally divided into day-students and night-students. The night-students work in the industries, largely at common labor, all day and every day, and go to school at night. . . . The day-school students . . . work in the industries every other day for three days a week and attend academic classes the remaining three days."[29] Academic studies also offered "incentives to good conduct and high thinking." "A school must . . . create in him abiding interests in the intellectual achievements of mankind in art and literature, and must stimulate his spiritual nature."[30] Washington felt that academic studies were important but that they should never become the exclusive concern of education.

After Washington's speech to the National Educational Association in Madison he began to receive numerous invitations

28. E. Davidson Washington (ed.), *Selected Speeches of Booker T. Washington*, 201.
29. Booker T. Washington (ed.), *Tuskegee and Its People: Their Ideals and Achievements* (Freeport, N.Y.: Books for Libraries Press, 1905), 62.
30. Washington, *Working with the Hands*, 84.

to address audiences in the North, but he also hoped to speak to representative white audiences in the South. In 1893 he was invited to address the international meeting of Christian Workers in Atlanta for five minutes. Of the occasion he would later write: "I spoke for five minutes to an audience of two thousand people, composed mostly of southern and northern whites. What I said seemed to be received with favor and enthusiasm."[31] As invitations to speak continued to increase, they came in equal numbers from Negroes and northern whites. This five-minute speech had started a chain of invitations which led to his most famous speech, the address delivered at the opening of the Atlanta Cotton States and International Exposition. It was the first time in history a Negro had been asked to speak from the same platform with white southern men and women on any important national occasion before an audience composed of the wealthy and cultured of the South, many northern whites, and a large number of Negroes.[32] With the delivery of this address on September 18, 1895, Washington won additional recognition as a Negro leader and for his ideas on education. He recorded the following description of his thoughts concerning the preparation of the address:

This seemed to me to be the time and the place, without condemning what had been done, to emphasize what ought to be done. I felt that we needed a policy, not of destruction, but of construction; not of defense, but of aggression; a policy not of hostility or surrender, but of friendship and advance. I stated, as vigourously as I was able, that usefulness in the community where we resided was our surest and most potent protection. In my opinion, the Negro should seek constantly in every manly, straight-forward manner to make friends of the white man by whose side he lived, rather than to content himself ·with seeking the good-will of some man a thousand miles away.[33]

On this occasion Washington demonstrated many of the

31. Washington, *Up from Slavery*, 204–205.
32. *Ibid.*, 211.
33. Washington, "Chapters from My Experience," 13633–34.

qualities that characterized his oratorical effectiveness and that won him recognition as a significant American speaker. One estimate is that he delivered between two and four thousand speeches. As Karl R. Wallace has observed, Washington demonstrated tact by appealing to the three distinct elements of his audience: southern whites, Negroes, and northern philanthropists.[34] He showed adeptness by opening with a striking anecdote about a distressed sailing vessel blown off course by a storm and running short of drinking water. A passing vessel signaled for them to "lower your buckets where you are." They were unaware they were sailing in the fresh waters where the Amazon River flows into the Atlantic Ocean and had not yet become thoroughly mixed with salt water. The application was for all groups in the audience to take advantage of jobs, people, and opportunities there in the South. The short figurative theme "cast down your bucket where you are." (repeated in various forms eight times) provided unity to his message and gave southerners a quotable premise upon which to build future racial relations. His simple but eloquent language possessed a moving and graphic quality, metaphorically depicting truths that give dignity to labor, earth, and spirit.

In this speech Washington presented in embryo form the policy that he was to follow throughout his life. He envisioned improvement through practical industrial education, designed to make the Negro a worthy, productive, useful part of society: "Our greatest danger is that in the great leap from slavery to freedom we may overlook the fact that the masses of us are to live by the productions of our hands, and fail to keep in mind that we shall prosper in proportion as we learn to dignify and glorify common labour, and put brains and skill into the common occupations of life; shall prosper in proportion as we learn

34. Karl R. Wallace, "Booker T. Washington," in William Norwood Brigance (ed.), *A History and Criticism of American Public Address* (2 vols; New York: McGraw Hill, 1943), I, 407–408.

to draw the line between the superficial and the substantial, the ornamental gewgaws of life and the useful."[35] This basic idea was similar to what he had been saying in his speeches all along, but this particular address was innovative in two ways. For the first time in public he talked specifically about social equality and consciously attempted to outline what the South and the nation had been searching for, a practical program of black-white relationships.[36] He so interlaced these two new ideas within the total text of the speech that it is difficult to point to any particular section where he developed one to the exclusion of the other. The following frequently quoted passage, known as the persuasive hand analogy, was included at the heart of the speech development: "In all things that are purely social we can be as separate as the fingers, yet one as the hand in all things essential to mutual progress." Later he expanded on that thought: "The wisest among my race understand that the agitation of questions of social equality is the extremest folly, and that progress in the enjoyment of all the privileges that will come to us must be the result of severe and constant struggle rather than of artificial forcing. No race that has anything to contribute to the markets of the world is long in any degree ostracized."[37]

Although reactions to the address were mixed, particularly among Negroes, it was generally looked on with favor. Letters, telegrams, and editorials proposed that he become "leader of the Negro people," a place left vacant by the death of Frederick Douglass.[38] The mantle of "leader of the Negro people" was assigned to Washington, not because he had just initiated a new proposal, but because he had phrased it so well for a national audience.

35. Harlan (ed.), *Booker T. Washington Papers*, III, 584.
36. Spencer, *Booker T. Washington*, 100.
37. Harlan (ed.), *Booker T. Washington Papers*, III, 585–86.
38. Washington, "Chapters from My Experience," 13634–35.

The "separate but equal" idea, implied in the Atlanta speech, became the yardstick of American race relations for the next half century. A year after the speech, the Supreme Court cemented this doctrine into the law of the land.[39] In a sense, that phrase, "separate but equal," was Washington's answer to integration. With that in mind it is easier to understand why he opposed segregation but never fought for the common use of facilities by both races. He opposed only the inequality in character and condition of the accommodations provided for the Negro. In an article written for the *New Republic*, December 4, 1915, he suggested that segregation was ill-advised for six reasons: "(1) It is unjust. (2) It invites other unjust measures. (3) It will not be productive of good, because practically every thoughtful Negro resents its injustice and doubts its sincerity. (4) It is unnecessary. (5) It is inconsistent. (6) There has been no case of segregation of Negroes in the United States that has not widened the breach between the two races."[40] Although in this statement he implied that segregation was not desirable, Washington never openly advocated integration of students and educational facilities. He approached "separate but equal" with a strong emphasis on industrial education.

A comparison of the oratory of Washington and Du Bois reveals that their main disagreement was over the type of education to be given the Negro. While Du Bois admitted the necessity for industrial training, at the same time he criticized the emphasis at Tuskegee. In a clever turn of the phrase he retorted, "I insist that the object of all true education is not to make men carpenters, it is to make carpenters men."[41] Du Bois claimed that Washington minimized the importance of higher educa-

39. Spencer, *Booker T. Washington*, 104–105.
40. Mrs. Booker T. Washington, "Are We Making Good?" in Anson Phelps Stokes (ed.), *Tuskegee Institute: The First Fifty Years* (Tuskegee, Alabama: Tuskegee Institute Press, 1931), 80–86.
41. W. E. B. Du Bois, "The Talented Tenth," in William Loren Katz (ed.), *The Negro Problem* (New York: Arno, 1969), 62.

tion and discouraged "philanthropic support" of it. Du Bois inferred that Washington's subordination of higher education to training in the skilled trades ignored the fact that many teachers in industrial colleges had received a higher education. He further indicted Washington: "We must lay on the soul of this man a heavy responsibility for the . . . decline of the Negro college and public school, and the firmer establishment of color caste in this land."[42] Other opponents of Washington suggested that his limitation of Negro education to industrial training tended to "re-enslave" them. In 1903 Kittredge Wheeler complained to Du Bois: "Washington's name, his work, his school, all are used here in the north, even as an argument against the education of the Negro. . . . The sentiment, 'Industrial Education for the Negro' is the shackle."[43] In an address to colored school children in Washington, D.C., Du Bois warned against training "black boys and girls forever to be hewers of wood and drawers of water for the cowardly people who seek to shackle our minds as they shackled our hands yesterday." He urged them: "loose yourselves from that greater temptation to curse and malign your own people and surrender their rights for the sake of applause and popularity and cash."[44] Amplifying this thought, he stated in one of his articles: "Earn a living; get rich, and all these things shall be added unto you. Moreover, conciliate your neighbors, because they are more powerful and wealthier, and the price you must pay to earn a living in America is that of humiliation and inferiority."[45] Since industrial education centered upon practical training and higher educa-

42. Du Bois, *Dusk of Dawn*, 68–72.
43. Aptheker (ed.), *Correspondence of W. E. B. Du Bois*, I, 58–59. Letter from Kittredge Wheeler to DuBois, dated July 20, 1903.
44. W. E. B. Du Bois, "The Joy of Living," in Francis L. Broderick, *W. E. B. Du Bois, Negro Leader in a Time of Crisis* (Stanford, Calif.: Stanford University Press, 1959), 71.
45. W. E. B. Du Bois, "The Negro Problem from the Negro Point of View," *World Today*, VI (April, 1904), 522, in Broderick, *W. E. B. Du Bois, Negro Leader in a Time of Crisis*, 71.

tion emphasized abstract knowledge, Du Bois felt that industrial schools did not adequately prepare students for advanced courses. Fostering a bitter offshoot from his disagreement with Washington, Du Bois felt that schools such as Tuskegee represented a selfish attitude toward other black schools in that they diverted revenue from them. Referring to the "Tuskegee Machine," Du Bois complained:

Not only did presidents of the United States consult Booker Washington, but governors and congressmen, philanthropists conferred with him, scholars wrote to him. Tuskegee became a vast information bureau and center of advice. . . . After a time almost no Negro institution could collect funds without the recommendation or acquiescence of Mr. Washington. Few political appointments were made anywhere in the United States without his consent. Even the careers of rising young colored men were very often determined by his advice and certainly his opposition was fatal.[46]

Du Bois objected to the notion that industrial training was sufficient for all Negroes. While still a student at Harvard, Du Bois began to develop his theory of the "Talented Tenth," a theory that any group could advance only through the racial leadership provided by a college-educated elite. In the following excerpt from one of his articles he explained the concept:

The history of civilization seems to prove that no group or nation which seeks advancement and true development can despise or neglect the power of well-trained minds; and this power of intellectual leadership must be given to the Talented Tenth among American Negroes before this race can seriously be asked to assume the responsibility of dispelling its own ignorance. Upon the foundation stone of a few well-equipped Negro colleges of high and honest standards can be built a proper system of free common schools in the south for the masses of the Negro people; any attempt to found a system of public schools on anything else than this—on narrow ideals, limited or merely technical training—is to call blind leaders for the blind.[47]

46. Du Bois, *Dusk of Dawn*, 73, 243.
47. W. E. B. Du Bois, "The Training of Negroes for Social Power," *Colored American Magazine*, VII (May, 1904), 333–39.

During the 1890s Du Bois pursued a conciliatory ideology that permitted him frequently to agree with Washington, but after the turn of the century Du Bois became increasingly critical of the Tuskegee educator. His first explicit public criticism of Washington appeared in *Souls of Black Folk*, a series of essays printed in 1903.[48] One chapter in particular, "Of Mr. Booker T. Washington and Others," dealt with the question of racial leadership and provided the opponents of Washington with a coherent argument which affected "a coalescence of the more radical elements and made them articulate, thereby creating a split of the race into two contending camps."[49] Although he tempered his censure with some praise of Washington, Du Bois was still harsh enough to faciliate a break which continued until Washington's death in 1915. When in November, 1903, Washington asked Du Bois for advice on matters relative to a proposed New York Conference, Du Bois clearly suggested the schism in his reply: "I do not think it will be profitable for me to give further advice which will not be followed. The conference is yours and you will naturally constitute it as you choose. I must of course reserve the right to see the final list of those invited and to decide then whether my own presence is worth while."[50] In a later, undated letter he became even more specific:

As to Mr. Washington, the people who think that I am one of those who oppose many of his ideas are perfectly correct. I have no personal opposition to him—I honor much of his work. But his platform has done the race infinite harm and I'm working against it with all my might. Mr. W. is today chief instrument in the hands of a N. Y. clique who are seeking to syndicate the Negro and settle the problem on the trust basis. They have bought and bribed newspapers and men.[51]

---

48. Du Bois, *Souls of Black Folk*.
49. James Weldon Johnson, *Black Manhattan* (New York: n.p., 1930), 134.
50. Aptheker (ed.), *Correspondence of W. E. B. Du Bois*, I, 54. Letter from Du Bois to Booker T. Washington, November, 1903.
51. Undated letter from Du Bois to Albert Bushnell Hart, *ibid.*, I, 111.

Declaring Washington's educational view as narrow, he charged that it had developed into a "Gospel of Work and Money" to the exclusion of philosophical and aesthetic values. He further claimed that Washington's protest of disfranchisement and lynching were so mild as to constitute surrender:

Mr. Washington distinctly asks that black people give up, at least for the present, three things,—First, political power. Second, insistence on civil rights, Third, higher education of Negro youth,—and concentrate all their energies on industrial education, the accumulation of wealth, and the conciliation of the South. . . . This policy has been . . . advocated for over fifteen years. . . . In these years there have occurred: 1. The disfranchisement of the Negro. 2. The legal creation of a distinct status of civil inferiority for the Negro. 3. The steady withdrawal of aid from institutions for the higher training of the Negro. . . . The question then comes: Is it possible, and probable, that nine millions of men can make effective progress in economic lines if they are deprived of political rights, made a servile caste, and allowed only the most meagre chance for developing their exceptional men?[52]

He found it not justifiable to shift the blame and responsibility for the condition of the Negro race completely to the Negro, while the rest of the nation became pessimistic spectators. He warned that he and thoughtful Negroes would support Washington's theories and leadership only so long as he was preaching "thrift, patience, and industrial training for the masses." "But so far as Mr. Washington apologizes for injustice, North or South, does not rightly value the privilege and duty of voting, belittles the emasculating effects of caste distinctions, and opposes the higher training and ambition of our brighter minds—so far as he, the South, or the nation does this—we must unceasingly and firmly oppose them."[53]

Souls of Black Folk received favorable notice from many literary critics, but Washington's prestige was too great to be significantly damaged by its criticism. Its appearance did, how-

52. Du Bois, *Souls of Black Folk*, 41–47, 49–59.
53. *Ibid*.

ever, provide some cohesion to the forming opposition and brought attention to Du Bois as a personality and leader. From the time of Washington's Atlanta Exposition Address in 1895, a small coterie of black as well as white intellectuals who declared that Washington had "sold out the Negro" grew in enthusiasm and gradually became more radical, especially between 1900 and 1905. Their activities eventually lead to the formation in 1909 of the National Association for the Advancement of Colored People, a more militant organization, in which Du Bois accepted the position of director of publications and research and became the editor of *The Crisis*.[54] At his disposal was placed a powerful medium through which to oppose Washington. But, discussing some of the restraints that he felt, Du Bois wrote:

> Many felt that I must not be allowed to direct its policy too openly against Mr. Washington. . . . This was in direct accord with my own desires and plans. I did not wish to attack Booker Washington; I wished to give him credit for much good, but to oppose certain of his words and policies which could be interpreted against our best interests; I wanted to do this through propaganda of the truth and for this reason I wished to continue in New York so far as possible my studies in Atlanta, and to add to this a periodical of fact and agitation which I should edit.[55]

In 1910 Washington delivered several speeches in England implying that the racial problem was on its way to being resolved in the United States. One of the founders of the NAACP, John E. Milholland, was in England at the time and wrote to Du Bois suggesting that the Washington speeches needed to be answered.[56] Du Bois agreed and wrote a pamphlet entitled *Race Relations in the United States: An Appeal to England and Europe*. In it he argued:

54. Spencer, *Booker T. Washington*, 151; Du Bois, *Dusk of Dawn*, 95, 225–26.
55. *Ibid.*, 224–25.
56. Aptheker (ed.), *Correspondence of W. E. B. Du Bois*, I, 172–73.

If Booker T. Washington, or any other person, is giving the impression abroad that the Negro problem is in process of satisfactory solution, he is giving an impression which is not true. We say this without personal bitterness toward Mr. Washington. He is a distinguished American and has a perfect right to his opinions. But we are compelled to point out that Mr. Washington's large financial responsibilities have made him dependent on the rich charitable public and that, for this reason, he has for years been compelled to tell, not the whole truth, but that part of it which certain powerful interests in America wish to appear as the whole truth. In flat contradiction, however, to the pleasant pictures thus pointed out, let us not forget that the consensus of opinion among eminent European scholars who know the race problem in America . . . is that it forms the gravest of American problems. We black men who live and suffer under present conditions, and who have no reason, and refuse to accept reasons, for silence, can substantiate this unanimous testimony.[57]

Shortly thereafter Du Bois went to England to the First Universal Races Congress, but he discouraged the arrangement of a lecture tour overlapping Washington's route. Aware of some conservative objections in England to his speaking, he wanted to avoid direct competition with Washington.[58] Statements and incidents of indirect opposition gave Washington good reason to remain suspicious of the NAACP and one of its major spokesmen, W. E. B. Du Bois.

Reactions to the Atlanta Race Riot of 1906 clearly demonstrated the differing attitudes of the two men. Both men were away from the South when the riot occurred, and they immediately canceled their engagements in order to return to Atlanta. Washington urged Negroes not to make "the fatal mistake of attempting to retaliate," but to "rely upon the efforts of the proper authorities to bring order and security out of confusion." He met with city authorities and helped organize a meeting of ten leading citizens of each race to discuss a course of action. He publicly advised Negroes to remember there was peace and

57. Du Bois, *Autobiography*, 262.
58. Aptheker (ed.), *Correspondence of W. E. B. Du Bois*, I, 172–73.

harmony in thousands of other communities. Some months later he reported that there was a general spirit of repentance and sorrow among the white people.[59]

On his way to Atlanta, Du Bois wrote "A Litany of Atlanta." The following excerpt from the poem expressed his hatred for the white race:

A city lay in travail, God our Lord, and from her loins sprang twin Murder and Black Hate. Red was the midnight; clang, crack and cry of death and fury filled the air and trembled underneath the stars when church spires pointed silently to Thee. And all this was to sate the greed of greedy men who hide behind the veil of vengeance!

Doth not this justice of hell stink in Thy nostrils, O God? How long shall the mounting flood of innocent blood roar in Thine ears and pound in our hearts for vengeance? Pile the pale frenzy of bloodcrazed brutes who do such deeds high on Thine altar, Jehovah Jireh, and burn it in hell forever and forever![60]

In reading these lines from "A Litany of Atlanta," it should be remembered that since his family was there Du Bois was deeply concerned for their safety. However, his hatred of the white man continued to grow, as is evident in another of his publications of 1921:

The white world's vermin and filth:
All the dirt of London,
All the scum of New York;
Valiant despoilers of women
And conquerors of unarmed men;
Shameless breeders of bastards
Drunk with the greed of gold,
Baiting their blood-stained hooks
With cant for the souls of the simple;
Bearing the white man's burden
Of liquor and lust and lies! . . .
I hate them, Oh!

59. Spencer, *Booker T. Washington*, 153–54.
60. W. E. B. Du Bois, "A Litany of Atlanta," *Independent*, LXI (October 11, 1906), 856–58.

I hate them well,
I hate them, Christ!
As I hate hell!
If I were God
I'd sound their knell
This day![61]

Du Bois saw no future in the South for ambitious young Negroes, since he did not believe that the average southern white
man had any desire to help the Negro. Therefore he directly
contradicted Washington's counsel and urged Negroes to go
north for freedom and advancement.

Kelly Miller summarized the positions of these two leaders
in an article entitled "Radicals and Conservatives" published
in 1908. He suggested that Washington stood for progress which
must begin with things as they are and move from that point
forward. The problem of Negro rights was a human one to be
solved by humans in the face of human opposition. The Negroes were a weak-child race which had to be strengthened in
the presence of white people who had fixed views, often not
fair nor equitable. The black man could not win in a fight with
the white man; therefore he needed to remain on friendly terms
with the stronger race. It was useless to demand his constitutional rights since the Negro was not yet capable of handling
them and his opponents would not let him have them. Therefore, the Negro should let politics alone and stress the most
powerful force on which all progress was based, economic progress. This could be done best through industrial education.[62]

Du Bois, on the other hand, said that the soul was more than
the body and he did not accept the gospel of material wealth.
Giving up the higher life and only seeking for riches was a back-

61. W. E. B. Du Bois, *Darkwater: Voices from Within the Veil* (New York:
n.p., 1920), 53–54.
62. Kelly Miller, *Race Adjustment: Essays on the Negro in America* (New
York: Neale, 1908), 11–18.

ward step. Acquisition of wealth should not have been placed before the development of culture. He chafed at the veil of Negro prejudice. If the white race needed higher education in order to develop its leaders, so did the black race. Those leaders, the exceptional "Talented Tenth," existed and the door of opportunity had to be kept open for them. Industrial education, necessary for a majority of blacks, could not provide the leaders who turn the tide away from the denial of rights for the Negro. Although Du Bois advocated neither violence nor patience, he might well have incited revolution if his approach had been followed at that time.[63]

One of the inevitable results of any debate is to either polarize the opposing factions or bring them closer together. Under the influence of the criticism of Du Bois and others and the continual deterioration of Negro rights and opportunities, Washington in later life moved toward an ideology which incorporated a much stronger stand on civil rights. He saw that discrimination had increased despite the Negro's economic and cultural advancement; as a result he became less conservative in his speeches.[64] He made the following comments before the National Colored Teacher's Association in 1911: "I do not overlook the wrongs that often perplex and embarrass us in this country. . . . I condemn with all the strength of my nature the barbarous habit of lynching a human being, whether black or white, without legal trial. I condemn any practice in any state that results in not enforcing the law with a certainty and justice, regardless of race or color."[65] Again in a speech in 1915 he said, "Regardless of state lines, whether the lynching occurs in one of the states of the Southland or in one of the states of the North, I believe the time is at hand when all true Americans,

63. *Ibid.*
64. Spencer, *Booker T. Washington*, 190.
65. E. Davidson Washington (ed.), *Selected Speeches of Booker T. Washington*, 206.

regardless of color, must recognize the fact that in the future we must have a government not by the mob, but a government administered by properly constituted courts of law." [66] Washington became even more upset with discrimination in public education and condemned more strongly the inequity in state appropriations between the white and black schools. In the last speech of his life he made the following comments: "There is sometimes much talk about the inferiority of the Negro. In practice, however, the idea appears to be that he is a sort of superman. He is expected, with about one fifth of what the whites receive for their eduction, to make as much progress as they are making. Taking the Southern states as a whole, about $10.23 per capita is spent in educating the average white boy or girl, and the sum of $2.82 per capita in educating the average black child." [67]

Always in his shadow and never able to influence the direction of the Tuskegee educator, Du Bois moved into the role of a protest propagandist. Thinking of himself as a member of the "Talented Tenth," he possessed self-assurance, outspoken boldness, and intellectual arrogance. In contrast to the calmness, patience, and compassion of Washington, Du Bois became revolutionary, pessimistic, and bitter with the passing years. The spirit of the man was reflected in the changing nuances of his rhetoric. In his speaking and writing, he became severe and extreme. Although his efforts continued through various writings, particularly in *The Crisis*, and through his speaking, Du Bois never completely attained the leadership role vacated by Washington's death in 1915. His Negro bias publicly reached a climax when he applied for membership in the Communist party and left America to spend the last few years of his long life in Ghana, where he died in 1963.

It is difficult to say who won the debate over the method and

66. *Ibid.*, 257.
67. *Ibid.*, 282.

direction of educational reform for the American Negro. Their debate was the result of distinct contrasts in their backgrounds, training, personalities, and work. One was born a slave in the South, the other free in an area of the North devoid of discrimination. One was rooted in the soil and the Bible, the other saturated in the agnostic liberalism of Europe. Washington disliked the tabulation of facts by a statistician, while Du Bois put faith in such surveys. Washington linked the facts he discovered to practical projects, while Du Bois expounded abstract ideas, expecting other men to act on them. Washington interpreted statistics and projects to men in order to win their financial support, and Du Bois rarely attempted money raising. Washington never expressed bitterness, but Du Bois admitted he could not control his "cold, biting critical streak."[68]

Perhaps the greatest difference between them was the comparative distances the two men had traveled from birth to manhood. Washington moved from slavery to freedom and national leadership. Since that great distance had been covered in such a few years, he reasoned that the Negro could afford to be patient in seeking full implementation of the promise of the Emancipation Proclamation. Du Bois could see relatively little progress from his birth in the North to his treatment in the South, rank with discrimination and cruelty. Late in life Du Bois gave credence to this idea when one evening in Ghana he summed up his controversy with Washington: "I think that maybe the greatest difference between Booker T. and myself was that he had felt the lash, and I had not."[69]

As a product of his environment, every man possesses myths of varying types and to varying degrees. Because of his different upbringing Du Bois did not share the prevailing racial concepts

68. Basil Mathews, *Booker T. Washington* (Cambridge: Harvard University Press, 1948), 277–78.
69. Leslie Alexander Lacy, *Cheer the Lonesome Traveler* (New York: Dial, 1970), 49.

of the South, was not the least sympathetic with them, and therefore could not compromise. Although he rejected some southern concepts, Washington had been so completely immersed in the southern tradition that he could not free himself from its world view. Rejecting some ideas, he often felt compelled to compromise out of necessity and expediency. Washington's contributions measured against those of Du Bois suggest the wisdom of the Tuskegee educator's adjustment to his contemporary environment, which really offered little choice in his program for education and civil rights. His successes partially resulted from and were magnified by his more capable and prolific speaking

History has proven that a new idea is generally first received by the public with skepticism if not open rejection. During the latter part of the nineteenth century, any proposals favorable to the improvement of Negro education and granting of Negro rights were likely to be rejected. To be successful in a tense atmosphere a speaker must frame the new, unfamiliar, and often unacceptable in terms of the known, familiar, and acceptable. To say that the Negro should be provided an opportunity for a publicly supported education, it was expedient to work from the assumption that the Negro is socially inferior and should not go to school with the whites. The balancing factor of the familiar at least gained a reasonably tolerant hearing of the unfamiliar until people became accustomed to and comfortable with the new. The only step remaining was the acceptance and implementation. Perhaps herein was the secret of Washington's speaking success. Du Bois would not compromise to the point of using any acceptable southern ideas on race; thus his rhetoric and writing were interpreted as too revolutionary, as asking too much under the circumstances. Hence he was relatively ineffective.

Reflection suggests yet another conclusion. Remaining in the South with the task of keeping support flowing to Tuskegee, Washington yielded to accommodation and provided an argument to rationalize Negro-white relations. He did not challenge the myth of white supremacy and made no attempt to expose the view of the happy docile Negro, so often portrayed in the rhetoric of Henry W. Grady and other southern orators. When Du Bois encountered pressures to submit to the myths he soon left Atlanta and the South. In the North and eventually outside the country he was free to voice an uncompromising rhetoric, bitter and defiant.

A speaker's words reflect his attitudes, which are the composite product of his family background, geographical origin, type of education, and experiences. Although sharing a common color and a common cause, Washington and Du Bois were polarized in their ideas relative to the issues of Negro education and to the oratory implemented in behalf of that cause. In their differences they both made lasting contributions. Through his conciliatory rhetoric of accommodation Washington started the Negro on the journey to self-improvement and acceptance. Du Bois introduced a black intellectual elite that he called the "Talented Tenth." The succeeding members of this group became increasingly uncompromising and defiant until their rebellion reached a peak in the middle of the twentieth century. Washington started the journey in the framework of the late nineteenth century and Du Bois continued the journey in the changing atmosphere of the twentieth century. Washington was a man for his time. Du Bois was a man slightly ahead of his time.

BIBLIOGRAPHICAL NOTE

Materials on W. E. B. Du Bois are found in Herbert Aptheker (ed.), *The Correspondence of W. E. B. Du Bois, 1877–1934* (Amherst: The University of Massachusetts Press, 1973), and in *The Autobiography of W. E. B. Du Bois* (n.p.: International

Publishers, 1968). Among Du Bois's other writings are *Dusk of Dawn* (New York: Harcourt, Brace and Co., 1968), and *Souls of Black Folks* (Chicago: McClurg Co., 1903).

There are numerous books on Booker T. Washington. Among his own writings are *Selected Speeches of Booker T. Washington*, edited by E. Davidson Washington (Garden City: N.Y.: Doubleday, Doran and Co., 1932), *Up From Slavery* (New York: Doubleday, Page, and Co., 1901), and *Working with the Hands* (New York: Doubleday, Page, and Co., 1904). *The Booker T. Washington Papers*, edited by Louis R. Harlan *et al.*, are being published by the University of Illinois Press (1972–). The first seven volumes have appeared.

Karl R. Wallace wrote a seminal article on Washington's speaking published in Volume I of *A History and Criticism of American Public Address*, edited by William Norwood Brigance (2 vols.; New York: Russell and Russell, 1960). Also valuable is Willis N. Pitts, Jr.'s "A Critical Study Of Booker T. Washington as a Speech Maker with an Analysis of Seven Selected Speeches" (Ph.D. dissertation, University of Michigan, 1952).

The Southern Lady Becomes
an Advocate *

On the occasion of her graduation from Wesleyan Female College in 1865, sixteen-year-old Mary Clare DeGraffenried discarded her "approved" valedictory address and "launched a scathing attack on the Federal occupation forces encamped nearby."[1] That she echoed the sentiments of her Georgia audience made her outburst tolerable and perhaps even heroic. Even so, such a departure from "propriety" was exceptional. The few women who spoke in public in the antebellum South met with little success. Northern women who appeared on southern platforms were dismissed as "yankees," and public opinion forced southerners like the Grimké sisters of South Carolina to leave their native states to gain a hearing. To escape censure, the rare women speakers had to adhere to strict standards of acceptability. Usually they restricted their remarks to "a few words" on a ceremonial occasion.

The prewar epideictic tradition that allowed women to read graduation addresses and present banners continued after 1865 with the advent of memorial associations. Even the most conservative critics deemed it "altogether fitting and proper" that women should honor their heroes and preserve the images of the Old South and the lost Confederacy. But advocacy of the New South from a platform was clearly suspect. Nevertheless,

* The research for this study was supported by the Research Grants Committee of the University of Alabama.
    1. Lala Carr Steelman, "Mary Clare DeGraffenried," in Edward T. James (ed.), *Notable American Women* (3 vols.; Cambridge: Belnap Press, 1971), I, 453.

southern women reformers agitated, cajoled, charmed, educated, threatened, and coerced through lobbies, petitions, newspaper articles, and editorials. By the early 1870s, they were speaking increasingly before southern audiences and exerting influence there far beyond that commonly imagined.

The purpose of this essay is to examine the public address of native southern women from 1870 to 1920, most particularly their reform speaking. The study identifies speakers and inquires into their motivation for invading the forum. It discusses obstacles to their entry into public affairs, describes their preparation for political involvement, examines issues, forums, and rhetorical strategies, and evaluates the effectiveness of their speaking.

The Speakers

Who were the women who dared defy convention to speak in public? Were they southern "ladies," or, as many charged, radicals, "pore white trash," and yankees?

A number of "outsiders" came South to advocate diverse causes. Although Anna Dickinson raised few eyebrows when she lectured on literary and cultural subjects, flamboyant Victoria Claflin Woodhull, champion of free love and spiritualism, was bitterly criticized in Montgomery, Alabama, when she defended women's suffrage. Mary E. Lease risked savage denunciation to further populism in Georgia.[2] Frances Willard argued in favor of prohibition from Louisiana to the Carolinas, while Anna Shaw and Susan B. Anthony orated on women's suffrage on many southern platforms.

"Foreign" speakers notwithstanding, native daughters of the

2. Trudy L. Hansen, "Anna Elizabeth Dickinson's Southern Speaking Tour, April, 1875" (M.A. thesis, Louisiana State University, 1973); Montgomery *Advertiser* (undated clipping), in Alabama Woman's Suffrage File, Department of Archives and History, State of Alabama, Montgomery, Alabama. See Robert T. Oliver, *History of Public Speaking in America* (Boston: Allyn and Bacon, 1965), 444; on Mary E. Lease see random clippings from the Felton Collection, University of Georgia Library, Athens, Georgia.

Old South did most of the speaking for reform in the region. The planter aristocracy continued to dominate life in the post-bellum southern communities. Because that tradition provided a privileged few opportunities seldom available to other southerners, most public-spirited women came from the upper class. Exceptions to that profile included proponents of economic reform who, through Grange, Farmers' Alliance, and People's party affiliations, found limited opportunities for public speaking.[3] However, the degree of power exercised by such women and the extent to which they acted as spokespersons for their organizations was not substantial. A number of black women also spoke out for reform, but their sphere of influence was largely in the black community itself or, as in the case of Ida Bell Wells-Barnett, one of the founders of the National Association for the Advancement of Colored People, in the states above the Mason and Dixon Line.[4]

Initially, relatively few "daughters of the Old South" embraced social reform, most being far more comfortable with rationalizing defeat and attempting to preserve the "glorious past." But the emerging "New Woman of the New South" battled complacency and ignorance to call for a new order. Lillian W. Johnson, acting president of the Southern Association of College Women, struck at these barriers in an address before

3. Clement Eaton, *A History of the Old South* (2nd ed.; New York: Mac-Millan, 1966), 388; Richard M. Weaver, *The Southern Tradition at Bay: A History of Postbellum Thought*, ed. George Core and M. E. Bradford (New Rochelle, N.Y.: Arlington House, 1968), 73; Robert Carroll McNath, Jr., "The Farmers' Alliance in the South: The Career of an Agrarian Institution" (Ph.D. dissertation, University of North Carolina, 1972), 236; Annie L. Diggs, "The Women in the Alliance Movement," *Arena*, VI (July, 1892), 163; Allan Nevins, *The Emergence of Modern America, 1865–1878* (New York: MacMillan, 1927); Solon J. Buck, *The Granger Movement* (Cambridge: Harvard University Press, 1913); William B. Hesseltine and David L. Smiley, *The South in American History* (Englewood Cliffs, N.J.: Prentice Hall, 1960), 427.

4. See Mary Magdelene Boone Hutton, "The Rhetoric of Ida B. Wells: The Genesis of the Anti-Lynch Movement" (Ph.D. dissertation, Indiana University, 1975); Annjennette S. McFarlin, "Hallie Quinn Brown—Black Woman Elocutionist: 1845(?)–1949" (Ph.D. dissertation, Washington State University, 1975).

the Eleventh Annual Conference on Education in the South. She charged:

We have so long looked back at that glorious olden time, and we have grown so sensitive over some of our problems that we have come to feel that we can develop within ourselves and from our own efforts without looking beyond the borders and seeing what others are doing.[5]

Journalist Josephine Henry's contemporary analysis provides insight into the disparity in goals. She divided southern women into two groups: those women "too ethereal to be troubled with [current] affairs," who confined their efforts to "devising ways . . . for retaining their social prestige," and those who realized their "potentialities" and had the "courage" to demand "action commensurate with their aspirations."[6] Mythmaking characterized the former's rhetoric; social issues dominated the speaking of the latter. Some southern women viewed reform and Old South romanticism as not necessarily contradictory ideas—at least until the suffrage issue surfaced. Ella Gertrude Clanton Thomas, for example, a "Georgia gentlewoman," served simultaneously as president of the state Woman Suffrage Association and as secretary and later as treasurer of the United Daughters of the Confederacy.[7]

That reform attracted "respectable women" lent credence to the causes they espoused. Josephine Henry, herself a suffragist, cited support of the ballot from southern women "of the highest intelligence and social standing, among them being many lineal descendants of the signers of the Declaration of Independence and the patriots of 1776, social leaders, noted wives, literary women, teachers, and taxpayers."[8] Caroline Merrick,

5. Lillian W. Johnson, "The Higher Education of Women in the South," in *Proceedings of the Eleventh Conference for Education in the South* (Nashville, Tenn.: Executive Committee, 1908), 134.

6. Josephine K. Henry, "The New Woman of the New South," *Arena*, XI (February, 1895), 353–54.

7. Mary Elizabeth Massey, "The Making of a Feminist," *Journal of Southern History*, XXXIX (February, 1973), 20–21.

8. Henry, "The New Woman of the New South." 357.

wife of the chief justice of the Supreme Court of Louisiana, led the fight for both suffrage and temperance in her state. Dixie Graves, wife of the future governor of Alabama and herself a future United States senator, advocated anti-convict-leasing laws and woman suffrage. Rebecca Latimer Felton, wife of a United States congressman, participated in a variety of reforms. Southern audiences found such prestigious names difficult to dismiss. These speakers were southern "ladies" and, as such, commanded respect, if not agreement.

Motivation for Speaking

What motivated these southern women to enter politics? Discriminatory statutory laws involving taxation and transfer of property aroused some. The personal magnetism of individual proponents of reform commandeered others. Caroline Merrick, for example, first president of the New Orleans Temperance Association, embraced the temperance movement not because of "deep conviction" but because of "the inspirations" of Frances Willard.[9] However, a more pervasive influence underlying women's entry into the political arena was prevailing community needs throughout the southern states. Specific inequities, arising out of social conditions and tempered by the economic and political context of the postwar South, provided the issues. Of particular concern were: the "shameless exploitation of Southern child labor by Northern industrial interests," health needs, prison conditions, care and treatment of the mentally ill, limited and inferior educational opportunities, temperance and, eventually, suffrage.

The progressive and humanitarian movements touched many southern women and provided a context and a rationale for their reform efforts. These women felt that social evils would not remedy themselves. Moved by "an impulse to set things

9. Caroline E. Merrick, *Old Times in Dixie Land* (New York: Grafton Press, 1901), 171.

right, rooted in their backgrounds and social stations," these women perceived reform to be divinely sanctioned. With holy fervor, they prepared to fight.[10] Consciences aroused and Christian idealism stirred, they labored directly and through joint efforts to remedy ills in their communities. Also a sense of noblesse oblige, inherited from their past, undergirded southern women's philanthropy. Though viewing those for whom they labored as "unfortunates" and taking a paternalistic stance toward them and their problems, southern women assumed responsibility for society's disadvantaged and entered the public forum on their behalf.

Obstacles

The obstacles that southern women speakers faced seemed overwhelming. The most formidable barriers emanated from long-standing stereotypes and prejudices about "woman's role." The archetype of the "Southern Lady" dictated her "proper sphere" as much in the New South as in the Old. A stringent, unwritten code prescribing the limits of propriety isolated women from politics and discouraged—and on occasion forbade—their speaking in public. As late as 1883, Jennie Grier, daughter of the president of Erskine College, was prohibited from presenting her graduating essay, written in French; consequently, she invited Francis Warrington Dawson, editor of the Charleston *News and Courier* to read it for her. In 1891 Julia Tutwiler, Alabama reformer, had to sit mute at a meeting of the Alabama Education Association and listen to her paper read "very badly" by a man.[11]

10. Richard Hofstadter, *The Age of Reform* (New York: Random House, 1955); Arthur S. Link, "The Progressive Movement in the South, 1870–1914," *North Carolina Historical Review*, XXIII (April, 1946), 193; Bruce L. Clayton, "Southern Critics of the New South, 1890–1914" (Ph.D. dissertation, Duke University, 1966), 237. Though Clayton is referring to social critics of the New South, his analysis is nonetheless appropriate.
11. Charleston *News and Courier*, May 3, 1883; Birmingham *News*, October 5, 1975.

Women were not only disenfranchised but limited in opportunities to observe politics. Not until 1866 were seats added in the Louisiana House of Representatives, an alteration that enabled ladies to attend debates.[12] What they could gain from newspapers and conversation dealing with politics provided little insight into the political process. For southern women formal training occurred primarily in seminaries, academies, and finishing schools whose purpose it was to instill "propriety" and to "turn out" ladies.

The conservative superstructure of the southern church imposed further severe restrictions. In contrast to Quaker women who occupied positions equal with men in church affairs, females were prevented from direct participation in most southern churches. Those who challenged the strictures were subjected to reprobation by ministers, church officers, the conference, and the congregation. Whether women should speak out in religious services was bitterly argued. In addition to having tradition on their side, the antagonists cited the authority of St. Paul, who had expressly forbidden the practice. Challenging both Baptists and Presbyterians on the issue, Mrs. Felton maintained that the apostle's words were "advisory, not mandatory."[13] When the Reverend J. B. Hawthorne of the First Baptist Church of Atlanta criticized Mrs. Felton for speaking publicly, her husband, Congressman Felton, defended his wife's honor and censured the minister. Stating "in plainest terms" that his wife spoke with his "knowledge, consent and approval," Dr. Felton vehemently countered, "I honor this true woman for her courage, as well as her fidelity to truth and honesty of purpose.

12. *Daily Crescent*, February 8, 1866, cited in Kathryn Reinhart Schuler, "Women in Public Affairs in Louisiana During Reconstruction," *Louisiana Historical Quarterly*, XIX (July, 1936), 726.

13. Scattered manuscripts and news clippings in the Felton Papers; Rebecca Latimer Felton, "Southern Presbyterians and the Woman Question" (Letter to *Woman's Journal*, May 27, 1893), cited in Josephine Bone Floyd, "Rebecca Latimer Felton, Champion of Women's Rights," *Georgia Historical Quarterly*, XXX (June, 1946), 84–85.

She has my approbation when she punctures frauds and shams in the pulpit, in the church or in the state."[14] Such "effrontery" and its defense were rare indeed.

So pervasive were the attitudes concerning what was and was not ladylike that women seldom questioned them. "Considering it improper for a lady's name to appear in public affairs," Ann Pamela Cunningham, founder of the Mount Vernon Ladies' Association of the Union, the first woman's patriotic society, signed her 1853 plea to the Charleston *Mercury* for the preservation of the historical landmark, "A Southern Matron." Captain J. M. Taylor, for one, approved of such "propriety." In a speech to the Opelousas Democratic Club, he complimented the "Southern ladies" for not outraging "the delicate retirement of their sex, by an open and active participation in the political issues of the day." Instead, he urged them to "inspire the sterner sex—their protectors—to a lively sense of their interest, happiness and safety."[15]

Gradually, however, changes in attitudes began to occur. By 1866, contemporary historian Frank Moore observed that "the boundaries which public opinion had placed on the legitimate activities and the proper sphere of woman have been enlarged." Commenting on the shift in thinking that allowed women's entry into public activities, he boasted: "They have shown that a wife, a mother, or a sister is never more truly lovely than when she pleads, even before a large and promiscuous assembly, the sacred cause of humanity, presenting reasons that flow from the fountains of charity, and descend from the celestial heights of religion."[16]

Less dramatic than it might appear, this transition from "ped-

14. Atlanta *Constitution*, December 15, 1893.
15. Wallace Evan Davies, "Ann Pamela Cunningham," in James (ed.), *Notable American Women*, I, 416; Opelousas (La.) *Courier*, August 22, 1868, cited in Schuler, "Women in Public Affairs in Louisiana," 731.
16. Frank Moore, *Women of the War: Their Heroism and Self-Sacrifice* (Hartford, Conn.: S. S. Scranton, 1866), 386.

estal to politics" involved not a reversal of roles for the southern woman but rather an extension and expansion of her former role as "mistress" of the plantation.[17] In reality plantation life had been hard and grueling for most of these women. Mistress of her own family and the entire community, the southern woman had a responsibility to settle disputes, mete out discipline, and preside over the sick room, and at times the classroom. As "keeper of the keys," she managed the stores, counted the silver, and doled out rations. The realities of war forced the southern woman to extend her "keeping" role beyond the single family unit and the plantation. Through the Soldier's Aid Society she gathered food, sewed uniforms and bandages, and raised money for war materials. She helped maintain morale, at home and abroad. Though some fathers forbade their daughters to become nurses, many southern women ministered to the wounded in the field and in hospitals. Economic necessity compelled "ladies" to carry out duties previously restricted to men. Serving as catalyst to a new order, war and its aftermath raised new questions about woman's "place."

The chaos wrought by war and reconstruction forced a broadening of the southern woman's traditional role and provided her with the wedge for participation in politics. Historians Francis Butler Simkins and James Welch Patton acknowledged that "out of the ruins of the defeated Confederacy there arose many hopeful and forward-looking women who were destined to have a vital part in creating the civilization of the New South."[18] But as Kathryn Schuler observed, "Instead of a sim-

17. Anne Firor Scott, *Women in American Life* (Boston: Houghton Mifflin, 1970), 88.
18. Francis Butler Simkins and James Welch Patton, *The Women of the Confederacy* (Richmond: Garrett and Massie, 1936), 259; Wilbur Fisk Tillett, "Southern Womanhood as Affected by the War," *Century Magazine*, XLIII (November, 1891), 12; Marjorie Stratford Mendenhall, "Southern Women of a 'Lost Generation,'" *South Atlantic Quarterly*, XXXIII (October, 1934), 337; Eliza-

ple *resumption* . . . a *re-creation* of the normal life was necessary." Continuing as overseers of the general welfare, southern
women realized that they could not isolate their homes from
their communities. Recognizing, as did Alice Ames Winter
(president of the General Federation of Women's Clubs), that
"government and social and health conditions invade its sanc-
tuary," the "New Woman of the New South" believed that she
must "go out from its walls for part of her time and do her best
to make government and social order and physical conditions
as fine as possible, that they may upbuild and not destroy." As
Sallie Cotten put it, "After her own home was clean she wished
for a clean town." [19]

Preparation for the Forum

Despite limited formal education, southern women did not
take to the platform without preparation. Largely through informal influences, women learned at home where they heard
significant issues discussed, sometimes by important person-
ages. They discovered new ideas in diverse family libraries.
Though barred from active participation, they had not been
isolated from hearing pulpit homiletics weekly, an occasional
lecture, and—sporadically—stump speaking. Some fathers, particularly those of the liberal spirit, encouraged their daughters to develop intellectually. A southern liberal, the father of
Sophonisba Breckinridge "repeatedly . . . urged his daughter to
uphold the family reputation 'for good thinking and courageous
utterance.'" Alabama reformer Julia Tutwiler's father, a disciple

beth Cady Stanton, Susan B. Anthony, Matilda Joslyn Gage, and Ida Hustid
Harper, *History of Woman Suffrage* (6 vols.; Rochester and New York: Susan B.
Anthony, 1881–1922).
    19. Schuler, "Women in Public Affairs in Louisiana," 692; H. Addington
Bruce, *Woman in the Making of America* (Boston: Little, Brown, 1933), 323;
Sallie Sims Southall Cotten (MS dated November 14, 1913), in Cotten Family
Papers, Southern Historical Collection, University of North Carolina Library.

of Thomas Jefferson, opened his own school, the Green Springs School, to neighbors' daughters.[20]

A few academically motivated women sought university educations comparable to those afforded their brothers. By 1876 twenty-seven colleges in the United States had admitted women, and numerous others provided private tutorial instruction.[21] Education reformer Lila Meade Valentine studied with professors from the University of Virginia and the University of Richmond; Julia Tutwiler "learned languages" from professors at Washington and Lee. Southern women enrolled in colleges, both North and South, and some even studied abroad.

For women not exposed to higher education, literary and culture clubs provided the major avenue for self-development. At their meetings women read their own carefully written papers and participated in discussions and debates. Often these gatherings were governed by standardized parliamentary procedure. In 1896 the Aesthetic Club of Arkansas adopted Roberts' *Rules of Order* and, in a move considered progressive, introduced "open oral discussions."[22] In 1912 the Alabama Federation of Women's Clubs incorporated "round table discussion" into its state convention program.[23] The Kettle-drum Club of Tuscaloosa, Alabama, established a prescribed formula for debating with a judge being appointed "to decide on the merits of the question at issue."[24]

20. Christopher Lasch, "Sophonisba Preston Breckinridge," in James (ed.), *Notable American Women*, I, 233; Dorothea E. Wyatt, "Julia Strudwick Tutwiler," in James (ed.), *Notable American Women*, III, 489.

21. Annie Meyer, *Woman's Work in America* (New York: Henry Holt, 1891); H. Clarence Nixon, "Colleges and Universities," in William T. Couch (ed.), *Culture in the South* (Chapel Hill: University of North Carolina Press, 1934), 229–47.

22. Jennie C. Croly, *The History of the Women's Club Movement in America* (New York: Henry G. Allen, 1898), 218.

23. Lura Harris Craighead, "The Alabama Federation of Women's Clubs: A History of the Third District, 1915–1925 with Background History, 1895–1915" (MS in Alabama Federation of Women's Clubs Collection), Department of Archives and History, State of Alabama, Montgomery, Alabama, 78.

24. The Kettle-drum Club was included in the *Directory of American*

Early in the development of culture clubs, papers and debates dealt primarily with literary topics, but by the turn of the century the activities of local women's clubs reflected the national shift of emphasis toward more involvement in education and philanthropy.[25] By 1914 Mrs. Littleberry James Haley, Alabama state president, proclaimed:

> The woman's club is a *social* force—first, because it develops the individual woman; second, because its influence is felt in family life; and third, because it furnishes a common meeting ground for all women. . . .
>
> The woman's club is a *civic* force—first, because it helps to mould public opinion; second, because it influences legislation; and third, because it is directly responsible for much civic improvement.[26]

Growing "out of the combination of old culture patterns of the South and new conditions of the South," these clubs "gave direction to the emergence of women into public life in the 1880's and 1890's when women were first beginning to realize the existence of usable leisure time." Their "great significance," it has been argued, was that they enabled "women to participate in public affairs while performing the duties of wifehood and motherhood." Caroline Merrick declared that "the Woman's Club was the initial step of whatever progression women have made through subsequent organizations." Agreeing, Josephine Henry called women's clubs "the primary schools which lead to the university of politics."[27]

Church-related organizations and associations also gave di-

Learned Societies issued by the Bureau of Education in Washington, D.C., 1895 (Croly, *History of the Women's Club Movement in America*, 232).

25. Craighead, *Alabama Federation of Women's Clubs*, 39, 92.

26. Ms. Littleberry James Haley, "The Woman's Club—A Factor in Social and Civic Progress," cited in Craighead, *Alabama Federation of Women's Clubs*, 86.

27. Margaret Nell Price, "The Development of Leadership by Southern Women Through Clubs and Organizations" (M.A. thesis, University of North Carolina, 1945), 168–70; Merrick, *Old Times in Dixie Land*, 217; Henry, "The New Woman of the New South," 355.

rection to women emerging into public life. The church not only provided a set of values that undergirded reform rhetoric but it also became a forum as well as a training ground for many southern women speakers. Though limited in their participation in the church hierarchy, women assumed leadership in the Sunday schools, pursued "charity" and other benevolent causes, and found opportunities for service in missionary societies and circles. Anne Firor Scott concluded that "the public life of nearly every southern woman leader for forty years began in a church society."[28] Through these groups, women sent prayers, money, and missionaries to foreign fields and, in spite of opposition, supported home missions. As southern church women involved themselves in settlement work, homes for unwed mothers, and day-care centers, they brought social concerns squarely into the sphere of the church and encouraged women to respond.

Efforts in behalf of temperance and suffrage provided models for budding female speakers as well as opportunities for speaking. Frances Willard, who traveled extensively in the South, proved a worthy example for imitation for her southern sisters. James Clement Ambrose thought Miss Willard "without a peer among women." Seeing "much of the Edward Everett in her language" and "more of the Wendell Phillips in her manner of delivery," he concluded: "She is wholly at home, but not forward on the platform, with grace in bearing, ease and moderation in gesture, and in her tones there are tears when she wills."[29] Some women reformers benefited from their participation in national and regional meetings. Belle Kearney described her first temperance convention as "a novel spectacle": "The delegates were massed together in perfect order, each looking

28. Anne Firor Scott, *The Southern Lady: From Pedestal to Politics, 1830–1930* (Chicago: University of Chicago Press, 1970), 141.
29. James Clement Ambrose, in *Potter's American Monthly*, May, 1882, cited in Frances Elizabeth Willard, *Woman and Temperance* (Hartford, Conn.: Park Publishing Co., 1883), 27–28.

so serious and intent; the stage was filled with women and decorated with flowers, while the walls were bright with banners. There were stirring debates and tactful engineering of parliamentary points. A beautiful Christian spirit, holy enthusiasm and sublime devotion for a great cause seemed to animate all."[30]

Temperance and suffrage groups made available special materials and instruction to local associations. "Suffrage schools," as well as short courses in public speaking, organizational methods, and campaign techniques were held in most southern states. Mrs. Frank Bonelli, graduate of the Emerson School of Oratory of Boston, conducted one such school in Birmingham. In its suffrage column the *News* explained: "She will give instructions in how to address an audience and hold its attention, how to marshall and present effectively the pro-suffrage arguments, how to answer "squelch" the "anti" arguments, how to organize new associations and preside over suffrage meetings. She will also deal with the history of the emancipation of women, and will give special care to the placing and control of the speaking voice."[31]

The Woman's Christian Temperance Union sent its members circulars on how to conduct a meeting, tendering such advice as: "Don't fail thoroughly to premeditate your 'impromptus'"; "Let the President of the WCTU preside and go forward, quietly to her duty, as a matter of course"; "Don't assume the role of Sir Oracle. Teach without seeming to do so"; "Carefully skip around all such 'hard words' as 'Take notice,' 'I call your attention,' 'Do you understand?' and on no account conclude a sentence with that irritating grammatical nondescript 'See?'" Miss Willard even suggested the following "general outline speech":

1. Very brief allusion to the origin and progress of temperance move-

30. Belle Kearney, *A Slaveholder's Daughter* (New York: Abbey Press, 1900), 141.
31. Birmingham *News*, October 25, 1914.

ments, with earnest acknowledgment of what has been done by the Church, the Washingtonian movement, Good Templars, Catholic Total Abstinence Society, etc.

2. Brief pictorial (not abstract) account of the Woman's Crusade.
3. Organization as its sequel—origin of National W.C.T.U., at Chautauqua in 1874.
4. Growth of the Society in the United States, in Canada, England, and elsewhere, evolution of its work, number and variety of its departments; notwithstanding this general uniformity, the National like a photograph of imperial size; the State a cabinet, the local a *carte de visite*.
5. Why we have superintendents instead of committees to insure individual responsibility. Illustrate by blackboard with our departments written out.
6. Reasons why women should join us. I have often given these in anecdotal form, telling just what women, old and young, grave and gay, had said to me about the convictions resulting from their own observation and experience which had led them into temperance work.
7. Appeal from considerations embodied in our motto 1. For God; 2. For home; 3. For native land.

This address, mixed with the Word of God and prayer both in its preparation and recital, should be followed by a humble petition for His blessing.[32]

The extent to which southern women speakers availed themselves of such training is difficult to determine. Certainly many worked to "perfect technique." Extensive notes, detailed outlines, and polished manuscripts found scattered in the personal papers of numerous southern women attest to care in speech preparation. Yet many, including Lila Meade Valentine, a southern speaker of national reputation, relied primarily on "fluency" and a "flair for the dramatic." And, as Belle Kearney shrewdly observed, it was often "fine clothes" that gained "a hearing for a speaker in an unpopular cause."[33]

32. Willard, *Woman and Temperance*, 616–17.
33. Lloyd C. Taylor, Jr., "Lila Meade Valentine: The FFV as Reformer," *Virginia Magazine of History and Biography*, LXX (October, 1962), 484; Kearney, *A Slaveholder's Daughter*, 158.

Issues and Forums

Culture clubs and church societies provided increasing opportunities for women to consider matters of social concern. Missionary societies included "departments" for child labor, prison reform, and temperance. The Alabama Federation of Women's Clubs promoted kindergartens, PTAs, and the admission of women to the state university. Louisiana club women worked for sanitation laws, improved working conditions for women, and public libraries.

That women advanced cogent arguments on pressing social issues and posed realistic solutions to these problems opened wider forums for public discussion on these issues. In the interests of reform, women talked to large and small audiences—at expositions, school commencements, private meetings, public meetings, conventions, and professional societies. They argued before state and national legislatures, particularly for suffrage. Mrs. Felton, "being a lady of superior intelligence, culture and brilliancy," was extended the "privilege" of addressing the Georgia General Assembly on "popular education, the injustices and imperfections of our Public School System with her views of the needed reforms and revisions thereof." Julia Tutwiler argued for prison reform before the Alabama legislature. Belle Kearney, the first woman elected to the state senate in Mississippi, addressed her fellow senators on numerous occasions. Rebecca Latimer Felton, though seated for only one day through a courtesy appointment to the United States Senate, took that occasion to make a speech.[34] Belle Kearney summarized her various speaking experiences over a three year period.

[She] traveled through nearly every Southern state in the interest of the Woman's Christian Temperance Union . . . speaking in halls, parlors, churches, theatres, school-houses and in the open air; to negroes

34. Joint Resolution of Georgia Assembly, Adopted November 5, 1901, concurred November 9, in Felton Papers; *Congressional Record*, 67th Cong., 3rd Sess., 23.

as well as to the white population; to audiences of children, young women, and mixed assemblies; in public and private schools, colleges and universities for both boys and girls; before conferences of ministers, chautauquas, schools of methods, State Teachers' Associations; State and National Conventions of the W.C.T.U., the Christian Endeavor, and Woman Suffrage Association, and . . . lobbied in the Mississippi legislature to secure the passage of the Scientific Temperance Instruction bill.[35]

Access to the pulpit was an important hurdle for women because, as one northern suffragist emphasized, "Here is where the sympathies of society center."[36] If the church opposed in principle the notion of women speaking in public, in practice it opened its doors to those reformers whose subject was deemed appropriate and just. At the Florida Methodist Conference, for instance, after he had refused to introduce reformer Juliana Hayes "because he thought women should be seen and not heard in public," a gentleman changed his opinion and became a strong advocate of women and their work."[37] Women's advocacy of benevolent causes and temperance helped to counter theological predispositions and traditional notions about woman's "place," thereby furnishing the leverage essential to transform the church from foe to forum. Even the Baptists encouraged involvement in reform activities, "as long as these efforts remain dissociated from the feminist agitation and politics."[38]

The identification of temperance with the church made membership in the WCTU not only palatable for many southern women but practically mandatory. Further, the movement's association with social concerns resulted in its becoming a fo-

35. Kearney, A Slaveholder's Daughter, 184, 235.
36. Stanton, Anthony, and Gage, History of Woman Suffrage, II, 849.
37. Noreen Dunn Tatum, A Crown of Service (Nashville: Parthenon Press, 1960), 25; Hunter Farish, The Circuit Rider Dismounts (Richmond, Va.: Dietz Press, 1938).
38. R. W. Sapin, "Attitudes and Reactions of Southern Baptists on Social Issues, 1865–1890" (Ph.D. dissertation, Vanderbilt University, 1961), 357, cited in Scott, The Southern Lady, 138.

cal point for a variety of reform efforts. Local WCTUs included within the framework of temperance: divisions for child labor, juvenile courts, industrial education, prison reform, and in some cases suffrage. As Mrs. Felton viewed it, the union was "a band of women devoted to God, Home and Native Land, united for home mission work among those who suffer and are in distress, especially among the victims of alcoholic drunkenness."[39]

Whereas temperance speakers relied on the church as a primary meeting place for public discussion, suffrage had no comparable institutionalized support. Most churches viewed the issue with horror. In Georgia both the WCTU and the Federated Women's Clubs refused to endorse suffrage. Initially, at least, it lacked "respectability." As Belle Kearney admitted, "I had to broach the work tentatively." On face, suffrage seemed inconsistent with a southern lady's role and image. Accordingly, a strong "anti" movement developed that prompted considerable speaking, particularly before legislatures. Nonspeaking became an issue in the 1919 Alabama hearings on the Anthony amendment. "Mrs. Pinckard's surprise," a "memorial" read by a male senator, explained that the Anti-Ratification League would take no part in the hearings since to do so would contradict its opposition to political involvement for women.[40]

To many southern reformers suffrage seemed the only way to ensure a better society. As Elizabeth Saxon, Louisiana suffragist, confessed to a congressional committee in Washington,

39. Rebecca Latimer Felton, "Woman's Relation to Temperance" (MS in Felton Papers); C. Vann Woodward, *Origins of the New South, 1877–1913* (Baton Rouge: Louisiana State University Press, 1951), 389, Vol. IX of ten volumes in Wendell Holmes Stephenson and E. Merton Coulter (eds.), *A History of the South*. Woodward pointed to the "close alliance" between the prohibition crusade and the progressive movement in the South.

40. A. Elizabeth Taylor, "The Last Phase of the Woman Suffrage Movement in Georgia," *Georgia Historical Quarterly*, XLIII (March, 1959), 14; *Woman's Journal*, XXXVIII (April 13, 1907), 60, cited in A. Elizabeth Taylor, "The Woman Suffrage Movement in Mississippi, 1890–1920," *Journal of Mississippi History*, XXX (1968), 12; Montgomery *Advertiser*, July 17, 1919. Specific attention to the speaking in the "anti" movement falls outside the scope of this chapter.

"I never realized the importance of this cause, until we were beaten back on every side in the work of reform." Pattie Ruffner Jacobs entered the movement because of "frustration over the recent defeat of a state prohibition amendment" and "a concern with the evils of child labor." Though specific—and often personal—injustices prodded some southern women into advocating suffrage, most saw in the ballot an opportunity to reform the world. Lila Meade Valentine's advocacy, for example, "stemmed from no feeling of persecution or militancy." Rebecca Henry Hayes, first president of the Texas Equal Rights Association, offered an objective assessment of the effect of the ballot in bettering society. Though viewing the vote as "a weapon, a power, a force whereby we may realize the highest form of self-government," she did not expect miracles. "I do not believe that the enfranchisement of woman will bring about an instantaneous radical change in the condition of political, social, or religious affairs," she said. "But it is a move in the right direction."[41]

Though their forums were limited, suffragists availed themselves of opportunities to speak wherever they found them. Their persistence in appearing before legislative committees and constitutional conventions led the Huntsville *Republican* to complain, "No matter how modest a constitutional convention is nowadays some female suffragist will find it out and insist on making . . . a speech." Suffragists spoke on street corners and in rented halls. Mary Winslow Partridge "delivered a masterpiece of eloquence standing in an automobile." At the state fair in 1914, Mississippi suffragists spoke as was their custom from the top of a cotton bale.[42] A number of confer-

41. Stanton, Anthony, and Gage, *History of Woman Suffrage*, III, 157; Lee Norcross Allen, "Pattie Ruffner Jacobs." in James (ed.), *Notable American Women*, II, 266; Taylor, "Lila Meade Valentine," 481; Dallas *Morning News*, November 7, 1893, cited in A. Elizabeth Taylor, "The Woman Suffrage Movement in Texas," *Journal of Southern History*, XVII (May, 1951), 197.

42. Huntsville (Ala.) *Republican*, June 15, 1901; *Report of the Organizing*

ences, congresses, and educational associations invited women to participate in collective action against society's ills. Southern women spoke from convention platforms and helped to shape organizational policy behind the scenes. In both the Southern Sociological Congress and the Conference on Education in the South, women reformers worked not only for the rectification of specific "wrongs" but also toward "the solving of the race question." The Southern Sociological Congress insisted on "the closest cooperation between the church and . . . social agencies for the securing of these results."[43]

Strategies

The primary rhetorical problem of southern women who spoke out for reform was credibility. Women speakers were suspect! Reform of any kind was subject to disapprobation. The appearance of "ladies" on public platforms speaking on political issues was shocking. To overcome the credibility problem, speakers pursued strategies not of confrontation but of accommodation. Specifically, they (1) adapted to traditional notions of woman's role, (2) defined social problems as moral ones, and (3) related reform to a southern renaissance.

Though the conditions of war and its aftermath had allowed an expansion of woman's "keeping" beyond the home to the community, the romanticized image of the southern lady and her appropriate "sphere" persisted well into the twentieth century. Southern women utilized these constructs to advantage. According to Belle Kearney, "Southerners, though tenacious of social traditions, are hospitable to new ideas and are chivalrous toward a woman who wishes their co-operation provided that

---

Committee, Birmingham Convention, February 12, 1917, in Alabama Woman's Suffrage File; Jackson (Miss.) *Daily News,* October 30, 1914, cited in A. Elizabeth Taylor, "The Woman Suffrage Movement in Mississippi," 21.

43. James E. McCulloch (ed.), *The Call of the New South* (Nashville: Brandau-Craig Dickerson, 1912), 9.

she comes to them also as a lady." Women played to the traditional myth through their attention to personal appearance, demeanor, and the thoughtful choice of issues and arguments. Contemporary writers used the adjectives *charming, lovely, dignified, cultured, poised,* and *refined* over and over again in describing female reformers. According to Anne Firor Scott, women advocates were "generally . . . the very model of Southern Ladies" in outward appearance. A biographer pictured Caroline Merrick as approaching the southern ideal: "Never aggressive . . . she had by her graciousness and social standing lent valued prestige to the suffrage cause. . . . [S]he demonstrated that a woman could be 'actively interested in public and benevolent activities' without abandoning 'her position as leader of the domestic circle.'"[44]

Speakers worked within the widely held attitudes about woman's "place." Miriam Howard Dubose, suffragist from Georgia, couched her arguments within the context of woman's proper role when she wrote, "I am a woman and a mother. I have a son to rear whose pure moral character I am powerless properly to mould and discipline without the ballot." Agreeing with that rationale, the president of the Alabama Suffrage Association contended, "To control the environment of her child is beyond the question of right or privilege, it is a duty."[45] Women rarely attempted to redefine their traditional role, and when they did they were usually speaking before partisans. To gain acceptance women sought to allay the fears of the white patriarchy that considered social reform, particularly suffrage, as an attack on male prerogatives. They did not wish to supplant their men, women argued, but to serve as "helpmeets" or, as Sallie

44. Kearney, *A Slaveholder's Daughter,* 185; Anne Firor Scott, "The 'New Woman' in the New South," *South Atlantic Quarterly,* LXI (Autumn, 1962), 475; L. E. Zimmerman, "Caroline Elizabeth Thomas Merrick," in James (ed.), *Notable American Women,* II, 531.
45. Henry, "The New Woman of the New South," 360.

Cotten proposed, "co-adjutors." Suggesting deferential if not reverential feelings toward men, "ladies" assured their listeners that they did not want "man's place or work in life." "Leave us our babies, our frying pans, and our brooms," they pleaded, "but arm us with fullest legal rights."[46]

Women reformers interpreted social problems as moral concerns. To lend credibility to and provide rationale for their strategy, they argued from the largely unquestioned tenet that "the glory of womanhood has been her purity, her superiority to man in the possession of a higher moral sense and standard."[47] Thus, concern for reform was consistent both with woman's traditional role and with her "humanitarian instinct." A correspondent to the Birmingham *News* observed that because men and women have different instincts, they have different traditional roles:

Because men produce and perfect property, and this is their traditional job, they will care for property and protect it by such laws as they deem wise. They have the commercial instinct, which is natural.

Because women produce and perfect human beings, and this is their traditional job, they will care for human beings and protect them by such laws as they deem wise. They have the humanitarian instinct, and this too is natural.[48]

A modified version of this argument praised the mutual creations of men and women but denounced the singular creations of men: "When men and women work together they build homes, schools and safeguards for the good of society, and men

46. Helena Holley, "What Woman Suffrage Will Do Toward the Conservation of Public Health," in James E. McCulloch (ed.), *The New Chivalry—Health* (Nashville: Benson Printing Co., 1915), 312.

47. John S. Ezell, "Minnie Ursula Oliver Scott Rutherford Fuller," in James (ed.), *Notable American Women*, I, 682–83; Annah Robinson Watson, "The Attitude of Southern Women on the Suffrage Question," *Arena*, XI (February, 1895), 366.

48. Birmingham *News* (undated clipping), in Alabama Woman's Suffrage File.

working alone build armies, navies, saloons and dens of vice and perpetuate the same with their ballots."[49]

Southern women posited their humanitarian bent as a divine trust. Sallie Cotten noted smugly that "since God made woman He has never made anything else. To her has been intrusted the evolution of the race."[50] To tie social reform to morality even more securely, women identified their topics with the virtues of justice and honor, emotional appeals long associated with chivalry. In an address on the care and training of children made to the Southern Sociological Congress, Cora Bristol Nelson, superintendent of the Bristol-Nelson School, declared it "a blot on the fair name of the chivalrous South to let this class of unfortunates be harbored in our poor-houses and insane asylums, and often, because they are misunderstood, incarcerated in our jails with hardened criminals."[51] Reformers labeled child labor and similar problems "injustices" that demanded remedy. Suffragists contended that—given women's humanitarian instinct —granting ladies the vote would ensure justice to the unfortunates. Arguing "justice" for the disenfranchised women speakers urged suffrage "not as a favor, not as a privilege, but as a right based on the ground that we are human beings, and as such, entitled to all human rights." One woman wrote, "It is but simple justice that I should have the suffrage."[52]

Consistent with the prevailing conservative theology that polarized good and evil, women presented social problems in terms of moralistic contraries: "the punch bowl" as an evil, prohibition as a good; ignorance as an evil, education as a good; child labor and the mistreatment of prisoners and the insane as

49. Cited in Henry, "The New Woman of the New South," 361.

50. Sallie Sims Southall Cotten, "Women and Social Service" (MS dated 1914), in Cotten Family Papers.

51. Cora Bristol Nelson, "The Care and Training of Feeble-Minded Children," in McCulloch (ed.), *The Call of the New South*, 43.

52. Stanton, Anthony, and Gage, *History of Woman Suffrage*, III, 828; Henry, "The New Woman of the New South," 358.

evils, legislative relief of these conditions as a good. In terms of tradition, such dichotomous rationale touched many sympathetic listeners.

Women found it necessary to reverse the good-evil paradigm when presenting the issue of suffrage. Southerners widely believed woman's "place" was a good and to venture outside that protected sphere was an impropriety, if not an evil. To overcome this contradiction, southern women orators identified suffrage as a means to an end acceptable to their audiences, specifically the amelioration of social wrongs. Mary Putnam Gridley of Greenville, South Carolina, believed—as did many —that, "woman's ballot means the enforcement of social purity and better government." Echoing the same theme, a Kentucky woman declared, "I wish to vote that I may aid good men to promote purity and justice in law and government, protecting the weak by placing in power those of known probity and honor."[53] Such identification of reform measures as means was not restricted to suffrage. Speakers advanced both temperance and education as vehicles of reform.

Women speakers couched their appeals in religious and other value-laden symbols and slogans. They identified temperance with the emotionally charged motto, "God, Home and Native Land." Southerners found the ambiguity of the term "Native Land" particularly fortunate since they had difficulty with a nationalistic bias. Antisuffragists of Alabama adopted as their call to arms, "Home Rule, White Supremacy, State Rights." The triumph of the political principles embodied in these terms would preserve morality, they argued, and would ultimately "save" the South.

Amid disruption, confusion, and chaos during the years following the war, the southerner held to an unshakable faith that the "South would rise again," a conviction that emerged in the

53. Henry, "The New Woman of the New South," 359, 362.

rhetoric of the New South as well as in that of a romantic South. Barriers to rebirth, though very real, were not impregnable. Whereas some southerners sought "renaissance" through a return to the old order, and whereas others promoted industrialization as the answer to the region's problems, women reformers focused on education as a means of guaranteeing to the young "good breeding, self-control, and a measure of skill sorely needed in the disorder of the times." On the occasion of the founding of the Richmond Education Association, Lila Meade Valentine made clear that position when she argued: "[The city's] growth will be greater and its foundations the surer, if our children, all of them, white and black, are trained in head and heart and hand, not only to do the work that cries out to be done in the material upbuilding of our city, but also to become the intelligent, self-respecting, law-abiding citizens who shall make impossible the inefficiency, bribery, and corruption that are disgracing so many American communities today." In her presidential address at the association's fourth anniversary celebration, she reiterated that objective: "Richmond can never be the great and beautiful city we all wish her to be, until her schools are so equipped as to train her boys and girls to be efficient, productive, law-abiding, beauty-loving citizens of the future."[54]

A generalized commitment to socialization through education provided rationale for radical departures in southern education. Women worked and spoke, particularly in support of the kindergarten movement and in the campaign for universal education. They lobbied for compulsory school attendance laws and the opening of state universities to women. Mrs. Felton

54. Mendenhall, "Southern Women of a 'Lost Generation,'" 343; Amory Dwight Mayo, *Southern Women in the Recent Educational Movement in the South*, Bureau of Education Circular of Information, No. 1, 1892, whole No. 186 (Washington: n.p., 1892); Taylor, "Lila Meade Valentine," 474; Lila Meade Valentine, "Address of the President," *Fourth Annual Report of the Richmond Education Association, 1903–1904* (Richmond: n.p., 1904), 6–7.

was active in a number of these efforts. In 1904 she addressed the Georgia legislature on the subject of a compulsory school law and took that opportunity to lecture that body on the wise use of taxpayers' money. Both Mrs. Felton and Miss Tutwiler led the fight for admission of women to their respective state universities.[55]

Recognizing that education served economic ends, women speakers demanded a system of comprehensive vocational training. At the third annual Conference on Education in the South, delegate Mrs. George Barnum argued for "obligatory industrial and technical training." Realizing that "wasted lives could be transformed into useful men," Miss Martha Berry founded a boy's industrial school in Rome, Georgia, and promoted it throughout the South as a model of "self-help."[56] Speakers sought to extend vocational education to juvenile offenders, women, and the Negro.

Those reformers committed to Negro education defended it as a tool of socialization and economic productivity. Further, they claimed that universal education would minimize, if not solve, the race problem. Or, as educator Grace House suggested in a speech before the Southern Sociological Congress in 1913, "With such schools at the foundation of the development of the negro race there will be no race problem to solve." She was not alone in her belief that "this 'schooling for the responsibility of freedom' . . . will win true freedom for the negro race."[57]

55. Anne G. Pannell and Dorothea E. Wyatt, *Julia S. Tutwiler and Social Progress in Alabama* (University, Ala.: University of Alabama Press, 1961), 98–104; Sara Bertha Townsend, "The Admission of Women to the University of Georgia," *Georgia Historical Quarterly*, XLIII (June, 1959), 156–69.

56. Mrs. George Barnum, "On the Industrial Upbuilding of Southern Cities and Communities," *Proceedings of the Third Conference for Education in the South* (Raleigh, N.C.: Printing Office, St. Augustine's School, 1900), 91; Martha Berry, "The Planting and Care of an Industrial School," *Proceedings of the Ninth Conference for Education in the South* (Richmond, Va.: Executive Committee, Richmond College, 1906), 90.

57. Grace House, "The Need and Value of Industrial Education for Negroes," in James E. McCulloch (ed.), *The South Mobilizing for Social Service* (Nashville: Brandau-Craig-Dickerson, 1913), 439–40.

The question of universal education was only a minor manifestation of the larger influence of the race question on southern thinking and strategy. The future of the South clearly was tied to the future of the Negro. Historian V. O. Key put it plainly: "In its grand outlines the politics of the South revolves around the position of the Negro."[58] Southern women advocating reform could not ignore that fact. Education would help to "solve" the race problem, they contended. Prohibition would control "drink-crazed Negroes." Suffrage, however, was more complicated, for it called attention to the South's effective disenfranchisement of black men and threatened to give the vote to black women as well. Women speakers sought to resolve that dilemma by identifying suffrage with the traditional rallying cries of white supremacy and states' rights. They argued the desirability of white supremacy and maintained that woman suffrage would ensure its continuation. In a letter to the editor of the Birmingham *News*, Pattie Ruffner Jacobs summarized the thinking: "[S]ince there are 150,000 more white women than negro women in Alabama, and four and a half million more white women than negro women in Southern States, the way to maintain it wwhite supremacyE is by ratifying the Suffrage Amendment."[59]

Similarly, southern women did not question the rights of states to determine who were the electorate. Such sentiment was sufficiently strong that a number of speakers worked for suffrage through state amendment *only*. So opposed to federal intervention was suffragist Kate Gordon that she "without hesitation joined the forces which had consistently opposed woman suffrage and worked to prevent ratification in Louisiana and

58. V. O. Key, *Southern Politics* (New York: Alfred A. Knopf, 1949), 5; Ulrich B. Phillips, "The Central Theme of Southern History," *American Historical Review*, XXXIV (October, 1928), 30–43; Carl Degler, *The Other South: Southern Dissenters in the Nineteenth Century* (New York: Harper and Row, 1974).

59. Birmingham *News*, June 8, 1919.

Mississippi."[60] Those reformers who lobbied for the federal amendment providing for woman's suffrage insisted that it would not interfere with a state's right to determine its voters. Boards of registrars and the newly instituted poll tax would continue to restrict the franchise. Further, the states had had their opportunity in constitutional conventions to grant the vote to women and, in failing to do so, had abdicated their rights. The question became one of balancing states' rights against justice for women. Women speakers argued that the latter was essential to the development of a New South.

Effect

Southern women orators met with indifference and ridicule but with some measure of support as they sought to solve social problems and claim equal rights under the law. Most often, these women speakers were politely, even solicitously received. According to contemporary characterizations, their audiences considered them "effective." Jean Gordon, Louisiana suffragist, was described as "clear-thoughted, direct of speech, charming of personality." Madeline McDowell Breckinridge, granddaughter of Henry Clay, was said to have "inherited much of her distinguished ancestor's talents and oratorical powers"; Frances Griffin of Alabama "captured the audience with her rich voice and southern intonation." Sophie Bell Wright, a New Orleans educator and welfare worker, was declared "an effective public speaker, direct and appealing in manner." The *Times-Picayune's* report of Mrs. Keating's suffrage speech at the Louisiana Constitutional Convention of 1879 typifies press reactions to southern women speakers: "The fair speaker had scarcely begun before it was seen she possessed a clear, slow enunciation and perfect confidence in her ability to enforce the doctrines of the

60. Kenneth R. Johnson, "Kate Gordon and the Woman-Suffrage Movement in the South," *Journal of Southern History*, XXXVIII (August, 1972), 392.

cause she was to advocate. She read from a written manuscript and showed no little knowledge of the rules of oratory." Incidentally, Mrs. Keating was "rewarded for her address by a round of applause which lasted some time."[61]

Most contemporary reports confirm that audiences considered women speakers intelligent, an impression women chose to cultivate. A clear, well-stated argument was to be expected of a "lady." As the Birmingham *News* said of visiting speaker Mrs. Desha Breckinridge, she combined "intellectual attainments with exalted womanhood." In reporting the 1900 state convention of the Alabama Federation of Women's Clubs, that same paper editorialized: "[It] has within its membership the most gifted, the most intellectual and the most advanced women in the state." Sallie Cotten thought the North Carolina federation's influence in the "uplift of the state" could be attributed to the fact that "its women are sane as well as progressive."[62] Such assessments indicate that audiences responded positively to women speakers and their talents. These descriptions, however, do not speak to the larger issue of the role of women's oratory in southern reform.

Although the specific effects of their rhetoric on the enactment of legislation is difficult to trace precisely, southern women's entry into the forum did have impact. It would be specious to contend that postbellum social legislation resulted solely—perhaps even largely—from their efforts. These speakers were notably unsuccessful in a number of causes they championed —most notably suffrage. Yet these women did contribute to

61. Birmingham *News*, May 24, 1914; Nashville *Banner* (undated clipping), Alabama Woman's Suffrage File; Stanton, Anthony, and Gage, *History of Woman Suffrage*, IV, 335; L. E. Zimmerman, "Sophie Bell Wright," in James (ed.), *Notable American Women*, III, 688; New Orleans *Times-Picayune*, June 17, 1879.
62. Birmingham *News* (undated clipping), in Alabama Woman's Suffrage File; Birmingham *News* (undated clipping), in Alabama Federation of Women's Clubs Collection; Cotten (MS dated November 14, 1913), in Cotten Family Papers.

sweeping social changes and, in so doing, expanded their own parameters of influence. They were instrumental in giving visibility to social issues and in raising the level of public discussion. Further, the record leaves little doubt that southern women speakers were efficient agents for legislative remedy of social ills.

Equally significant was the effect political involvement had on those women who campaigned for social justice. In their efforts on behalf of society's "unfortunates," women reformers attuned themselves to their own potential and to the statutory laws which limited it. Through clubs, church societies, and temperance and suffrage movements, they became involved in the political process and sought full participation through the ballot. Though Mississippi reformer and political leader Belle Kearney probably overstated the case for the WCTU's role in the development of southern women, her analysis is nonetheless thoughtful. "The Woman's Christian Temperance Union was the golden key that unlocked the prison doors of pent-up possibilities," she said. "It was the generous liberator, the joyous iconoclast, the discoverer, the developer of Southern women."[63] Similar claims have been made for suffrage, women's clubs, and church societies in the movement of southern women from "pedestal to politics." As Caroline Merrick remembered, the decision to speak was, in itself, liberating. "Fearing" that she could not be heard, Mrs. Merrick had asked her son-in-law to read her speech on suffrage before the Louisiana convention delegates. "But Mrs. Saxon said: 'You do not wish a man to represent you at the polls; represent yourself now, if you only stand up and move your lips.' 'I will,' I said. 'You are right.'"[64]

Seeking ways to better society, these proponents of "pragmatic radicalism," as Anne Firor Scott characterized the "'New Woman' in the New South," challenged both the "philosophy of

63. Kearney, *A Slaveholder's Daughter*, 118.
64. Merrick, *Old Times in Dixie Land*, 128.

ANNETTE SHELBY

retrenchment" and the prevailing doctrine of laissez faire that, as Woodward observed, had become "almost a test of Southern patriotism."[65] They approached their task with optimism, determination, and a zeal that, on occasion, bordered on fanaticism. Yet the rhetoric that emerged was a rhetoric of adaptation. Speaking at the state capitol on behalf of sending a Georgia exhibit to the Chicago World's Fair, Rebecca Latimer Felton was careful to associate her interests with those of her audience. "I come before you tonight as a Georgian interested in the success of our grand old Commonwealth," she declared. "I am not here to advocate Chicago's interests or the interests of anybody, except Georgians. . . . Whatever I am, or fail to be, I am a Georgian—a Southern woman—bound to you by every tie of interest and affection."[66]

Working within women's "sphere," but extending the role of "keeping" to the larger society, southern women orators identified New South reform with the values and symbolism of southern tradition. In so doing, they earned credibility for themselves and their causes. Though not alone in their efforts, these speakers focused on and provided direction for social reform in the New South. The results, written into the legal statutes of every southern state, provided a better life for those entrusted to "women's care."

BIBLIOGRAPHICAL NOTE

Bibliographic sources include an essay in Anne Firor Scott's *The Southern Lady: From Pedestal to Politics, 1830–1930* (Chicago: University of Chicago Press, 1970) and entries in *Notable American Women*, edited by Edward T. James (Cambridge, Massachusetts: Belknap Press, 1971). Marjorie Stratford Mendenhall's "Southern Women of a 'Lost Generation,'" *South Atlan-*

65. Scott, "The 'New Woman' in the New South," 483; Woodward, *Origins of the New South*, 65.
66. Felton (undated MS), in Felton Papers.

tic Quarterly, XXXIII (October, 1934), and Kathryn Reinhart Schuler's "Women in Public Affairs in Louisiana During Reconstruction," *Louisiana Historical Quarterly*, XIX (July, 1936), analyze women's perceived "place" and role.

Autobiographies by Belle Kearney, *A Slaveholder's Daughter* (New York: Abbey, 1900), and Caroline Merrick, *Old Times in Dixie Land* (New York: Grafton, 1901), offer a "first person" viewpoint. Biographies include Margaret Evelyn Gardner's "Sophie Belle Wright, 1866–1912" (M.A. thesis, Louisiana State University, 1959), Sophonisba T. Breckinridge's *Madeline McDowell Breckinridge: A Leader in the New South* (Chicago: University of Chicago Press, 1921), and Anne G. Pannell and Dorothea E. Wyatt's *Julia S. Tutwiler and Social Progress in Alabama* (University, Alabama: University of Alabama Press, 1961).

The History of Woman Suffrage, edited by Susan B. Anthony, Elizabeth Cady Stanton, Matilda J. Gage, and Ida Hustid Harper (6 vols.; Rochester and New York, 1881–1922), gives an overview of the suffrage movement. Elizabeth Taylor's essays on suffrage published in regional journals provide a more complete and objective assessment of the movement. Records of the Woman's Christian Temperance Union are scattered. The national library in Evanston, Illinois, and state and local libraries have scrapbooks, manuscripts, minutes and some published materials. Jennie C. Croly's *The History of the Woman's Club Movement in America* (New York: Henry G. Allen, 1898) and Margaret Nell Price's "The Development of Leadership by Southern Women through Clubs and Organizations" (M.A. thesis, University of North Carolina, 1945) have documented the development of the woman's club movement.

Manuscript sources and newspapers provide most of the speech materials. Major manuscript collections include: Hallie Q. Brown Papers, Central State University, Wilberforce, Ohio; Sallie Sims Southall Cotten Papers, North Carolina and Southern Historical Collections, University of North Carolina; DeGraf-fenried Collection, Southern Historical Collection, University of North Carolina; Felton Papers, University of Georgia; Breck-inridge Family Papers, the Library of Congress; Ethyl Hudson Collection, Tulane University; Patty S. Hill Papers, Filson Club, Louisville, Kentucky; Martha Carey Thomas Papers, Bryn Mawr; Julia Strudwick Tutwiler Papers, University of Alabama; Sue Shelton White Papers, Schlesinger Library, Rad-cliff College; Sophie Wright Scrapbook, Howard-Tilton Library, Tulane University; and Valentine Papers, Valentine Museum, Richmond, Virginia.

VIII

Educational Reformers in North Carolina: 1885–1905 *

To the campus of the University of North Carolina in the late 1870s and early 1880s came several young men who were destined to influence the course of education in North Carolina and the entire South. Using their rhetorical abilities, Charles B. Aycock, Edwin A. Alderman, James Y. Joyner, Charles D. McIver, M. C. S. Noble, and Robert W. Winston fomented an educational revolution. Three of these men—Alderman, Aycock, and McIver—were the most prolific and effective speakers in the effort to revitalize public education in the "Old North State." Later their efforts extended beyond their native state and they were recognized throughout the South as leaders in educational reform. Because of their state and regional importance, this essay centers upon the efforts of these three prominent protagonists in the educational reform movement in North Carolina from 1885 to 1905.

Rhetorical Training

A quick look at the training of the three men provides some insight into their later speaking. Undoubtedly their experiences prior to their arrival at the university shaped their interests and rhetoric. During the period when Aycock, Alderman, and McIver were growing up, few schools in North Carolina received

* The author wishes to express his appreciation to the University of North Carolina at Chapel Hill for a faculty research grant which supported this research effort.

237

public support. It is ironic that men who were to exert important influence in strong public schools themselves missed the opportunity of public school education.

Aycock and his six brothers walked miles to attend a school operated by the citizens of Nahunta, who pooled their resources to employ a teacher. Later he attended the Wilson Collegiate Institute, where he excelled in declamation and debate under the direction of a Mr. Hassell. Aycock's biographers in *The Life and Speeches of Charles B. Aycock* describe his elocution as a student to be clear evidence of his talent as a speaker: "'His voice,' we are told by one of his youthful rivals, 'was not melodious, and he was rather awkward in his movements, but when he rose to speak, every person within reach of his voice listened until his conclusion.' His earnestness, sincerity, and directness in debate compelled attention. . . . On Friday afternoons, when declaiming some of the old masterpieces . . . he seemed to make them his own, and to be able to get hold of his audience as well as if he were making a speech that he had composed, suitable for the occasion. The teachers and children of other schoolrooms would throng the hall to hear him." A classmate in Hassell's school recalled that Aycock "was a leader in his studies and the first *debater* in the school."[1]

Alderman attended two private schools in Wilmington, the Burgess Military School and the Catlet School, "which appears to have been the only place in town where a sound classical training could be obtained." In addition, he was tutored by his sister Alice and his mother, who "was austere in the training of her children and her word was law. . . . It is not without significance that she could repeat lectures and sermons verbatim and that she set Alderman to memorizing and delivering orations.

1. R. D. W. Connor and Clarence Poe, *The Life and Speeches of Charles B. Aycock* (New York: Doubleday, Page, 1912), 18–19. D. Peacock to Connor and Poe (n.d.) in Aycock Collection, North Carolina Department of Archives and History, Raleigh.

Conversational ability, which was so marked in him, was conspicuous in her."[2]

Not much is known about McIver's early schooling except that he attended a school built by several families at a central site about a mile from his home. Staffed by a teacher paid out of the pooled resources of the families, the school apparently had no speech activities.

Coming to Chapel Hill in 1877 and 1878 (Alderman), all three became active in the literary societies: Alderman and McIver in the Dialectic Society, and Aycock in the Philanthropic. On the first night that Aycock attended a Philanthropic meeting, he surprised everyone by responding to an invitation extended to the initiates to speak at the conclusion of a debate. He analyzed the arguments that had been presented and then introduced new ones. At one point he declared that his opponent's speech "reminded him of the fellow who was looking for a black cat in a dark cellar, on a dark night, with no light, when the cat was not there." A classmate reported that Aycock "made decidedly the best speech [sic] of the night, and was roundly applauded, and at once took the first debater's place in the Society."[3]

Although McIver was an enthusiastic member of the Dialectic Society, he never matched Aycock and Alderman's enjoyment of the speaking activities. Noted as a skilled conversationalist, he found it difficult to think on his feet in front of an audience. In a speech at the university a few years after his graduation, McIver reported: "During my four years at this institution I made no appearance before the public as a speaker

2. Dumas Malone, *Edwin A. Alderman* (New York: Doubleday, Doran, 1940), 7, 12.

3. Robert W. Winston, *Aycock: His People's Genius* (Founder's Day Address, October 12, 1933), published as a supplement to University of North Carolina *Alumni Review*, XXII (November, 1933), 4, 9; J. R. Rodwell, "Some Incidents in the College Life of C. B. Aycock by His Classmate and Chum," in Aycock Collection.

when the payment of fines . . . could relieve me from that duty." Although not entirely clear, the intent of this comment may be that he never spoke at a Dialectic meeting. Outside the hall of the literary society, however, McIver was known as a popular conversationalist. "Whenever Mac stopped at the Old Well he was quickly surrounded by a crowd. He loved to talk; he talked well. Others liked to listen because he made everything funny in the telling, gave even the most serious matter a humorous fillip, and convulsed them with his mimicry, whether of farmer Clark on his donkey or an august university professor."[4]

Another program at the university that was to further their speaking skills was a debating society in connection with a summer teachers' normal school the university had begun in 1877. A classmate who later became a professor of education at the university notes that their attendance, their "interest in the classwork and public lectures," and their participation in "the debating society were, no doubt, the starting point of their . . . devotion and labor in behalf of public education in North Carolina and throughout the South." In 1880 Aycock won the Mangum medal for oratory, given to a senior. Two years later, Alderman received the same recognition. Although he won honors in Greek, McIver gained no similar recognition in oratory and requested to be excused from the customary speaking appearance at his commencement in 1881.[5] Later overcoming his reluctance to speak, McIver became known for his powers of persuasion.

After graduation in 1880 Aycock studied law and was admitted to the bar. Making his home in Goldsboro, he became a

---

4. Rose H. Holder, *McIver of North Carolina* (Chapel Hill: University of North Carolina Press, 1957), 49–52.
5. M. C. S. Noble, *A History of the Public Schools of North Carolina* (Chapel Hill: University of North Carolina Press, 1930), 416; Kemp P. Battle, *History of the University of North Carolina* (2 vols.; Raleigh: Edwards and Broughton, 1912), II, 175; Michael G. Martin, Jr., Archivist, to Bert Bradley, April 29, 1975, in possession of the author.

member and later chairman of the school board. Through his concern for education, he persuaded the board of trustees of the Goldsboro public school to grant the first pension ever given to a public school teacher in North Carolina. Wanting the public schools to have a democratizing influence on the community, he opposed education of the factory operatives' children in separate schools because he thought it "tended to create and develop a caste system, and that offended his ideals of democracy." Meanwhile Alderman and McIver accepted teaching positions. Alderman became a teacher in Goldsboro, and by 1885, at twenty-four, he was superintendent of the schools. His biographer Malone suggests that "his meteoric rise" resulted chiefly from "his effectiveness on the platform."[6] McIver first took a teaching post in Durham and in 1884 moved to a new school in Winston. In the summer of 1886 he conducted a summer normal school at Yadkinville and that fall moved to the Peace Institute in Raleigh.

Major Speaking Campaigns in Behalf of Education

These three men participated in three major speaking efforts in behalf of education. The first was the teacher training institutes involving primarily Alderman and McIver. The second was the struggle to establish the State Normal and Industrial School for women led by Alderman and McIver. The third effort, featuring Aycock, included the gubernatorial campaign of 1900 and the educational campaign of 1902–1903.

Teacher Training Institutes

In 1889 after the legislative assembly established two conductors of state teachers' institutes, Alderman and McIver were chosen for the two positions. In pursuing this assignment they had to deal with the deplorable conditions in the public schools.

6. Connor and Poe, *Life and Speeches of Aycock*, 112–13; Malone, *Edwin A. Alderman*, 31.

They found that many teachers were academically unqualified, that a school term lasted "on the average, sixty days," and that the teachers received only "seventy-five dollars in wages."[7]

The conductors were to hold week-long training sessions for teachers in each of the county seats in the state. Schools were suspended, and teachers were required to attend. Monday through Thursday the conductors gave instruction in teaching techniques as well as presenting substantive knowledge on English, history, and other subjects. On Friday morning they delivered public lectures. In actuality these presentations were persuasive in purpose and were intended to muster greater community support for public education.

"A happier choice of crusaders for a great cause was not possible," observed a biographer of Alderman, for "neither [Alderman nor McIver] suggested the imagined staidness of the scholar." Instead, they impressed their associates with "a feeling of joyousness in life and eagerness for performance."[8] The enthusiasm of Alderman and McIver for their new assignments as conductors of the state teachers' institutes is clearly demonstrated in Alderman's recollection of commencement night with McIver at Chapel Hill in 1889 when the two men were revisiting the educational mecca of North Carolina.

We were to start out in a few days on a new and untried experiment in North Carolina or the South, a deliberate effort by unique campaign methods to create and mold public opinion on the question of popular education, involving taxation for the benefit of others. We were in the twenties, and there were young wives and children at home, and the work we were undertaking was a temporary creation, due to the sug-

7. E. A. Alderman, "Reports on Conductors of County Institutes in North Carolina," in *Public Documents of the State of North Carolina, Session 1891* (Raleigh: Josephus Daniels, 1891), 3–4. Hereinafter cited as Alderman, "Reports on County Institutes."

8. John S. Patton, *Dr. Edwin Anderson Alderman* (pamphlet in folder entitled "Alderman's Biographical Sketches"), in Alderman Collection, Edwin A. Alderman Library, University of Virginia.

gestion of the State Superintendent of Public Instruction, and the good impulses of the legislature, which could not quite make up its mind to have done with us once and for all. There was no precedent for what we were trying to do, except Horace Mann, and he seemed so far off and so great, that each one of us would have laughed at the other for mentioning the comparison. I remember that we talked about our plans and purposes and difficulties until the cocks began to crow. I told him to let me say one more word and then let us both go to sleep. He replied, in his hearty, wholesome way, that he did not propose to be put to sleep and let me have the last word at the same time. We then decided to make a night of it, and talked on until the sun rose. I am inclined to think it about the best night I have ever spent, for an intelligent and unselfish idea held our youth under its spell, and bound us for life to a service, which was not the service of self. As I think of it today, the grim old room in the inn at Chapel Hill, and the silent watches of that night are lit with the light that never was on land or sea.[9]

The two men needed all their enthusiasm and idealism to sustain them in the next three years as they traveled separately and together throughout the state. Coming into "contact with people who had no more than heard of educational institutes," they continually surprised "the natives with new points of view." Seldom moving far from the railroads, Alderman and McIver coaxed the people to their meetings, "and by eloquent expositions . . . and good, gripping stories, they kept courageously at their task of convincing men and women that the school house is of more importance than the circus on a vacant lot, or a revival in a country chapel, and that it is the doorway of opportunity through which their children were to reach usefulness, power and success." One historian noted that "the whole procedure might well have been a flash in the pan, a gesture without results, had it not been for the fortunate choice of

9. Edwin A. Alderman, "In Memoriam: Charles Duncan McIver," reprinted from Fiftieth-Anniversary Volume (N.p.: National Education Association, 1907), 313–14.

the two young men, both of whom had a flair for the platform and public contacts."[10]

The act establishing the teacher's institutes provided the two conductors with some help: (1) It charged the state board of education to adopt rules and regulations for holding the institutes, to decide how often they should be held, and to use the money appropriated to meet the necessary expenses. (2) It designated the county board of education to provide quarters for the institute and to bear all local costs, including the board of the conductor. (3) It required the county superintendent to assist in holding the institute and, with the conductor, to examine any teacher applying for certification. Participants passing the examination at the end of the week received either first- or second-grade certificates which were honored for three years in any county of the state.[11]

From July 1, 1889, to July 1, 1890, Alderman reported that 8,500 people attended his Friday lectures. "In seven other addresses, and in my daily talks, it is fair to claim that I reached 3,500 more, making a total of 12,000." The average attendance at each institute during the first year was: "teachers 45, committeemen 22, citizens 283." Over the span of three years, Alderman held 84 institutes, taught 3,607 teachers, and spoke to approximately 35,000 citizens.[12] For his part McIver reported in 1891 that "nearly 15,000 people have attended these Friday exercises in my Institutes since July 1, 1889. The number of teachers attending the Institutes was nearly 1,500, which is about 50 per cent. more than attended all the eight summer Normal Schools each year." For the three years he served as institute conductor McIver presided over 86 institutes, instructed approximately 3,800 teachers, and addressed approxi-

10. Patton, *Dr. Edwin Anderson Alderman;* Henry McGilbert Wagstaff, *Impressions of Men and Movements at the University of North Carolina* (Chapel Hill: University of North Carolina Press, 1950), 68–69.

11. Noble, *A History of the Public Schools of North Carolina,* 428–29.

12. Alderman, "Reports on County Institutes," 1891, p. 4; 1893, p. 53.

mately 30,000 North Carolinians.[13] Of the 3,607 teachers attending institutes conducted by Alderman, only 148 received
certificates; McIver awarded certificates to a mere 75 of the almost 1,500 teachers he instructed in the first year.[14] One is
hard pressed to imagine the level of competence of the teachers
not receiving certificates when he reads Alderman's statement
that "many of the questions given were taken from examina-
tions given to twelve- and thirteen-year-old children in our city
graded schools."[15]

McIver was less precise than Alderman in recording activities but he indicated that he lectured "on the different branches
taught in the public schools; on school organization: discipline,
methods of teaching, and methods of studying; on school law,
and on the proper use of books on the State list." He planned
the exercises on Friday, which he designated "People's Day," to
interest and instruct the local citizens "in the work of public
education." In this address he dealt with "the necessity for education by taxation" and answered "objections to it commonly
heard among the people."[16]

Alderman spent "five hours—three in the morning and two
in the afternoon" on Monday, Tuesday, and Wednesday lectur-
ing mainly on methods of teaching, of which he made the following outline:

I. THE TEACHER

1. His daily preparation
2. His professional preparation
3. His general preparation
4. His social preparation
5. His moral preparation

13. C. D. McIver, "Reports on Conductors of County Institutes in North
Carolina," in *Public Documents of the State of North Carolina* (Raleigh: Josephus Daniels, 1891), 1891, p. 15, 1893, p. 50. Hereinafter cited as McIver, "Reports on County Institutes."
14. Alderman, "Reports on County Institutes," 1893, p. 53; McIver, "Reports on County Institutes," 1891, p. 15.
15. Alderman, "Reports on County Institutes," 1891, p. 8.
16. McIver, "Reports on County Institutes," 1891, p. 15.

		1. Attendance
		2. School-room
2. HOW TO ORGANIZE		3. Text-books
		4. Classification
		5. Opening Exercises
		6. Programmes
		7. School Devices
		1. Discipline
3. HOW TO GOVERN		2. Punishments
		3. Purposes of Punishment
		1. Reading
		2. Spelling
4. HOW TO TEACH	METHODS IN	3. Language
		4. Arithmetic
		5. History
		6. Geography

Each subject was presented for treatment and discussed under five heads, as for example:

Arithmetic.   1. What is arithmetic?
2. Why do we teach arithmetic?
3. What are its essentials?
4. What is the rational method of teaching arithmetic?
5. The best books on arithmetic?

The topics considered were "necessarily varied with the character of the teachers." Alderman devoted most of Thursday "to the non-compulsory examination of teachers for the three-year Certificate." On Friday morning he gave a public lecture to which all citizens in the surrounding area were invited.[17]

Alderman's records and McIver's letters to his wife indicate moments of exhilaration and of discouragement that faced the two "crusaders." After one institute, Alderman wrote that "the public address fell rather flat."

17. Alderman, "Reports on County Institutes," 1891, p. 3–8.

I did my best but couldn't stir things much. What between crying babies, squealing pigs, badly behaved children, "Sam" the village idiot,
& an ill-conditioned Supt. my oratorical task was rather heavy. The
Supt. did me very little good—a man of whisky habits, with the con-
ceit of ignorance & the courage of stupid convictions, large-red-faced-
bulldozing-blundering, his civilities were obnoxious. My first *real* un-
pleasant colaborer.[18]

In a letter to his wife, McIver complained about the meeting
place of one institute, calling it "the most Godforsaken place
I've struck."

In some respects this place is worse than Columbia. I'll have a worse
time here than at Troy because Will was at Troy. . . . There is no court-
house. I suppose ¼ of the lights are broken out of the windows. . . .
How I shall rejoice when Friday comes!!!

There was not even a fire in the stove today . . . when we opened.
There were 6 teachers present, which number was afterwards increased
to 8 & about as many other people were also present. There were
barely enough seats provided for these.[19]

At Alleghany, Alderman said the teachers assembled were
"untrained" and "unfit to teach truly children."

Three or four bright men the rest as usual—largely ungainly young
lads with slim notions of manners, politeness or culture. I do not
mean to say they were not kind. . . . They need teaching themselves.
. . . The teachers were very attentive & prompt, tho many of them
sought to return to their farm work. I did my best to do them some
good, to really help them. But I frankly fear & say that I doubt if much
real good can be done to people who only spend ¼ of their time in
teaching.[20]

In another instance, reacting to small attendance, Alderman
wrote: "The Institute was poorly attended—& seemed to at-

18. E. A. Alderman, "Institute Statistics" (notebook), in Alderman Collection.
19. C. D. McIver to Mrs. McIver from Bayboro, March 16, 1891, in McIver
Collection, University of North Carolina at Greensboro.
20. Alderman, "Institute Statistics."

tract very little attention." At Caswell, Alderman noted the negative responses of the local citizens to his final speech. He said that "the crowd on Friday . . . was hard to interest or arouse. I butted against their solidity for about 1½ hours, but I fear did little save expend nervous force. There were appreciative people, of course."[21]

Reflecting his personal problems and loneliness, McIver wrote to his wife: "I was sorely disappointed tonight, when I found that I had no letter from you. I am sick too. I haven't had any panacea water since last Friday. I feel sore in every joint & am in rather low spirits. I not only have to drive myself to work, but when I begin to lecture I find my mental joints as stiff as my physical & I have to lash myself into an appearance of life. My vacation is coming none too soon." However, in spite of uninviting accommodations McIver seemed to have retained a sense of humor, describing his landlady on one occasion as a widow whose "snuff stains ornament her mouth in wreaths." Turning next to the food, he said "Winton coffee, no milk, messed eggs, sick children, dingy grease, evergreen collards, aged butter, and spoilt-child was the bill of fare for dinner. I forgot to mention raw biscuit."[22] In another letter (n.d.) McIver reacted lightly:

No news this morning except that the wind blew the old rags & socks out of my window during the night and let the breezes in. I had a pretty good night's rest, however, and am not feeling so bad as I expected.

I can appreciate the situation now of the boy who couldn't pronounce g-l-a-s-s until his teacher said it was what you put in windows, when he brightened up & said: g-l-a-s-s "daddie's old britches."

The hardship of travel contributed to the weariness of the two men. Not all county seats were accessible by train. Alder-

21. *Ibid.*
22. McIver to Mrs. McIver, December 10, 1890, December 14, 1890, in McIver Collection.

man wrote to McIver (September 5, 1891) that he had spent "seven hours of hard riding" to cover twelve miles over a high mountain to reach "Robbinsville . . . an awful place about a third as large as Lillington. . . . We went in a ordinary spring-less wagon used for other 'substances.'" But despite the difficult travel, miserable living conditions, and sometimes indifferent response, the two men reported moments of joy from their accomplishments. On January 1, 1890, from Raleigh, McIver wrote to his wife: "My Institute [is su]cceeding beyond my expectations. The cou[rtho]use was fuller than ever today and I have no idea that it will hold the crowd tomorrow. . . . Everybody expresses surprise at the interest manifested here. I don't believe the old town has been so much interested in anything in a long time."

From Albemarle on September 19, 1890, McIver reported to his wife that he "had a good Institute taking it all together" with the "courthouse full of people—70 teachers, 30 school officers . . . & about 200 other people. I have been told by a number of people that my speech today was much stronger than Alderman's. I suspect he is hearing the same thing wherever he goes about his being better than mine was last year. Binns, the Co. Supt. says mine is much stronger."

Also encouraged by favorable responses, Alderman reported that "the Court-House was full" in Durham. He said that two of the people "were kind enough to say that it was the best educational address they had ever heard. This encourages me, but does not turn my head, I trust. I know my limitations." He also expressed enthusiasm about the institute at Statesville that had been very well attended. He wrote: "Large crowds of citizens attended daily & great interest and curiosity manifested in the work. Teachers seem to be more than ordinarily good. Many women fortunately are employed." He concluded that the institute at Albemarle had been "a marked success. The largest attendance yet found in the state—74 bona fide teachers in daily attendance. The Ct. House was crowded every day. The public address was largely attended—a *full* house. These teachers were the most *punctual* & attentive I have yet encountered."[23]

According to Josephus Daniels, "holding the teachers' institutes was the smallest thing" Alderman and McIver did. In truth, they became "the two chosen educational evangelists of the State." Placing these teachers' institutes in perspective, the respected editor of the Richmond *Times-Dispatch*, Virginius Dabney, labeled them as "an epochal and unprecedented crusade for public education which . . . did much to arouse widespread interest in better public schools for the entire" South. "And paradoxical as it may appear," Alderman, who was "president of three Southern universities may have achieved most enduringly for his section" by these efforts "as a young North Carolina school teacher."[24]

The State Normal and Industrial School

"The original idea of the establishment of the State Normal and Industrial College in North Carolina was born in the brain of Charles McIver. He did not borrow the idea from Massachusetts or New York. The whole scheme forced itself upon him out of the dust of injustice and negligence right under his eyes."[25] So testified Alderman at McIver's death. A number of responsible educators, including Alderman and McIver, recognized the need for a normal school because of the dearth of qualified women teachers in North Carolina. As a result of "a stirring speech" by McIver in 1889 before the Teachers' Assembly, the statewide organization of teachers, the group appointed

23. Alderman, "Institute Statistics."
24. Josephus Daniels, *Tar Heel Editor* (Chapel Hill: University of North Carolina Press, 1939), 370; Virginius Dabney, review of *Edwin A. Alderman: A Biography by Dumas Malone*, in *New York Tribune Books*, November 10, 1940.
25. Edwin A. Alderman, "In Memoriam: Charles Duncan McIver," 313.

a committee, composed of McIver as chairman, Alderman, George T. Winston, and Edward P. Moses, "to appear before the Legislature at its next session and personally present and urge the adoption of a bill for the establishment of a training school for teachers." Together Alderman and McIver prepared the first memorial to present to the legislature in behalf of such an institution. After the senate passed the bill "by a large majority," the house defeated it, perhaps because it called for a coeducational institution. In 1891, omitting the coeducational feature of the bill, McIver and Alderman again went to the legislature which passed it with almost no opposition.[26]

The board of directors faced a dilemma when the choice for the president of the new institution was quickly narrowed to Alderman and McIver. Learning of the board's problem, McIver wrote to Major Sidney M. Finger, chairman of the board:

I had a free talk with Alderman as to the presidency of the State Normal and Industrial School. He feels just as I do about the matter. Neither of us could afford to be *candidates*. And the selection of either would mean no reflection on the other. He would accept a position under my management as I should not hesitate to do under his, if the Board saw fit to elect him, and should offer me an agreeable line of work. . . . What we want is that no personal relations of friendship should affect the choice. That only the highest interest of the Institution should be considered. Would it be better to have Alderman president and me a professor, or me president and Alderman a professor is the question before the Board. Either of us will submit cheerfully to action of the Board.[27]

McIver was chosen, and in retrospect, it would seem that this decision was a wise one. The two men had spoken frequently in favor of the education of women and had worked hard from

26. William C. Smith, "Charles Duncan McIver," in *Biographical History of North Carolina from Colonial Times to the Present*, ed. Samuel A. Ashe (8 vols.; Greensboro, N.C.: Charles L. Van Noppen, 1906), V, 212–30.
27. "Founder's Day Address, October 4, 1941," Women's College of the University of North Carolina, Greensboro, North Carolina, in McIver Collection.

within the Teachers' Assembly to persuade the legislature to establish the institution for female training. But, according to one source, McIver was "the man who had done most to mold public sentiment in its favor";[28] and he seemed to be more intensely dedicated to the education of women as teachers and for other occupations as well. And he did so for a compelling reason. McIver became imbued with his wife's yearning for greater educational opportunities for women. She was good in mathematics and science but was prevented from becoming a doctor because at that time there was no institution in the state where a white woman could obtain an inexpensive or free higher education. Under her influence, "he made his first public speech in behalf of the higher education of women" in the summer of 1885 "at a teachers' institute held in Winston." From the day he was named president he set out to make the State Normal and Industrial School the best available for women in the South and the entire country. Walter H. Page wrote that "twice McIver had a chance to possibly become President of the State University, but he considered his work in building a college for women, of greater importance." With a broad concept of the education of women, McIver believed "that too little stress was laid upon the thorough and rounded education that made the woman able to take the place in the home and the world that he thought she ought to occupy."[29]

True to McIver's prediction, when the institution opened in 1892 Alderman accepted a position as professor of history and English and helped to make the school a success. In 1893 Alderman was appointed professor of education at the University of North Carolina, and in 1895 became its president.

28. Charles L. Coon, "Charles Duncan McIver and His Educational Services 1886–1906." in *Report of the Commissioner of Education* (Washington: Government Printing Office, 1908), 333.

29. William C. Smith, "Charles Duncan McIver," 212–30; Walter H. Page, "Charles D. McIver," *South Atlantic Quarterly*, V (1906), 391; Raleigh *News and Observer*, September 23, 1906.

The Educational Campaigns of 1900 and 1902–1903

At the turn of the century the banner shifted to Charles B. Aycock, who in 1900 and 1902–1903 led campaigns to improve public education statewide. During the years that McIver and Alderman were guiding the destinies of the State Normal and Industrial School and the University of North Carolina, Aycock, who had developed his law practice and served on the school board of Goldsboro, became more and more involved in politics. Along with many Democrats, he was dissatisfied with the state government which, since the election of 1894, had been under the control of the Fusionists—Republicans and Populists. Since the Fusionists were able to stay in office only through the support of the Negroes, the Democrats sought a way to eliminate that vote.

Finally in 1898 the Democrats gained control of the legislature and prepared an amendment to the state constitution which disqualified from voting any person who could not read and write, unless that person had voted prior to 1868 or was a lineal descendant of one who had. This amendment, presented for ratification at the general election of 1900, became a crucial issue in the gubernatorial campaign. Because Aycock had been instrumental in the success of the Democratic party in 1898, he became the Democratic nominee for governor in 1900. He based his campaign on the issue of education. Although he advocated the literacy requirement for voting and made no attempt to hide his belief in white supremacy, he also made it clear that he supported "public taxation for the education of all children of both whites and Negroes as a basis for increasingly more equal opportunity of all people, white and black, to learn, to earn and to vote as the common rights of the citizens of the commonwealth."[30]

30. Frank P. Graham, "Charles Brantley Aycock of North Carolina" (typescript of address to Joint Session of N.C. Legislature, April 9, 1951) in Aycock Collection. Hereinafter cited as Graham, "Aycock of North Carolina."

Despite the efforts of Alderman and McIver some ten years earlier, North Carolinians only provided enough tax money to keep the schools "open only seventy-three days in the year, and . . . less than one-third of the children of school age attended them." Within the state, only thirty districts, "all urban, considered education of sufficient importance to levy a local tax for the support of schools." When Aycock was inaugurated on January 15, 1901, the situation began to change. According to Frank P. Graham, "the man, the place, the cause, and the opportunity came together in North Carolina in 1900 in Charles Brantley Aycock when he committed the people of North Carolina to public taxation for the education of all the children of all the people."[31]

The 1902–1903 educational campaign resulted from Aycock's success in subduing the divisive, and sometimes acrimonious, competition that existed between public and private education at all levels in the state. At McIver's instigation, Aycock called and presided over a conference of educators, February 13, 1902, whose purpose was to initiate a cooperative program for both public and private education. Some believed that Aycock was the only "man in the State who could have brought together all these warring factions and accomplished" the purpose of uniting them.[32]

The conference set up the Central Campaign Committee for the Promotion of Public Education in North Carolina. The three members appointed to the committee were Aycock, McIver, and Thomas F. Toon, the state superintendent of education, who died shortly thereafter. James Y. Joyner, who was a student at the university at the same time as Aldermn, Aycock, and McIver, filled the vacancy by virtue of being appointed

31. Connor and Poe, *Life and Speeches of Aycock*, 114–15; Graham, "Aycock of North Carolina," 11.
32. "Proceedings of the Fifth Conference for Education in the South," *Bulletin of the Southern Educational Board*, I (1902), 21; Connor and Poe, *Life and Speeches of Aycock*, 119.

Toon's successor. The work of the committee was to conduct a systematic campaign for local taxation, consolidation of districts, better buildings, and longer school terms. At the conclusion of the conference, Governor Aycock reported as follows:

The Educational Conference held in Raleigh this week resulted in bringing together the forces which have heretofore worked separately in the fight against illiteracy. In the past we have been wanting in the power which comes from unity of action. We have always had among educators a common purpose, now we are going to join in the actual work. . . . We know now that 20 per cent. of our white population over ten years of age cannot read or write. Knowing this we determined that each year should show a decrease in this number. To this end a systematic campaign will be organized. Speakers will be sent out over the State, the newspapers—always on the side of popular education—will be asked to devote more space to educational matters, and the preachers are invited to join in the great work.[33]

To help the committee, the Southern Education Board gave four thousand dollars annually for two years to help finance a statewide campaign for local school taxes. During the following summer people assembled in open-air meetings, courthouses, churches, and schoolhouses to hear "two hundred or more speeches." In fact, McIver claimed that the audiences at "the educational meetings in June, July, and August were larger than" those "that attended the political speakings in the months of September and October preceding the November election." Nevertheless, the speaker "whom the people were most eager to hear was Charles B. Aycock." McIver reported that Aycock himself said "that his audiences at his fifteen speeches in the educational campaign were larger than [those] he addressed at any fifteen political gatherings."[34]

Aycock rightly earned the sobriquet "North Carolina's edu-

33. Raleigh News and Observer, February 16, 1902.
34. Ibid., February 14, 1902; Charles D. McIver, "Report from the Field," in Proceedings of the Conference for Education in the South: The Sixth Session (New York City: Committee on Publication, 1903), 66–67; Connor and Poe, Life and Speeches of Aycock, 122.

cational governor" because he "talked and preached education in every county . . . and in states from Maine to Florida as a flaming evangel sent from God for the education and redemption of all the children of men. *For every day of every year of his administrtion as governor, a new school house arose in North Carolina.*"[35]

One resident said that Aycock was regarded "as almost a messiah who would lead their children into a new and finer life, of which they had dreamed."

My father had served as County Superintendent of Schools in Yadkin County for many years in the early 1900's. It was a completely rural county; no town of any size, the largest having less than 300 population; no railroad of any description; no improved roads. The schools were operated a maximum of 4 months and sometimes as short a term as 2 months. The buildings were largely one-teacher, miserable frame buildings, and a few log ones left. . . . [M]y father saw . . . in Aycock, a spark of hope for better educational advantages for even this backwoods county. As a boy I travelled with him to every school in the County—there were over a hundred—and heard him make literally hundreds of talks telling the people of Aycock and what he was trying to do for their children.[36]

Frank H. Curtis, president of Reidsville Seminary and a personal friend of Aycock, observed that "only eternity will ever reveal the good he did in helping to strike off the shackles of ignorance from tens of thousands of helpless little children, and to plead so eloquently in their behalf and for their emancipation."[37]

As noble and effective as were his efforts, Aycock was suc-

35. Graham, "Aycock of North Carolina," 15; Charles D. McIver, "Forward Movement of Education in North Carolina," *Southern Educational Association, Journal of Proceedings and Addresses*, XV (1904), 96.

36. Leroy Martin to Clarence Poe, September 21, 1955, in Aycock Collection.

37. Frank H. Curtis to Connor and Poe, April 24, 1912, in Aycock Collection.

cessful only because he came, as Graham observed, at the climax of "the long gathering momentum of the crusades of Alderman and McIver and their valiant cohorts in North Carolina." Dumas Malone, Alderman's biographer, suggested that Alderman and McIver "prepared the way" for Aycock and that they also "initiated campaign methods which were to be followed in other states under their direction and by which, in the first decade of the new century, the educational life of the entire Southeast was to be stimulated." Josephus Daniels claimed that "the educational revival in North Carolina may be dated truly from those evangelistic meetings" of Alderman and McIver. Even Aycock admitted: "If I have taken up the cause of education it was because the work was made ready to hand by those who have gone before."[38]

The improvement of education in North Carolina during the twenty-year period covered by these three campaigns becomes apparent by comparing its status in 1905 with that of 1885. Many of the rural districts had been consolidated. Still, the total schools had increased from 6,600 to 8,193. The number of teachers had risen from 6,700 to 9,687. The net worth of public school property had moved from $700,000 to $3,182,919. By 1905 teacher employment increased from an average of sixty days a year to eighty-eight. Instead of $80 teachers received an annual stipend of $136.29. The number of towns and cities levying local school taxes had grown from nine to sixty-three. In 1886 no county districts levied local taxes for schools; 354 did in 1905.[39] Undoubtedly, many factors contributed to these changes; but clearly the persuasive efforts of these men were important in promoting improvements during this twenty-year period.

38. Graham, "Aycock of North Carolina," 15; Malone, *Edwin A. Alderman*, 47; Daniels, *Tar Heel Editor*, 371; "Education Day in Reidsville" (unidentified newsclipping, no author) in Aycock Collection.
39. Coon, "Charles Duncan McIver," 331.

Persuasive Power

Using an axiological rhetoric, these three speakers attempted to introduce a new set of human values into the thinking of the citizens of North Carolina and the South. On several occasions, after reciting the names of outstanding southern leaders in politics and war, and acknowledging that the South had "never been long without successful leadership in agriculture, at the bar, and in the pulpit," McIver declared that it had not, however, "produced a group of educational leaders among its great men in high public places." He promised, however, that the next ten years would "witness the development of a group of men who will go upon the hustings and fight out for our children the real battle of liberty and independence." Indicating that the real struggle was over values, McIver suggested that the battle could be "won only by a revolution in popular thought, resulting in a recognition of a paramount importance of securing for every child in the South a thorough public school education."[40]

Alderman, Aycock, and McIver all emphasized that a first value of universal education was its worth or benefit for the people. To develop this value, Aycock employed these arguments: (1) It would advance the prosperity and glory of North Carolina. (2) It would eliminate ignorance, which is the enemy of liberty and progress. (3) It would provide trained leadership. (4) It would develop the competition that causes full development of an individual.[41] Moreover, it was argued, universal

40. See Ralph T. Eubanks and Virgil L. Baker, "Toward an Axiology of Rhetoric," *Quarterly Journal of Speech*, XLVIII (1962), 158; Charles D. McIver, "Presidential Address to North Carolina Teachers Assembly," in *Proceedings of the Eighth Annual Session of the North Carolina Teachers Assembly*, VIII (June, 1891), 471–78; "Educational Statesmanship," *Southern Educational Association, Journal of Proceedings and Addresses*, XI (1901).

41. Based on speeches delivered 1900–1903. See Connor and Poe, *Life and Speeches of Aycock*, 222–88; Charles B. Aycock, "Address before Charlotte Chamber of Commerce, 1902" (typescript), "Speech at Boone, 1902" (typescript), "Education Day at Reidsville" (newspaper clipping), all in Aycock Col-

education met a responsibility of the state. In a period when many people believed that the acquisition of learning was an individual matter and hence no legitimate concern for the state, Alderman and McIver forwarded as a second value that schools were a responsibility of North Carolina. Alderman argued that since a child had a *right* to an education, the state had a *duty* to establish schools. McIver charged that they were a necessity because they provided the only sources of education for most.[42]

Probably the value that stirred the greatest opposition among North Carolinians was the contention that women should have opportunities for higher education. McIver was the most enthusiastic proponent of this position, but Alderman maintained that the absence of colleges for women was discriminatory. On at least one occasion Aycock praised advanced training of women and implied that he recognized the value of female education.[43] Apparently, however, McIver developed these arguments more often and in a more complete form than his two colleagues. McIver contended: (1) Woman is the natural teacher of the race. (2) There is more illiteracy among women than among men. (3) The refusal to educate women is grounded in the idea that masses do not need a liberal education, only a few educated leaders do. (4) Woman is the fountainhead of civilization. (5) In no section of the country have women been treated justly in educational matters. (6) The state gives aid in educating young men "while the girl—weaker and more dependent

lection; Charles B. Aycock, "Education and the Voluntary Tax," *Conference for Education in the South, Proceedings*, V (1902), 4; Charles D. McIver, "Two Open Fields for Investment in the South," in *Proceedings of the Fourth Conference for Education in the South*, Winston-Salem, N.C., April 18–20, 1901, p. 31; "The Education of the White Country Girl" (manuscript), and "Speech at Columbia, S.C.," December, 1901, in McIver Papers.

42. Alderman, "Reports on County Institutes," 1891, p. 4; Fayetteville *Observer*, July 17, 1890; Wilson *Advance*, May 29, 1890.

43. Charlotte *Chronicle*, August 17, 1889; "Governor Aycock to the Moravians" (unidentified newspaper clipping) in Aycock Collection.

. . . is left to fight her way, alone and unassisted."[44]

As unpopular as was the issue of taxation, either local or state, these men faced unflinchingly the cost of their proposals and sought approval of taxation by emphasizing the human values involved. As usual, McIver presented the most elaborate and the most sophisticated case, involving six premises: (1) Liberal taxation is the chief mark of a civilized people. (2) People find money to spend for what they believe to be a supreme necessity. (3) The world cannot afford not to tax itself to the utmost to secure leaders of thought. (4) Taxation is simply an exchange of money for something better—civilized government. (5) General education is possible only by self-imposed taxation. (6) North Carolina is not too poor to do better than she has been in the cause of universal education.[45]

Alderman tried "to show that education in a free government is legitimately a tax on protected property." Aycock simply admitted that public education would be expensive, that the money would have to come from taxes, and that the best way to accomplish his program was through local taxation.[46] Realizing that the opposition to taxes was deep and strong, Aycock attempted to shift attention from the issue to a higher value—the people's love for their children. An instance in which Aycock included an anecdote to bring the argument to a personal level was recalled by Dr. Clarence Poe in 1959:

Yes, I am asking you to pay more taxes for schools—and I know just how much you hate taxes. I can never forget the anguish and distress

44. Charles D. McIver, "Two Open Fields for Investment in the South," "Speech at Columbia S.C.," "Education of the White Girl" in McIver Collection; Fayetteville *Observer*, July 17, 1890.

45. Charles D. McIver, "Speech at Columbia, S.C.," "The Teacher as a Citizen," Peoria, Ill., 1905, "Address on Local Taxation," in McIver Collection; Fayetteville *Observer*, July 17, 1890.

46. Alderman, "Reports on County Institutes," 1891, p. 4; Based on speeches delivered in 1902–1903. Connor and Poe, *Life and Speeches of Aycock*, 2–8, 284–94.

on the face of an old farmer as he goes into the sheriff's office and asks, "Sheriff, Sheriff, how much is my taxes?" Then drawing out an old, half wornout billfold tied all the tighter with four or five strings, he unwraps each string as painfully as if he were having a tooth pulled, then counts over the whole amount of money three or four times to make sure he has not paid the state one extra penny, parting with each coin or bill as dolefully as if he were bidding the last farewell to a friend . . . and finally leaves the sheriff's office looking as if he had been to a funeral. Yes, I know how deep is your aversion to taxes but I know one thing deeper—and this is your love for your children.[47]

A second distinctive feature of the rhetoric that the three men shared was that, with one exception, they eschewed the use of myths in attempting to recast the educational environment. Many southern speakers in the postbellum period employed to advantage such myths as those of the Old South, the Lost Cause, white supremacy, the Solid South, and the New South. As Professor Braden has explained, these myths were persuasive because "the belief in certain 'mind pictures of his world or of the larger world around him—images that he wants to believe' permitted southerners to forget and to view the present and the future in a more favorable light."[48] As conductors of the teachers' institutes, Alderman and McIver had no time for such myths; they made certain that North Carolinians "heard not flattery nor the glorification of a dead past," but that they heard of "the shame and blighting effects of illiteracy."

They heard a new doctrine of the spiritual and economic meaning of education; they heard how necessary it was that the teachers of little children have the best training for the most important work of civilization; they heard how for a century the State had been aiding men to secure the blessings of higher education and denying the same privilege to women; and they heard for the first time in their lives men plead that taxes be raised instead of lowered. This campaign marked a new epoch in North Carolina history, for it was a campaign with-

47. Clarence Poe, "Governor Aycock's Approach to Voters when Advocating School Taxes," (typescript, 1959), in Aycock Collection.
48. See pp. 8–9 herein.

out appeal to race prejudice, without appeal to dead issues; it was a campaign free from the quarrel words of the past; it was an appeal for broader vision.[49]

Instead of appealing to a myth-encrusted past, these speakers were forward looking and sought to create conditions to promote education. And they admitted that progress would bring changes in southern life, that is, as Alderman noted, it might "lose an element of charm and picturesqueness, but . . . gain in wealth and productive energy."[50]

Avoiding other popular myths, the three reformers did accept and appeal to white supremacy to promote their arguments. Slyly, Aycock suggested that universal education would keep the whites in advance of the Negroes. Although he accepted white supremacy, McIver rejected the argument "that education is not good for the negro, and that when you educate one of them, you spoil a field hand." Instead he insisted that "the proper kind of education hurts no one." In his view "it would be a good thing for this country if we could convert half of our field hands into artisans, who could erect our buildings and convert our raw material into profitable products."[51] Despite his progressive stance on Negro education, McIver said that the white race was "the thoroughbred among races and stands among inferior races as the thoroughbred animal stands among scrubs." Thus he justified greater effort in educating whites. To amplify his contention he argued that, "if you feed the thoroughbred and the scrub animals on poor diets the scrub will suffer less than the thoroughbred; and only when there is a liberal provision of food and care will the thoroughbred's blood fully assert itself; and that similarly on a starvation educational diet an inferior race has a comparative advantage, while on a

49. Coon, "Charles Duncan McIver," 333.
50. Edwin A. Alderman, "Higher Education in the South," *National Education Association: Journal of Proceedings and Addresses* (1895), p. 981.
51. Charles B. Aycock, "Speech before Charlotte Chamber of Commerce, 1902" (typescript) in Aycock Collection.

liberal diet the advantage is with the superior race."[52] Except for their advocacy of white supremacy these men were too busy trying to improve education to be concerned with romanticizing the Old South and the Lost Cause.

A common source of their rhetorical effectiveness was that the three men were perceived as men of good character—honest, sincere, interested in the welfare of others. One of his listeners reported that Aycock "got hold of the crowd at once and held its attention throughout the two hours or more. The effect was wonderful, magical, marvelous. His perfectly apparent honesty, and sincerity, his utter lack of sham and pretension completely. He spoke fervidly, eloquently, and triumphantly."[53] In comparing Aycock and Zebulon B. Vance, another popular leader, Aycock's law partner, who had been a classmate at the university, declared that they both "had deep convictions and their heart was in every word they spoke."[54] "The people had faith in his honesty," said the Raleigh *News and Observer* (January 12, 1905). Even political opponents testified as to Aycock's goodness. C. S. Wooten recalled that in 1892 when he was making Populist speeches, they "met in joint debate on two occasions in Pitt and Wayne Counties. During the discussion not a word was uttered by him to wound any body's [sic] feelings, but he was amiable in disposition, gentle in spirit and kind in his manner. He illustrated fully what Shakespere [sic] said, 'A smile secures the wounding of a frown.'" Senator Marion Butler, who faced Aycock in a series of public debates, later wrote that Aycock "was a high type of man who could meet a strong opponent in the fiercest kind of contest and yet command the

52. Charles D. McIver, "Speech at Columbia, S.C., December 1901" in McIver Collection (see footnote 45 above).

53. T. Gillam (?) Windsor (typewritten page) May 21, 1912, in Aycock Collection.

54. Robert W. Winston, "Vance and Aycock," Speech delivered at Memorial Hall at the University of North Carolina on October 11, 1951 (printed copy, Aycock Collection).

respect of his opponent more at the end than at the beginning."
Apparently, from the first of his career he had the ability and
willingness to sting an opponent, however, for a classmate from
Hassell's school testified that in debating Aycock would occasionally "*cut*, it is true, but it was rather the wound of a benefi-
cial surgeon than a willful shedder of blood."[55] Alderman's
rhetorical success apparently came primarily from similar rapport with listeners. On one occasion, the Fayetteville *Observer*
(November 14, 1889) reported that he was "earnest and impressive. His heart and sympathies . . . are evidently thoroughly in
his great work."

The perception of McIver as a "good man speaking well" was
likewise a significance in his rhetoric. Attributing his effectiveness to his sincerity, Josephus Daniels said that McIver
"became eloquent because he had a message that impelled him
to carry it to his fellows." Daniels continued that "if he had not
been possessed by an idea, he would never have developed as a
speaker, for he had no natural gift for public speaking as we understand the gift of oratory. He never did learn to speak unless
his heart was in his subject."[56] "He has the public educational
interest at heart and is enthusiastic in his work," said the Windsor *Ledger* (April 2, 1890). One who attended an institute at
Concord wrote to the Raleigh *Daily State Chronical* (August
31, 1890) that McIver had "what so few men" had, "the courage of his convictions. . . . Now I love him for his great love
of North Carolina's best interest and his great work in that
cause." More than one reporter described McIver as an "earnest" speaker. *The Outlook*, a national periodical, called him
"a man of intense earnestness." Noting McIver's rapport, Alder-

55. C. S. Wooten, "Charles B. Aycock" (handwritten sheets) April 15, 1912,
in Aycock Collection; Frank A. Daniels, "Address at the Presentation and Unveiling of Memorial Tablet, Charles Brantley Aycock," Goldsboro, N.C., November 1, 1929 (typescript) in Aycock Collection; D. Peacock to Connor and
Poe, April 25, 1912, in Aycock Collection.
56. Raleigh *News and Observer*, September 23, 1906.

man claimed that "a crowd always interested him and stirred his powers no matter how weary he was, and he moved about the crowd with a vast human interest in his face." Alderman declared an audience "dull and senseless . . . that did not respond to his earnestness." Friend and editor of the Raleigh *News and Observer*, Josephus Daniels commended McIver along with William Jennings Bryan for "their transparent sincerity and honesty." Joyner, a classmate at Chapel Hill and professor under McIver at the normal school, thought that McIver "without any of the arts of the orator . . . was the most convincing, the most irresistible speaker" that he had heard. "He was too intense, too earnest to employ paltry decorations of speech. He spoke directly and simply as one having authority. He had a message and seemed to feel—'Woe is me if I do not deliver it.' He forgot himself in his message."[57]

A second source of the rhetorical effectiveness of the three men was their skill in adjusting their presentations to specific audiences. Aware of the importance of adaptation, Aycock explained that eloquence "was simply the response of the *common sense* to what the speaker was saying. Slumbering in the minds of men there is a sense of right and justice, and the man who can interpret this feeling and give it expression is the eloquent man, and this is why he can so mightily move men." In comparing the two politicians, Robert Winston said that Vance "was with the people, Aycock was the people. . . . Vance amused and edified the boys, Aycock was one of the boys."[58]

To relate to rural people McIver suggested that "the teacher is the seed corn of civilization and none but the best is good

57. Greensboro *North State*, July 10, 1890; Concord *Standard*, August 29, 1890; "Public School Leaders," *Outlook*, LXXX (1905), 737–38; Alderman, "In Memoriam: Charles Duncan McIver," 314, 316; Daniels, "Charles Duncan McIver," in W. C. Smith (ed.), *Charles Duncan McIver Memorial Volume* (Greensboro: Jas. J. Stone and Co., 1907), 230; James Y. Joyner, "Memorial Address," *Charles Duncan McIver Memorial Volume*, 160, in McIver Collection.

58. Archibald Johnson to Connor and Poe, April 15, 1912, in Aycock Collection; Winston, "Vance and Aycock."

enough for me." McIver impressed rural listeners when he said that "the farmers' daughters, in this State, ought to do most of the teaching, and they would be glad to do it if they had a chance. What we need is a training school for women, helped by the State." Perhaps some fathers considered putting their daughters in the classroom to free their sons for work in the fields. McIver increased his effectiveness when he asked the members of one audience to raise their hands if they "had heard their children recite during the last winter." When only sixteen responded, McIver chided his listeners, "Why you would take more interest in your hogs and cattle than that."[59]

Alderman too identified with his audiences. One biographer noted how well he "could tell a story" and turn it "to the advantage of his cause; he was intensely folksy and democratic. His power to interest equally men with the bark on and polished men in a king's council helped him to do a wonderful work."[60] The farmers, steeped in Jeffersonian democracy, were delighted to hear Alderman pay honor "to Thomas Jefferson, the morning star of democracy[;] because he had the wisdom to embody in the grandest constitution of the world, 'All men are created free and equal.'" Applying his admiration of Jefferson to education, he observed: "Man was made to rule and not to be ruled, and public education is the prime enemy of despotism. The safest security and prosperity of any country, rests upon the education, intelligence, and character of its citizens, and only in a State where education is free to all, can Democratic institutions be preserved." To make clear the destitute condition of the schoolhouses Alderman declared in a speech that "our schoolhouses are sometimes so poor that a farmer wouldn't put his hogs in them."[61]

59. Coon, "Charles Duncan McIver," 337, "Speech at Columbia, S.C.," December, 1901; Charlotte *Chronicle*, August 18, 1890; Concord *Standard*, August 29, 1890.
60. Patton, *Dr. Edwin Anderson Alderman*, 2.
61. Charlotte *Chronicle*, August 17, 1889.

The sources of their effectiveness involving preparation, language, and delivery are difficult to crystalize into common pattern because of the variety of reports about the methods and habits of the three men. These elements probably reflect their individual personalities. Upon one occasion when he received a request for a copy of a speech Aycock responded that it was "entirely offhand and that he had neither copy or notes."[62] At another time a listener observed that Governor Aycock was "at his best" when "he had no notes" and "spoke extemporaneously." In a figurative statement Winston suggested that "words came to his lips in torrents, as freely indeed as water flows down Morgan creek after an August Freshet." On several occasions Aycock himself indicated how he prepared and delivered his speeches. For example, he wrote to a friend that "writing speeches is, as you know, a difficult task for me. I much prefer to make them as the boys say, 'hot from the shoulder.' Of course, in delivering the speech, I shall not use my manuscript, nor follow too closely the matter contained therein, but I think it well to write it out so as to get the general line of thought." On one occasion Aycock wrote to another friend that he had finished his speech and had "it ready for delivery, subject to the revision of such of my friends as I can submit it to before delivery."[63]

Winston, Aycock's last law partner, indicates Aycock's "manner" in his speech preparation:

It was Edgar Allen Poe who taught him to give his thoughts totality, to waste no words on the immaterial, to cut out externalities. . . . Aycock went about the preparation of his speeches as deliberately and analytically as Poe constructed his weird phantasy, "The Raven." Poe's essay on the art of composition and his logical detective stories lay upon Aycock's desk. Whether preparing a simple speech for a county

62. J. Allen Holt to Connor and Poe, April 24, 1912, in Aycock Collection.

63. B. B. Dougherty (unaddressed, unsigned statement), January 23, 1941, in Aycock Collection; Winston, *Aycock: His People's Genius*, 8; Aycock to S. S. Royster, March 26, 1912, Aycock to H. G. Chatham, April 1, 1912, in Aycock Collection.

jury or an elaborate address for the Supreme Court of the United States, he went to his Poe.[64]

How Aycock prepared and delivered his acceptance speech for the Democratic nomination in 1900, perhaps the best he ever made, is under considerable question. When an admirer suggested it was extemporaneous, "Aycock laughingly broke in, 'Ex tempore? Why I sat up all night, three live-long nights, committing that ex tempore speech to memory! I have been writing on that speech for the last three months.'"[65]

Yet another friend gave an entirely different account concerning the acceptance address. Pleased because his friend had committed about half the speech to memory, Aycock confided that he "experienced more difficulty in preparing that speech than any other" he had ever made. He explained:

I had every reason to believe that I would be nominated, but what to say in accpeting [sic] I just seemed unable to get up satisfactorily. So things went on until just before the convention and still I was unprepared, I had retired for the night, and it must have been after two oclock in the Morning when it all came to me like a flash.
I got up out of bed and wrote that speech and made no material changes in it before it was delivered.[66]

Adding to the confusion about Aycock's customary speech habits, is a report by a newspaperman who covered Aycock's campaigns. In his account of Aycock's first speech of a campaign, the reporter included Aycock's jokes. Looking up the reporter immediately after the next speech, Aycock exclaimed: "I saw your report in the Charlotte *Observer* today, and you not only reported my speech, but told my jokes. That will never do. You must not do it again." Aycock then "explained that at the beginning of a campaign he prepared a speech to suit the is-

64. Winston, *Aycock: His People's Genius*, 17–18.
65. *Ibid.*, 14.
66. F. A. Macon to R. D. W. Connor, April 25, 1912, in Aycock Collection.

sues, interspersed it with appropriate jokes, stories and anecdotes, and changed it little as he went along."[67]

Aycock probably wrote many of his speeches in advance, but adapted them to the specific situation. Supporting this explanation is a report given by Aycock's childhood teacher, Sylvester Hassell, who heard him in 1904 make two political speeches: "one in the grove of Smithwick's Church, ten miles south of Williamston, and the other the same night in the Court-House at Williamston." Aycock had advised him not to go to the speech that night because "in the same campaign, he made substantially the same speech everywhere." Hassell went anyway and said that he "heard interesting new matter, as well as some of the things said in the day."[68]

Lending credence to reports that Aycock generally spoke extemporaneously, but did write his acceptance speech in 1900, his law partner revealed that "Aycock was what is known as an extempore speaker and after his graduating speech, never wrote a speech except an address on Joan of Arc delivered by him, in 1881, before a school for young ladies, in Tennessee ... until he wrote his speech accepting the nomination for Governor in 1900."[69]

In contast to what is known about Aycock's platform manner, the evidence on how McIver prepared and delivered his speeches is scant. Providing little insight into the man's speaking, reporters employ such phrases as a "masterly speech," "graphic force in the presentation of his views," being an "able speaker," and never failing "to impress an audience."[70] But

67. H. E. C. (Buck) Bryant, "My Memories of Charles B. Aycock," Charlotte *Observer*, April 6, 1952 (clipping, Aycock Collection).

68. Sylvester Hassell to Connor and Poe, April 17, 1912, in Aycock Collection.

69. Frank A. Daniels, "Address at the Presentation and Unveiling of Memorial Tablet" (see footnote 55 above).

70. Wilson (N.C.) *Advance*, May 29, 1890; Fayetteville *Observer*, July 17, 1890; Greensboro *North State*, July 10, 1890; "Professor Charles D. McIver," *North Carolina Teacher*, IX (September, 1891), 29.

none of these writers speak of McIver's actual preparation. The McIver collection, however, includes several speech manuscripts that show signs that they went through revisions. For example, one copy has penned changes on it. Another version, however, includes the penned changes in the typescript. In one instance the existence of a manuscript and an outline indicates that for some he prepared outlines in advance. In fact, his secretaries report that "a peculiar characteristic of Dr. McIver was that he could not make a set speech from a prepared manuscript and *be himself*. So, more often than otherwise, the manuscripts he had carefully prepared in the office remained unused in his pocket while he spoke."[71]

Alderman's habits concerning how he assembled and presented his speeches are as confusing as the reports about Aycock. Alderman probably wrote carefully some speeches in advance, but he had the ability to extemporize. One biographer observed:

There is not a great deal of difference between Dr. Alderman's style as a writer and his style as an orator. Matthew Arnold seems to have influenced it, but not greatly. There is nothing of Burke in it, nothing of Webster, and no more than a suggestion of Wendell Phillips. He is not a phrase-monger, like Arnold. He does not rely on flashes, but on heat and light. The whole paragraph is the unit with him. It scintillates throughout, whether the paragraph be in an essay, an oration or used in casual conversation.[72]

Concerning his speaking for education in North Carolina, one reporter declared Alderman to be "elegant and polished. . . . Bright, witty, elegant and faultless in diction, it was a literary treat that could not fail to please all lovers of 'English undefiled.'"[73] In later years, one critic acknowledged that his

71. E. J. Forney, Fodie Buie Kenyon, Emily Semple Austin, *Leaves from the Stenographers' Note Books* (Greensboro: Harrison Printing Co., n.d.), 14.
72. Patton, *Dr. Edwin Anderson Alderman*, 4.
73. Raleigh *Daily State Chronicle*, December 6, 1890; Raleigh *News and Observer*, December 6, 1890.

"phrases were always carefully turned; literary allusions were felicitous and imagery was fitting," but he observed that Alderman was sometimes "not sufficiently artful in concealing the fact that he had used much midnight oil." The editor of the Richmond *Times-Dispatch* also noted that "no one ... could be unaware of his highly visible pomposities, or could overlook the occasionally stilted quality of his rhetoric." Charles W. Dabney, president of the University of Tennessee, said that McIver and Alderman were "distinctly opposite types, especially in their manner of public speaking. McIver was humorous and interesting, but he was ponderous in argument, awkward in manner, and without special literary gift, while Alderman had beautiful diction, was graceful in delivery, and magnetic and eloquent."[74] Agreeing with Dabney, Daniels observed:

No man lived in my day in North Carolina who was quite in [Alderman's] class. At first, his speeches smelled of the lamp and he was so careful of his diction that he did not always strike fire. McIver never cared about forming his sentences and was in no sense in Alderman's class as a finished orator. Alderman held in reserve his enthusiasm, but it was at the basis of things and gradually he could lose himself, but always you felt when you heard him that he had said the last word and had polished every sentence until it shone. He was the best classical scholar in the State. He had broad statesmanship and never in any assembly was he outshone. ... McIver loved folks and loved to speak in country school houses and to have intimate touch with the farmers and people. Alderman was quite as devoted to their welfare but had a certain aloofness. He loved time to read and to write and to fill his mind with the best in literature. McIver was a born democrat; Alderman had an aristocratic air, but to see them together was like seeing two boys at play.[75]

These comments may explain why the terms "earnest" and

74. Lindsay Rogers, review of *Edwin A. Alderman: A Biography by Dumas Malone, New York Times Book Review*, October 27, 1949, 4; Virginius Dabney, *New York Herald Books*, November 10, 1940 (clipping, Alderman Collection, University of Virginia); Charles W. Dabney, *Universal Education in the South*, I, 193.

75. Daniels, *Tar Heel Editor*, 460–61.

"sincere" were so seldom used to describe Alderman's speaking, and so often applied to the speaking of Aycock and McIver. Of course, over the years Alderman changed from an intense, dedicated young advocate of educational state reform to a more confident spokesman for one of the outstanding universities in the South. Too, the early reporters covering the Carolina crusade were less sophisticated than the later critics and may have failed to reflect adequately upon his rhetorical style.

In developing their arguments, these speakers incorporated "the available means of persuasion." As pointed out earlier, their credibility constituted an important factor in their effectiveness. The three also included affective appeals, but Alderman and Aycock seemed to use them more than McIver. Alderman lauded McIver for his "homely humor." But Coon explained that McIver "impressed no one as a mere 'funny man;' he was earnest." Alderman and Aycock evoked laughter, but they also could move listeners to tears. One paper noted that Alderman's "plea for the children—for all the children was heart-moving and not a few eyes were moist."[76] On one occasion a hearer reported:

Governor Aycock spoke eloquently about equal opportunity and education for the children of North Carolina. There were tears among the women at the story of the poor boy who was so eager for an education that he went to school with only green apples for his lunch. Mamas were wishing they could have fed that little boy. The men swallowed the lumps in their throat and resolved anew that their children were going to have the opportunity and the education the Governor was talking about if it took their last dollar.[77]

The three men reasoned with great skill. Reports suggested

76. Alderman, "In Memoriam: Charles Duncan McIver," 314; Coon, "Charles Duncan McIver and His Educational Service," 134; D. Peacock to Connor and Poe, April 25, 1912, in Aycock Collection; Raleigh *Daily State Chronicle*, December 6, 1890.

77. Bernice Kelly Harris, "Fragment from my autobiography, in preparation, with compliments" (typescript), in Aycock Collection.

that Aycock's rhetoric was "logical and persuasive," and as being, "only common sense rationalized." In a similar vein Alderman was described as "strong and forcible and convincing," a rare instance of specific reference to Alderman's ratiocination.[78] On the other hand, reporters frequently described McIver as "forcible and logical in argument," as using "clear and forceful presentation of facts to accomplish a definite result," and being able "to clinch an argument as effectively as Vance." Indirect references to his logical appeal were to "the undeniable utterances of the Professor," "his extraordinary fund of information," "the brainiest man we ever had here on education," "the truths and principles that Prof. McIver presents," and his "common sense."[79] McIver's speeches suggest why listeners responded favorably to his cognitive discourse, because he inundated them with evidence.

Alderman, Aycock, and McIver took full advantage of what Aristotle called the "available means of persuasion." They assembled well their arguments and evidence and through their personalities and their skill as communicators they won respect and furthered the cause of education in North Carolina.

When Alderman, Aycock, McIver, began their work in the early 1880s, they were confronted with a poorly developed system of public education fraught with limitations and a record of failing to educate youngsters. The state led its neighbors in the percentage of native white illiterates; it had the fewest high schools, the smallest number of students enrolled, and the smallest average number of days of recorded attendance.

78. D. Peacock to Connor and Poe, April 25, 1912; C. Alphonso Smith to Clarence Poe, April 29, 1912, in Aycock Collection; Raleigh *Daily State Chronicle*, December 6, 1890.

79. "Professor Charles D. McIver," *North Carolina Teacher*, IX (September, 1891), 29; Smith, "Charles Duncan McIver," 212–40; Josephus Daniels, *Charles Duncan McIver Memorial Volume*, 230; Montgomery (Troy, N.C.) *Vidette*, September 11, 1890; Fayetteville *Observer*, July 17, 1890; Raleigh *Daily State Chronicle*, August 31, 1890; Concord (N.C.) *Standard*, August 29, 1890; "Public School Leaders," *Outlook*, LXXX (1905), 737–38.

Eschewing the myth-encrusted rhetoric typical of many other southern speakers of the period, these three North Carolinians offered an axiological rhetoric that embraced a new set of values for the state. The change in popular thought that they sought did not come quickly, for certain aspects of their vision have not been completely attained to this day. Nevertheless, Alderman, Aycock, and McIver were instrumental in starting important developments in North Carolina and the South.

BIBLIOGRAPHICAL NOTES

The McIver papers are located at the University of North Carolina, Greensboro. The materials, uncatalogued as late as 1973, include correspondence (especially several bundles of letters between McIver and his wife), manuscript copies of various speeches, and records from his administration of the State Normal and Industrial School.

The Library of Tulane University has most of the papers connected with Alderman's tenure as president of Tulane. The bulk of Alderman's papers, especially the papers related to the period of this study, are housed in the Alderman Library of the University of Virginia. Included are manuscript copies of some speeches and outlines of others.

Most of the Aycock papers are at the North Carolina Department of Archives and History in Raleigh. Included are a number of manuscript copies of speeches, many of which were used in the educational campaigns covered by this study.

Miscellaneous items on all three men may be found in the North Carolina Collection and the Southern Historical Collection at the Louis R. Wilson Library at the University of North Carolina, Chapel Hill.

A substantial bibliography of materials about and by McIver can be gleaned from the "Notes" section at the end of Rose Howell Holder's biography of McIver.

An extensive bibliography of Alderman's speeches and writings is available at the University of Virginia Alderman Library. The excellent biography by Dumas Malone is also an important source of materials about Alderman.

A detailed bibliography of materials on Aycock is provided at the end of the exhaustive biography by Oliver H. Orr, Jr., *Charles Brantley Aycock* (Chapel Hill: University of North Carolina Press, 1961).

A Selected Bibliography

This bibliography is a supplement to the one that appeared in *Oratory in the Old South* (Baton Rouge: Louisiana State University Press, 1970). It continues the practice of assembling only items that consider or reflect upon the composite southern oratory and related concepts. No attempt is made to duplicate the items of southern history and biography listed in the excellent bibliographies that appear in such books as Paul M. Gaston's *The New South Creed: A Study in Southern Mythmaking* (New York: Knopf, 1970), 281–98. Of course specific entries that support essays in this volume are included in the "Bibliographical Notes" at the end of each chapter.

Blassingame, John W., *Slave Testimony: Two Centuries of Letters, Speeches, Interviews, and Autobiographies*. Baton Rouge: Louisiana State University Press, 1977. Part II is devoted to speeches, 1837–1862, gathered from fugitive sources.

Blyton, Gifford, and Randall Capps. *Speaking Out: Two Centuries of Kentucky Orators*. Winston-Salem, N.C.: Hunter, 1977. Chapters are devoted to fourteen speakers: Barton W. Stone, Henry Clay, Ben Hardin, John J. Crittenden, Richard Hickman Menefee, Cassius M. Clay, John C. Breckinridge, James P. Knott, Henry Watterson, Carry A. Nelson, Laura Clay, Augustus O. Stanley, Alben W. Barkley, and A. B. "Happy" Chandler.

Boulware, Marcus H. *The Oratory of Negro Leaders: 1900–1968*. Westport, Conn.: Negro University Press, 1969. The book is not specifically about southern speaking, but it identifies many prominent black speakers.

Braden, Waldo W. "C. Alphonso Smith on 'Southern Oratory Before the War,'" *Southern Speech Journal*, XXXVI (Winter, 1970), 127–38. The article discusses the influence of a prominent professor of English who delivered a lecture through the South from 1895–1923. The lecture had much to do with promoting the myth of southern oratory.

————. "Myths in a Rhetorical Context," *Southern Speech Communication Journal*, XL (Winter, 1975), 113–26. The article applies theories of the social myth to public address with special reference upon southern speakers.

————. *Oratory in the Old South, 1828–1860*. Baton Rouge: Louisiana State University Press, 1970.

————, and William Strickland, comps. "Southern Public Address: A Bibliography of Theses and Dissertations." *Southern Speech Communication Journal*, XLI (Summer, 1976), 388–408. The bibliography lists about four hundred graduate studies devoted to public address of the eleven states of the Old Confederacy and of Kentucky. Orators are listed by states.

Brooks, James T., Jr. "A Rhetorical Study of Campaign Speaking of Selected Southern Reform Governors During the Progressive Era." Ph.D. dissertation, University of Florida, 1974.

Byrd, Gale K. "The Contribution of *The History of Southern Oratory* to the Concept of Southern Oratory." M.A. thesis, Louisiana State University, 1977. The study presents a critical analysis of Thomas E. Watson's *History of Southern Oratory*, Volume IX in the thirteen-volume set *The South in the Building of the Nation*.

Clark, E. Culpepper. "Henry Grady's New South: A Rebuttal From Charleston." *Southern Speech Communication Journal*, XLI (Summer, 1976), 346–58. The article presents views of Francis Warrington Dawson, a South Carolina editor who was critical of Grady's New South advocacy.

Day, Edith H. "A Rhetorical and Content Analysis of Florida Gubernatorial Addresses, 1845 to 1971." Ph.D. dissertation, Florida State University, 1973.

Dorgan, Howard. "A Case Study in Reconciliation: General John B. Gordon and the Last Days of the Confederacy." *Quarterly Journal of Speech*, LX (February, 1974), 83–91. The article presents an account of the delivery and reception of famous popular lectures.

————. "The Doctrine of Victorious Defeat in Rhetoric of Confederate Veterans." *Southern Speech Communication Journal*, XXXVIII (Winter, 1972), 119–130. The article discusses the ceremonial speaking of veterans at their annual encampments.

———. "Southern Apologetic Themes as Expressed in Selected Ceremonial Speakings of Confederate Veterans, 1889–1900." Ph.D. dissertation, Louisiana State University, 1971. Analysis is made of the numerous apologetic rationales and their influence upon a Confederate myth.

Huff, A. V., Jr. "The Eagle and the Vulture: Changing Attitudes Toward Nationalism in Fourth of July Orations Delivered in Charleston, 1778–1860." *South Atlantic Quarterly,* 73 (Winter, 1974), 10–22.

Jordon, Daniel P. "Mississippi's Antebellum Congressmen: A Collective Biography." *Journal of Mississippi History,* XXXVIII (May, 1976), 157–82. The article identifies many little-known figures.

Kirkpatrick, Edith Kay. "The Contribution of *The Library of Southern Literature* to the Concept of Southern Oratory." M.A. thesis, Louisiana State University, 1970. The study assesses the orations and critical comments included in the seventeen-volume set published in 1907 and 1909.

Logue, Cal M. "Gubernatorial Campaign in Georgia in 1880." *Southern Speech Communication Journal,* XL (Fall, 1974), 12–32. The article discusses the campaign of Alfred H. Colquitt, incumbent, against Thomas M. Norwood, a minority Democratic candidate.

———. "Rhetorical Ridicule of Reconstruction Blacks." *Quarterly Journal of Speech,* LXII (December, 1976), 400–409.

———. "The Rhetorical Appeals of Whites to Blacks During Reconstruction." *Communication Monographs,* XLIV (August, 1977), 241–51.

Saxon, John D. "Contemporary Southern Oratory: A Rhetoric of Hope, Not Desperation." *Southern Speech Communication Journal,* XLI (Spring, 1975) 262–74. The author argues that contemporary southern speaking "is characterized by an aversion to the past rhetoric of desperation and lost cause by a spirit of renewal and with a focus which is decidedly futuristic."

Scott, Anne Firor. *The Southern Lady: From Pedestal to Politics, 1830–1930.* (Chicago: University of Chicago Press, 1970). The book describes woman's clubs, temperance societies, and suffrage movements. Although not specifically addressed to speaking, it provides much important background material.

Bibliography

Starr, Douglas P. "Secession Speeches of Four Deep South Governors Who Would Rather Fight Than Switch." *Southern Speech Communication Journal*, XXXVII (Winter, 1972), 131–41. The article discusses speaking to legislatures of governors in Florida, Georgia, Louisiana, and Mississippi in 1861, advocating secession.

Terry, Ronald R. "A Rhetorical and Historical Analysis of Texas Populist Lecture Bureau, 1895–1896." M.A. thesis, Louisiana State University, 1973. This study discusses speaking of H. S. P. Ashby, James H. Davis, Jerome C. Kearby, and John B. Rayner.

Towns, Walter Stuart. "Ceremonial Speaking and the Reinforcing of American Nationalism in the South, 1875–1890." Ph.D. dissertation, University of Florida, 1972. "This historical-descriptive study examines twenty-six post Civil War ceremonial speeches delivered by Southerners to Southern audiences."

——, *et al.* "Bibliography of Speech and Theatre in the South for the Year . . ." *Southern Speech Communication Journal*, annually, usually the fall issue. It lists southern histories and biographies of southern speakers, theses, dissertations, and rhetorical criticisms. It is an excellent source of fugitive materials published in state speech journals.

Walsh, Barbara H. "The Negro and His Education: Persuasive Strategies of Selected Speeches at the Conference for Education in the South, 1898–1914." Ph.D. dissertation, Louisiana State University, 1974. The study considers "selected speeches on Negro education delivered to the Conference for Education in the South" (1898–1914).

Warner, Ezra J., and W. Buck Yearns. *Biographical Register of the Confederate Congress*. Baton Rouge: Louisiana State University Press, 1975. This work provides sources to identify many remote figures.

Contributors

Waldo W. Braden (Ph.D., University of Iowa, 1942) is Boyd Professor of Speech at Louisiana State University. He has served as executive secretary (1954–1957) and president (1962) of the Speech Communication Assoication and as president of Southern Speech Communication Association (1969–1970). He edits the annual volume of *Representative American Speeches*, and was principal editor of *Oratory in the Old South* (1970).

Bert E. Bradley (Ph.D., Florida State University, 1955) is chairman of the Department of Speech Communication at Auburn University. He has served as president of the Southern Speech Communications Association (1977–1978) and as editor of *Southern Speech Communication Journal* (1972–1975). He coauthored one of the essays that appeared in *Oratory in the Old South*, has written textbooks, and has contributed numerous articles to speech communication journals.

Danny Champion (M.A., and a doctoral candidate at Louisiana State University) is coordinator of the Department of Speech at Carson-Newman College, Jefferson City, Tennessee.

Howard Dorgan (Ph.D., Louisiana State University, 1971) is professor of speech at Appalachian State University and co-director of the annual Conference on the Rhetoric of the Contemporary South. His essay grew out of a dissertation directed by Waldo W. Braden.

Contributors

Cal M. Logue (Ph.D., Louisiana State University, 1967) is professor of speech Communication at the University of Georgia and has served as president of the Southern Speech Communication Association (1975–1976). He is a textbook writer and author of *Ralph McGill, Editor and Publisher* (1969).

Harold D. Mixon (Ph.D., Florida State University, 1964) is associate professor of speech at Louisiana State University. He is a former book review editor of *Southern Speech Communication Journal* (1972–1975) and has served as associate editor of the *Speech Teacher, Southern Speech Communication Journal*, and the *Bibliographic Annual* (SCA).

Annette N. Shelby (Ph.D., Louisiana State University, 1973) is assistant professor of business communication in the Department of Management and Marketing at the University of Alabama. She is a member of Phi Beta Kappa.

W. Stuart Towns (Ph.D., University of Florida, 1972) is associate professor of speech communication and departmental chairman at the University of West Florida. He is the present executive secretary of the Southern Speech Communication Association. His essay grew out of a doctoral dissertation completed under the direction of Donald E. Williams.

Index